Global Financial Meltdown

Also by Colin Read

INTERNATIONAL TAXATION HANDBOOK – Policy, Practice, Standards, and Regulation, *edited with G. Gregoriou, 2007*

Global Financial Meltdown

How We Can Avoid the Next Economic Crisis

Colin Read

palgrave
macmillan

Softcover reprint of the hardcover 1st edition 2009 978-0-230-22218-2

First published 2007 by
PALGRAVE MACMILLAN

Palgrave Macmillan in the UK is an imprint of Macmillan Publishers Limited, registered in England, company number 785998, of Houndmills, Basingstoke, Hampshire RG21 6XS.

Palgrave Macmillan in the US is a division of St Martin's Press LLC, 175 Fifth Avenue, New York, NY 10010.

Palgrave Macmillan is the global academic imprint of the above companies and has companies and representatives throughout the world.

Palgrave® and Macmillan® are registered trademarks in the United States, the United Kingdom, Europe and other countries.

ISBN 978-1-349-30770-8 ISBN 978-0-230-59518-7 (eBook)
DOI 10.1057/9780230595187

This book is printed on paper suitable for recycling and made from fully managed and sustained forest sources. Logging, pulping and manufacturing processes are expected to conform to the environmental regulations of the country of origin.

A catalogue record for this book is available from the British Library.

Library of Congress Cataloging-in-Publication Data

Read, Colin, 1959–
Global financial meltdown : how we can avoid the next economic crisis / Colin Read.
p. cm.
Includes index.
1. Finance. 2. Economic policy. 3. Monetary policy. 4. International finance. 5. International economic relations. I. Title.

HG173.R36 2009
332′.042—dc22 2008029930

I would like to thank Natalie and Blair for their inspiration and how they challenge me to do my best, and Herb and Mary Carpenter, both as friends and confidants.

Contents

List of Illustrations

Figures

Tables

About the Author

Colin Read is a Professor of Economics and Finance and the Dean of the School of Business and Economics at SUNY College at Plattsburgh. He has a PhD in Economics, JD in Law, MBA, Master's of Taxation, and has taught economics and finance for 25 years. Colin is a prolific writer, having published a book on international taxation, and written dozens of papers on market failure, volatility, and housing markets. He produces a monthly column in a business trade journal and appears monthly on a local PBS television show to discuss the regional and national economy. He has worked as a research associate at the Harvard Joint Center for Housing Studies and served the Ministry of Finance in Indonesia under contract from the Harvard Institute for International Development. He operates Economic Insights (www.economicinsights.net) to advise clients on long term trends affecting their enterprises. In his spare time he enjoys floatplane flying from his home on Lake Champlain that he shares with his partner, Natalie, daughter, Blair, and dog, Walter.

1
Introduction

The world is fast becoming a complicated place. The number of interactions each of us has each day would boggle the mind of someone living a few generations ago. And more than at any other time in our history, many of these interactions are economic transactions. From the purchases we make each day, to the bills we pay online, or even to the range of tasks we perform for others in return for a wage, our lives now seem marked by our bit parts in a world economy.

At the same time as our economic lives have become more complicated, global finances have begun to affect us all, with a level of subtlety and complexity that could not have been imagined a generation ago. At no other time have so many people interacted so frequently with something that baffles us so completely. This book will delve into the mysteries of the world economy and will unravel for the lay leader the mysterious ways of the major financial markets. We shall see that our tacit acceptance to leave financial market management to the experts has cost us – dearly.

The primary purpose of this book is to provide an economic education for the educated reader who does not have a college major or minor in economics. The issues are complicated, the history is extensive, and the future is very fluid and dynamic. The concepts we discuss in these pages are only those that play an important role on the economic health of the world. Indeed, we cannot treat all the relevant various economic forces without filling volumes. The issues are very complex and inter-related.

Even if we have stripped down the analysis and commentary only to those variables that are most significant, it is these same variables that are constantly invoked in the popular and the financial press. Most financial reporters have communications or journalism degrees rather than economics degrees. I had to complete a Ph.D.

in economics, a lifetime of research and teaching, and years of contemplation of economic issues to make sense of the modern economy.

I wanted to write a book that would empower readers to understand market economics. Current events have made the telling of this story even more compelling. Gone are the days when we knew the local shopkeeper by name or assumed that the pension we earned over a lifetime of service would be there when we retired. We have learned it is necessary to take hold of our own economic futures, but we have not been given the tools to understand an economy or marketplace that grows more complicated every day.

And, so, we have entrusted our economic future to our favorite politicians and public figures, even though they likely have no more profound economic insights than we do. This book is meant for those of you who feel more comfortable understanding for yourselves how this vast economic machine works. I hope this knowledge will allow you to seize your own economic destiny and perhaps, articulate your needs and expectations for the next generation of politicians and economic leaders.

I also hope my background will offer you a well rounded perspective of the global economic travails. I have been a practicing economist and professor for 25 years, having stepped into the field of economics from an undergraduate degree in physics. I have always enjoyed understanding how things work. But while a small boy can take apart an old radio to see what makes it tick, there is a lot more to unravel in understanding a modern economy.

In my academic career, I soon realized that economic theory cannot tell the whole story. So after my Ph.D. in real estate economics and finance, I completed a Master's in Business Administration to better appreciate the economy from a businessman's perspective. I also became fascinated with the legal and public policy institutions underpinning any modern economy, and went on to complete a Juris Doctor degree in Law. Finally, because I realized that I could not understand the modern economy until I understood how it interacts with the labyrinth of rules we call the tax code, I donned my green eyeshades and studied for my Master's of Accountancy in Taxation. All the while, I continued to research and write in these various fields, both in specialized journals and in the popular press. Now as the dean of a business school, I have had the opportunity to gain knowledge in the other business disciplines of marketing, management, and production, to round out my training in economics, finance, accounting, and law. I have come to realize that this multidisciplinary approach is necessary to understand the increasingly complex economic landscape.

As the story unfolds, I believe you will find that the workings of the global economy are not nearly as difficult as they might seem. You will also begin to notice that those who report on the economy often know little more than you do, and cannot afford the air time or column inches to give you the whole story. The better you understand the workings of the modern marketplace, the more likely you will be able to avoid problems that seem vexing, frequent, and threatening to your own economic future.

The book is divided into parts that will take you, the reader, from basic economics to a description of policies that can correct a number of market failures we are currently experiencing. The first part delves into why the free market system has evolved as the center of the modern economic model. In part 2, we discover the emerging middle class and the creation of a new financial market participant, known as the Consumer-Investor. Part 3 indicates how the economic world as we know it will change dramatically in the next two generations. In part 4, we take a look at the role of central banks and the Federal Reserve system as referees in an increasingly complicated global financial world. Part 5 recaps some of the significant financial failures that have brought about untold economic pain to many. In part 6 we consider the role of politics in creating, or frustrating, economic prosperity and stability. Finally, we close with some recommendations on how we might avoid the calamities that have threatened our economic security.

As you read the chapters that follow, I hope your interest is piqued. I certainly want you to read these chapters as part of a bigger mystery, with each chapter illuminating an unnecessarily opaque landscape. At the end of the book, you may realize that you are much more capable of understanding world economies.

You may also realize that our leaders don't necessarily know much more than we do, and some even less, of the workings of a modern economy. I hope you will come away feeling as though you can ask questions of our candidates, demand good stewardship from our leaders, and challenge those that make millions, but cost us billions.

Our economic future is too important for us to entrust to others hoping to profit or grind a political axe. So trust your intuition, don't be afraid to ask questions, and expect simple, straightforward answers to your reasonable economic questions. And be mistrustful of answers that appear too trite or simplistic, while reinforcing the well-being of the economic soothsayer. In short, follow the money. If an economic theory seems too good and too easy to be true, it surely is. The world is nuanced, and the economy is complex. If we can understand these nuances and see our very important role as economic citizens in the global marketplace, the entire economy will function much better. The journey is worth the while, and all of our economic futures are at stake.

Part I

Evolution of the Modern Economic System

We begin with a primer on markets and competition. Much of what we will subsequently discuss is premised on the notion that markets are an amazingly efficient device to channel resources. We will also discover, though, that the ideal of a competitive market can fail in a number of ways. Of course, some would have us discard markets for perhaps even more unworkable allocation mechanisms. However, so long as we understand what can cause markets to fail, perhaps our insights can allow us to fix them before they fail. Readers less interested in the evolution of the market system, and more concerned about the state of our modern economy, can skip forward to Part II.

2
The Beauty (and the Beast) of Free Markets

Fire is an amazing innovation. It keeps us warm, gives us light, allows us to sustain ourselves, and makes our food safer to eat. It can also do damage if used improperly. Fire can be mishandled and it can be used as a weapon by and against us. We have learned from experience to understand and respect fire, which allows us to protect ourselves from its misuse.

Markets are equally remarkable. The first markets allowed us to access goods and services with amazing diversity in time, location, and characteristics. We were freed from the toil of producing everything we needed and we benefited from the skills of others as they benefited from ours.

As long ago as 1776, Adam Smith described in *The Wealth of Nations*[1] how markets create surpluses that could not exist otherwise. Markets allowed us to concentrate on those endeavors we most enjoy or in which we are most accomplished, knowing that the wealth our skills created would allow us to enjoy the artisanry of others.

The market also acts as a tool to solve the double coincidence of wants, freeing us from having to find for ourselves those individuals that produce the goods or services we desire, while at the same time desiring the goods or services we ourselves produce. The marketplace does this matching for us, miraculously adjusting prices to balance supply and demand.

This invisible hand that determines prices is a beautiful thing. Self-interested humans magically come together in this complicated exercise to ensure that everyone can produce something of some value, with prices reflecting the relationship between how many individuals have the skills to produce a good and how many individuals want the good that is produced.

This mechanism is deceptively simple. It is precisely our natural human desire to advance our own self-interest that makes the market function. And no other human made process could work any better to signal what should be produced and consumed at a given time – usually.

While the remainder of the book is devoted to this dance of self-interest, and the missteps that can occur along the way, let me digress for a moment to describe some alternative mechanisms to satisfy human wants and needs.

Alternatives to free markets

Perhaps the most elusive alternative to the market is the collective. A varied group of individuals, possessing all the skills necessary to take care of their individual needs, comes together and provides for each other. Resources and the fruits of their labors are divided relatively equally. Some trading can still occur if we wish to trade something we have been given but do not much value, in exchange for someone else's share of a different good.

This system can work pretty well as long as the number of participants remains manageable. With too many players, envy sets in, and those that produce what is highly valued may become resentful that they are not afforded a greater slice of the pie in reward for their hard work or their "marketable" skill. Subsequent side trading between participants becomes the norm rather than the exception, creating a de facto underground economy, but without the legitimacy of a traditional marketplace.

As the appealing notion of the collective breaks down under the onslaught of human nature, a benevolent dictator often steps in to maintain order and to ultimately determine who will produce and who will consume which products or services. This "centrally planned" economy imposes an untenable requirement on the benevolent dictator. The dictator would have to somehow know how much each individual values the various possible goods and services and must then tweak production to somehow maximize the happiness of the citizenry.

However, in the absence of a free market, there are no accurate signals to guide these insights of benevolent dictators. Instead, they must guess what pleases their constituents. If I were a citizen in the collective, and someone asked me what I need, I would have every personal incentive to over-represent my preferences if I felt it would translate into a greater share for me. Even more problematic is the fact that the benevolent dictator would have to find a way to induce me to produce for the common good. Sufficient coercion to prevent shirking is difficult even in a family, and nearly impossible for anything but a trivially small economy.

Might makes right and takings

Another mechanism to allocate resources is "Might Makes Right." Such a system does not protect the property rights of the individual. Those with strength merely take what they want. A version of this method is still used, but with compensation. Expropriations under the "takings clause" of the Amendments to the US Constitution[2] allows the US government to take property from its citizenry if it is deemed in the public interest. It is also used, without compensation, in international quarrels, and often over natural resources.

While the takings clause remains controversial, especially when the property is subsequently turned over to private developers, it is still the law of the land. You might argue that a "taking" mimics the marketplace because fair compensation – presumably market compensation – is offered in return for the property. However, unlike voluntary markets, few want to be the subject of a taking. Invariably, an owner's valuation of the property will differ from the valuation of the taking authority. This is because the owner is typically cognizant of the fair market valuation at any time, and has not volunteered to sell up to this point.

Before we return to the beauty and the beast of the free market, let's recognize the coercive element in each of these allocation mechanisms. Under the collective alternative, often known as communism, individual preferences are subjugated to the somehow-determined needs of the masses. In the second alternative, the powerful offer the weak no choice.

The best and worst of free markets

Interestingly, the free market shares some of these characteristics. The invisible hand of the marketplace determines the valuation of all goods and services, not unlike the valuation dictated by the collective. And the free market also relies on economic might, also known as wealth, to exert a disproportionate influence on the marketplace. However, unlike the other alternative allocation mechanisms, this wealth is proportional to one's innate skills, as valued by the marketplace. And at least the market permits some element of control for the individual to develop those valuable skills.

Within this free market system, inherited wealth remains controversial because it exerts the same influence as earned wealth, but without any requisite skills on the part of the individual. This asymmetry is the basis of the argument for high levels of taxation for inherited income. However, the free market system typically respects inheritance because it is the embodiment of free choice to permit individuals to do as they wish with their hard earned income and subsequent estate.

Now let's turn to some reasons why this otherwise superior free market system may fail to perform as well as we would like. Variations of these themes will be addressed throughout the remainder of the book. As we develop our market intuitions, we will begin to recognize the circumstances that cause markets to fail. The ability to identify these circumstances will allow us to repair market imperfections. In turn, we will be able to preserve the other advantages of the marketplace, and not have to abandon free markets for a system that cannot recognize free will and self-interest.

Economists typically hold up the perfectly competitive model as the holy grail of economic interactions. If economists appear to be enamored of free markets, we are more correctly enamored with the intrinsic beauty of a perfectly competitive market. It is characterized by a large number of buyers and sellers exchanging a commodity in an environment of such transparency that all participants know all prices and all relevant information about the commodity. These assumptions are so extreme that it is unlikely that any market is truly competitive. Failures abound, and each failure mitigates the beauty of the market, to the extent that some still argue we should abandon the free market altogether and adopt instead one of the alternatives described earlier.

Until now, though, no alternative allocation system has teased the best efforts out of producers, or accurately gauged the preferences of consumers. Until an alternative system can, we should instead try to remedy the failings of the free market system. Here are the circumstances by which the free market may fail.

The competitive ideal

First, the competitive ideal assumes that information we receive about the price, value, and characteristics of a commodity is perfect. Modern information technologies help with this assumption. We can now determine prices for a myriad of comparable goods, seemingly anywhere in the world. For instance, it seems like a price for almost all commodities can now be found on the Internet. It is much more difficult, though, for goods that are not easy to describe, or for services that are as varied as individuals.

Interestingly enough, the stock market may come closer to realizing some of these necessary qualities. A stock is a well-defined commodity, with property rights well described, and with a common price that can be observed anywhere in the world, instantaneously. And regulatory agencies such as the United States Securities and Exchange Commission (SEC) work to ensure that buyers understand the property right they are purchasing, and that a level playing field is maintained. There is probably no market more carefully scrutinized. Ironically, there may be no market more manipulated either.

Asymmetric information

A major theme of this book is that even this most perfect of all markets can be rife with market failures. While part of the assumption of perfect information is in the instantaneous and accurate listing of the price of a security, it is still a matter of constant diligence to ensure that all information affecting the value of the security is made available to all buyers and sellers at the same time. If this assumption is violated, buyers and sellers of a security may make choices they may not have otherwise made, had they access to the same information. Imperfect information distorts the market price, and an incorrect market price frustrates the beauty of the free market. Whole chapters to follow will be devoted to the problems that can arise when participants try to profit on inaccurate or hidden information.

A large number of buyers and sellers

A second failure can arise if the premise of a large number of buyers and sellers is violated. While technology has made prices easier to discover, undue influence from a small number of powerful buyers or sellers is still problematic. If market participants can somehow impose undue influence on the market, they can manipulate the market price to their advantage.

For instance, if small buyers or sellers of stock incorrectly believe that all necessary information is incorporated into the price of the stock, they can be induced to sell a security whenever they see a small but sudden drop in its price. This strategy can create mischief. A large seller could dump a small amount of shares, causing the price of the share to drop, which in turn causes a large number of small stockholders to also sell. This large seller can then buy the stock up at a bargain basement price and watch as the small stockholders come to their senses, realize the stock is incorrectly priced, and bring the price back up to where it ought to be (and perhaps was originally). The large seller makes a handsome profit in return.

Another extreme example of this phenomenon is in the behavior of a monopoly, defined as one seller of a market good, or a monopsony, defined as a single buyer who dominates the market. By withholding their participation, the monopoly can force smaller players to accept less than desirable terms for fear of not receiving any terms at all. Of course, it is in the nature of human activity that some have sets of skills that are unique and highly valued. For instance, Alex Rodriguez, to anybody except a Boston Red Sox fan, has a unique combination of baseball skills that no one else embodies. As a consequence, he can auction his services until he usurps almost every bit of value and the buyer (renter) of his services is almost indifferent to his hiring. Actually, the New York Yankees do not have to sacrifice every bit of surplus. As in any auction, they are still able to extract the surplus over what they would have been willing to pay and what the next highest bidder would have paid.

A monopoly is always at least partly objectionable. However, it is most troubling when it is not the natural monopoly just described, but rather is artificially created for strategic reasons. A company that maintains its monopoly, and hence its undue market power, by building a better mousetrap is productive. However, a company that maintains its market power through such anti-competitive behavior, such as buying out competing firms, is destructive. These companies are also in violation of good public policy and of anti-trust laws.

Such destructive competition against the interest of a well-functioning marketplace is difficult to distinguish from other sound and reasonable corporate strategies. Because of the difficulty in detecting and prosecuting such transgressions, US anti-trust laws, and their international counterparts, typically deter and punish anti-competitive behavior by fining those successfully prosecuted treble damages, or three times the ill-gotten gains.

A distorted market is a terrible thing to waste

A third problem can arise if there are incomplete markets. If it is too costly to fully bring to the marketplace all the various characteristics we might enjoy from a product we purchase, we may be forced to buy only some of the desired characteristics. Or perhaps the packaged good is bundled in a way that includes some things we want, but cannot exclude some things we do not want. For example, the cable television company may give us a bundle of channels, in effect forcing us to buy some we do not wish to have.

Bundling of characteristics also occurs with financial products. For instance, when we buy a security, we are purchasing the flow of future profits accruing to the owner of the security. We may also inadvertently be buying risk. Some buyers are purchasing just the right amount of risk and can somehow manage that risk. Others may prefer to accept a lower return but also face less risk. However, there may not be a secondary market that can take some of the risk from the buyer in exchange for some of the return.

There are simply too many characteristics embodied in the huge variety of goods and services to be able to create a unique market for each unique packaging of the good or service. However, as we shall see later, modern financial markets have become amazingly adept at tailoring these characteristics to ensure as broad a potential market as possible.

We don't know everything everywhere

We stated the perfectly competitive model assumes perfect and complete information. Actually, it turns out that this assumption can be relaxed somewhat. So long as there are enough sufficiently well-informed buyers and sellers, the market can be self-policing. For instance, if there is a certain cost of bringing items to market, and if sellers cannot profit from a sufficiently high number of uninformed buyers, they will not try to engage in non-competitive behavior. The informational threshold is still rather high, though. A sufficiently large number of buyers and sellers with good information on the price and quality of all goods brought to market keeps the market honest and competitive for the rest of us.

It is unlikely that the requirement of full information can always be met. For instance, you may buy a car once in a decade. The car dealer sells a number of cars every week. It is reasonable to assume there are significant information and negotiation asymmetries in such transactions. These asymmetries will violate our assumption of perfect information.

Here the Internet comes to our rescue. Its ability to quickly provide the consumer with the price and availability of comparable goods performs an important service to the marketplace. Sellers are forced to try harder to differentiate their goods and services from others to prevent us from so easily making those apples-to-apples comparisons.

The tragedy of the commons

A problem related to incomplete markets is when a private market cannot efficiently provide a good we all collectively value. Garret Hardin eloquently described the tragedy of the commons in his 1968 essay.[3] Consider our various simultaneous uses of a town square. All of us value this public good, and government often provides such goods on our behalf. Under the theory of "the more the merrier," we should make such goods broadly available, perhaps even for free.

If I chose to enjoy the town square by allowing my goat to graze on its grass, you may not appreciate the odor and may stop enjoying the park. This problem of abusing common property because something that belongs to everyone is ultimately protected by nobody may hasten the demise of public goods.

Society has gone through waves of privatization of public goods, especially in times when government faces a budget deficit. However, while taxes allow a government to provide public goods, a private firm may not find it profitable. Private providers must set an admission fee to help defray maintenance costs and provide for a profit commensurate with their investment. In doing so, they restrict use to those that value the experience more than the entry price. This price barrier creates a market distortion because some are excluded from enjoying something they value but which imposes little or no cost on society. For instance, it costs nothing to allow one more person to enjoy a beautiful view from a scenic lookout. If the private provider charges a price, it can make a profit, but ultimately it must exclude some that value the view but are unwilling to pay the price. And society loses because of the enjoyment foregone.

Others enjoy what you enjoy

Related to this tragedy of the commons is the problem of externalities. If one's consumption benefits others, society is better off. However, this "positive externality" often goes unrewarded, inducing consumers to do less of this activity than is optimal because they do not receive the side benefits accruing to others.

For instance, you might be willing to pay more for a compact disc if you factor in the enjoyment your neighbors receive when you play your music. On the other hand, if you play music others detest, you create a negative externality and consume too much of this music rather than too little. In this case, society should impose upon you a bad-taste tax. Either way, externalities distort markets, in one direction or another, and create inefficiencies.

Transactions costs

Finally, there are costs of bringing goods to market, separate from the value of the good or service itself. These transactions costs, such as marketing or legal expenses, act as a friction in the marketplace, preventing some goods from being otherwise exchanged because their value is small relative to the transaction costs. This distortion limits the number of otherwise willing buyers and hence distorts the true market price.

Obviously, almost all markets suffer from one or the other of these problems, to some degree. It is likely that there is no single competitive marketplace. And a subtle, but beautiful, proof in economics declares that all markets are distorted if any market is distorted.[4] The best we can do is second best, as we try to reduce distortions, so that the market is not too imperfect.

This recognition of the problems of the theoretical perfect competitive marketplace elicits a number of responses. Some would conclude that markets are inherently flawed, and would have us revert to another perhaps more flawed allocation mechanism. Others would doubt the ability of any enlightened public policy do-gooder to somehow repair these imperfections, under their belief that the cure is worse than the disease.

The exact response is more than a matter of political tastes. The market system is a terrible system, until we consider the alternatives. So we are left with two philosophies – to do nothing, or to roll up our sleeves and try to repair these problems.

Some of the problems seem rather easy to fix. For instance, we have made great inroads in improving the information about the price and availability of commonly purchased commodities. We witness this in the ubiquitous ways in which new techniques are adopted to give participants better market information. These innovations are offered voluntarily and eagerly adopted – presumably, because some innovations, indeed some innovations offered by or sponsored by government, make our exchanges more efficient.

If you accept we cannot throw the market baby out with the bath water, and we recognize that there is some low hanging fruit that can help improve the efficiency of the market, the real issue is just how much market fixing we should permit or promote.

A legitimate role for government as a market watchdog?

Many argue that government is the anathema to efficiency. This conclusion, perhaps borne out of long lines at the local Department of

Motor Vehicle office, is a politically dogmatic conclusion rather than a pragmatic one. Obviously, a government-imposed remedy must somehow balance the cost of the problem with the cost of the solution.

The difference between the benefits created by a well functioning market and the costs of a poorly performing market can be quite sizeable. This difference, expressed as a share of these unfortunate costs compared to the overall market benefits, is known as a deadweight loss. Such losses have been measured to consume upwards of 10% or more of market benefits, and are quite typically of the range of a few percent. Even a few percentage points of the fourteen trillion dollar economies of the United States or the European Economic Community is comparable to the size of their federal budget deficits, and certainly deserves our attention.

Before we leave this discussion of the categories of market failures and jump into its practical implications, let's describe what we cannot do. All of our discussions have to do with market efficiency. We propose market innovations so that people may benefit from surpluses that would otherwise contribute to deadweight losses. We have said nothing about whether the outcome is fair.

I want your piece of the pie

Fairness is an elusive concept. Ask any five year old to do something they do not want to do, and you will likely hear "that's not fair." Fairness or equity, in the economic rather than the financial sense, is a beauty in the eyes of the beholder. In the absence of a universally agreeable definition of equity, economists avoid this concept and instead leave it to democracy or some other messy political innovation to somehow determine the haves and the have-nots.

It is actually possible to create a market for equity. If we have a number of different "solutions" to the division of economic benefits, we can create an entire spectrum of these solutions, perhaps dispersed across the land. If we do not like the solution one jurisdiction comes up with, presumably we can move to the choices established by another. This is called "voting with your feet."[5] However, if each of these jurisdictions caters to just the right number and mix of participants, my voluntary move to your neighborhood may at some point frustrate the Nirvana you are trying to establish.

That said, if we create the tools to solve inefficiencies, and if we create the jurisdictions – (and perhaps even the membership fees) – to provide the right balance of equity that different groups demand, everyone can benefit within this market system. The art then remains. How do we first recognize the problems, how can we fix the problems, and do we have the wisdom to know when we ought to "fix" the problems? I focus on the financial markets because in these markets today, retirements are earned and lost, and whole livelihoods may be destroyed. We need to know why.

Of course, you would not be this far into the book if you did not subscribe to the philosophy of identifying and then fixing problems. For the remainder of the book, specific characteristics of marketplace will be presented, and innovations proposed in the hope of increasing market efficiency and market participation. However, with each innovation comes some displacement, some reaction, and ultimately responses by some to capitalize on, or undermine, public policy prescriptions.

You have seen a glimpse of the importance of good market information. We next describe the evolution of markets, from simple farmers' markets of millennia ago to the modern complex financial markets that are now so often in the news.

3
The Post-Industrial Revolution and the Transforming Economies

Markets were an incredible innovation. So robust and efficient, they were also versatile, adapting to new trade routes on land and over water, and accommodating new currencies and other mediums of exchange. But the essential role of the marketplace, as a location to exchange goods and services for a common currency, has remained unchanged, up to the Renaissance.

The first major innovation in the development of the market was the movement toward agrarian societies and urbanization. Once people became fixed in one location, rather than following the herd, they could accumulate surpluses and sell these surpluses in the market. Markets became established in place, and associated with the cultural hubs of early cities. This model remains essentially unchanged, even if markets today may be at the local mall, the New York Stock Exchange, or increasingly, a page on the World Wide Web.

The Industrial Revolution created the second wave of urbanization. The steam engine and water wheels allowed us to harness power in place of human toil. This permitted one unskilled laborer to produce as much as could a cottage of skilled guildsmen. And with railroads and large ships, we could move goods from one end of the globe to another cheaper than we could produce these same goods locally.

Today, every 30% decline in transportation costs doubles the area of the world that can profitably trade with us. But, while we can transport goods with increasing efficiency, we cannot import a haircut, a nurse, or a car mechanic. Most of the things we enjoy are necessarily local even today, perhaps made up of some combination of goods or services that originated elsewhere, but were ultimately brought here, sold here, and enjoyed here.

The circular flow of income

These simple economies are not too difficult to understand. For thousands of years, production equaled consumption and income equaled spending. Through taxation, government exacted a share of production, to be diverted to the ruling class and sometimes partially distributed to peasants in exchange for their support of this two-class society. The ruling class and the church were allied in this precarious balance, and after centuries and much bloodshed, everyone eventually understood their place.

Then something changed. With the Industrial Revolution and the rise of the middle class, savings and investment were added to this simple economy. Financial markets and intermediaries took in the savings of the emerging middle class, and pooled financial capital that allowed new companies to expand, through debt or through the issuance of equity shares to intermediaries and eventually to the public. We shall see that this simple and modest innovation of capital formation drastically changed the basic functioning of the market – for better and worse.

Savings and wealth are created when individuals produce more than they consume. Efficiencies and surpluses created by the Industrial Revolution expanded the economic pie and created the middle class. These savings required instruments that could act as a store of value. Financial equity, the modern publicly traded corporation, and financial markets quickly arose.

While the transition from a simple economy to one with savings, and hence investment, seems like a minor innovation, the economy has not been the same since. It created new types of markets, a new role for government, and new opportunities for the economy to come to a grinding halt, as we shall see. And it created the Consumer-Investor, who earned greater labor earnings than they could consume, and invested the rest.

Let's ignore for now the opportunity for unscrupulous financial intermediaries. We'll have time to return to that later. Instead, we'll focus on how this innovation of savings and investment hampered market coordination and changed the way economic decisions were made.

The principle and the agent

First, by separating producers from investors, we suffer from a new economic disease – the principal-agent problem. When producers created and invested their own capital, there was no doubt that all of the producer's investment decisions were made in the best interest of the

Producer-Investor, and catered to the Producer-Investor's tolerance for risk, preference for timing of cash flow and profits, and expectations of a return. If the returns were not sufficient, the Producer-Investor could always work harder to produce more.

Under the new entities that emerged during the Industrial Revolution, a producer was monolithic but the investors were not. Instead, investment capital was mobilized from many individuals, each with a slightly different tolerance for risk, ability to comprehend the balance sheet, expectations of returns, and preference for the timing of their return to capital. One way to solve the heterogeneity of investors was to package investment into market instruments so that units of investment (shares of stock) could be easily traded if individual investors felt the instrument's patterns of return and risk no longer suited their needs.

Unfortunately, commoditization of investment instruments must necessarily oversimplify investment. The emphasis went from the intricacies of the enterprise to the simplicity of quarterly returns, return on equity, and the risk/return tradeoff. A sophisticated investor could try to judge if the market was properly measuring the subtleties of the enterprise. If not, there were profits to be had – either way. If the market was overvaluing an enterprise, an investor could sell short, in essence borrowing some shares, selling them, and buying shares back later at a lower price to return to the original lender. If the market undervalued the enterprise, the investor could buy shares low, and sell them at the higher price once the market "caught on" to the true valuation. Either way, there are profits to be had.

Notice that, for the first time, we use the term investor in two new and different ways. Historically, the investor was the producer who actually mobilized the capital to create the machines and build the production process. Investment meant machines and productive capacity. With the creation of financial markets, the investor became the faceless provider of financial capital, used to purchase not new machines but, more likely than not, shares previously owned by another "investor." No longer would investment necessarily mean an increase in an economy's capacity to produce. Only in the case of Initial Public Offerings or the sale of newly minted shares to raise funds for a new factory, for example, would new-style investment be synonymous with old-style investment. And such truly new investment is quite rare, especially when compared with the volume of shares exchanged each day.

Recessions and depressions

We can now see why this decoupling between investment and production can give rise to recessions and depressions. Let's hypothesize that investors get wind of some news that could damage the economy. The value of stocks fall because investors fear that stockholders' share of the flow of profits from publicly traded companies may decline. This depression of stock values instantly wipes out paper wealth, which in turn depresses the part of our investor's spending related to their perceived wealth.

Notice that the actual production line remains independent of this emerging train wreck – so far. But, with the decrease in spending and consumption by stockholding Consumer-Investors, who suddenly feel poorer, production inventories rise. Any prudent producer will be forced to lay off some workers until inventories decline to more manageable levels. Wage-earning line workers will then reduce consumption because their wages have become uncertain, while laid-off workers dramatically reduce their consumption. This recession started reasonably enough because of some bad news. However, true or untrue, the news became a self-fulfilling prophecy because of the wealth-effect drop in consumption on the part of investors, and the lay-off-led drop in consumption on the part of wage-earners.

A recession is popularly defined as two consecutive quarters of negative growth. If the economic growth arising from technological improvements and population increases is out-swamped by the declines in consumption for two quarters, a recession results. Unfortunately, because the data of quarterly growth is known only some time after the quarter ends, we discover that we are in a recession only after we are deep in one, making a subsequent quarter of negative growth quite likely. If a recession becomes sufficiently prolonged, we label it a depression.

Why is this scenario less likely with the old "Producer-Investor?" Before financial intermediation, Producer-Investors would only feel poorer if consumers on average were no longer buying their products. But, if workers were still employed, they would still have to spend their income somewhere, and one producer's loss is likely to be another's gain. So long as Producer-Investors, in the aggregate, are paying workers, these workers can continue to buy the producers' goods, in the aggregate. Production supplied and income created results in demand for products that, in turn, allow producers to pay workers, and so on. This phenomenon is known as "Say's Law," after the eighteenth/nineteenth century economist Jean-Baptiste Say who first described the self-fulfilling law that supply creates its own demand.[1]

The old school

There is a premise of "old school" economics that postulates even an increasingly sophisticated and linked economy will not suffer the arbitrary swings of human economic irrationality. If a group of economic actors began to behave irrationally, a more rational actor could profit from this irrationality and, in doing so, move the market back toward equilibrium.

Take for instance the "old school" classical school response to an irrational fall in stock prices described a moment ago. In such a case, smart money would move in, buy up the depressed stock, and profit by selling the stock once the market returns to normal. This model of "arbitrage" would suggest that the irrationally induced recession should quickly return to normal, the smart money would profit, and the irrational money would suffer. Through economic Darwinism, eventually the irrational players would go away, making future recessions all the more unlikely.

While this model of arbitrage may make some sense in the very long run, how long is a piece of string? There is nothing in economic theory that guides our understanding of the dynamics and timing of the arbitrage process. We will return to failings of the simple arbitrage process later when I offer an explanation of the wild gyrations recently experienced in international equity markets. Suffice to say for now that the old adage "an economist will tell you what will happen, or when it will happen, but cannot tell you both" has honest roots.

Houston, we have a problem

The "old school" of classical economics fails if Producer-Investors and Consumer-Investors are decoupled. If the separation between the Producer-Investor and the Consumer-Investor repealed Say's Law, is there a credible way to get us out of this bind? If you recall, the industrial evolution spawned surpluses, allowed for savings by the middle class, and created the first middle class investors. The middle class was motivated to save for and invest in the future, and developed a thirst for education as investment in its own human capital.

Producers, the Industrial Revolution's version of the Nouveau Riche, had no interest in, or the capacity to provide the education infrastructure their skilled workers demanded. Indeed, without the ability to forcibly retain their workers, producers would not want to invest in their human capital for fear workers would demand a commensurately higher salary, or worse, would defect to work for a competitor. The only entity that could credibly provide this infrastructure to the emerging middle class was government.

And this required a new theory of government. Before the government of the Industrial Revolution, royalty and the church modestly provided for the needs of peasants. There was no need for education, and the guilds took care of the training and apprenticeship of their own. Now a new style of government was emerging, and it was firmly interjected between the urban middle class and the elite.

We learned earlier that taxation was not an innovation discovered during the Industrial Revolution. Now the transformed economy accepted taxation, mostly borne by Producer-Investors, to create the educational and industrial infrastructure industry needed, but refused to do themselves. Education was a public good, and as we saw in Chapter one, public goods are not well provided by the private sector.

Government did not stop there though. As the benevolent defender of the middle class, government took on health and safety on the factory floor, passed laws to protect Consumer-Investors, and at the same time created the property infrastructure that would benefit workers and producers alike. And when government was unwilling to play its new-found role at times, unions were formed to work on behalf of labor, to provide, in the words of John Kenneth Galbraith, the countervailing power against the extensive power of the Producer-Investors.[1]

So all of a sudden we have Consumer-Investors (Savers), Producer-Investors (the economist's definition of Investors), and Government. The simple world of Say's Law became much more complicated, and hence much more difficult to coordinate. And we went from depression to depression, with fair regularity. We saw depressions and panics in 1819, 1832, 1836, 1857, 1869, 1873, 1893, 1901, 1907, and of course the Great Depression of 1929. This increasingly complicated economy was just too difficult to coordinate, especially with little knowledge of its functions, and no economic theories to guide policy makers.

At first, our faith in everything scientific may have been a curse rather than a cure. The emerging scientific-economic thought of the nineteenth century was based on faith of a self-regulating economy. Like the doctor without a clear explanation of the cause, the economist's best cure for everything was patience. The trouble with doing nothing though is that the affliction often gets worse.

The trouble with normal is it always gets worse

It was not until relatively recently that an economist came along with a new way of thinking about this perplexing problem. Just as in the early part of the twentieth century Albert Einstein looked at the same old physics experiments with a fresh set of eyes, John Maynard Keynes offered the observation that, at times, a depression is not merely a troublingly persistent disequilibrium, but rather is a new type of equilibrium arising from markets that are too complex to be effectively coordinated, at least with the tools then at hand.[2]

Keynes' brilliant observation that the complex and fragile links between markets mean that they may not necessarily or quickly heal themselves was not well understood at first. Indeed, some are still reluctant to abandon their blind faith in the self-regulating ability of markets. To do so would beg the question – if markets cannot always coordinate themselves to avert panics, who or what can?

These recessions, depressions, and panics that so interested Keynes often began when consumption sneezed. As the sneeze infected related investment and production markets, and was retransmitted to and reinforced by the consumer once again, it was natural to ask how we might cure the economic illness. First, we can ask Consumer-Investors not to sneeze. But this is not sustainable because while I would appreciate it if you don't sneeze, I may not heed my own pronouncements. Do unto others as you would have them do unto you was replaced by anything goes, in the new and uncoordinated economy.

Failing the prevention of their involuntary economic response, we could then implore Producer-Investors to continue to invest in new plants and equipment, even in times of economic gloom. Of course, we would not be surprised if they do not heed our prescription. Their symptoms are real – in the form of mounting inventories and declining sales. Who would blame them for doing precisely the wrong thing? By laying off their workers for a few days or a few weeks, they are only doing what their Consumer-Investors stockholders would demand. But now with no income coming in, their worker-Consumer-Investors cut back on purchases, and the few days or few weeks lay-offs stretch out to a few months or a few years. Try to tell the Producer-Investors they did precisely the wrong thing.

We started with jobs lost by the Consumer-Investor inducing reduced spending destined for the Producer-Investor. This feeds into further lay-offs of the Consumer-Investor, and so forth. But we are missing one very important player. Remember government? – the entity that had invested in our human capital because producers, understandably, would not?

Few would claim that the government should collectively ride up on its white horse and show capitalists how to run the marketplace. And perhaps on the verge of a recession or depression, our skeptical guard would be up even higher over a perceived government intervention. So why would we seem to naturally turn to government at this, and only this, time? For one reason only – because we know that there is not a single other credible entity that has nearly the capacity, the taxpayer funded bankroll, or the bully pulpit to induce us to do the right thing.

Enter government

It is the Paradox of Thrift that the government is in the best position to solve. When times become uncertain, Consumer-Investors, representing 70% of all spending in our economy, respond to the uncertainty by becoming overly cautious. And this often-irrational fear creates a self-fulfilling prophecy. The paradox is that their thrift brings the economy down. What Consumer-Investors should do instead is accelerate spending, if only they felt they have any capacity to do so. But this would defy human nature. Of course, the Producer-Investors could also spend more. They too have the same human instincts of conserving in risky times though.

By taxing us in the past, present, or future, and ensuring that the tax revenue is spent right now, we can augment consumption, enhance spending, and get the train back on the track. An already astute reader might ask what the best form of spending might be, and this question is best left for a later chapter. What is important, though, is the necessity of a quick and effective shot in the economic arm, sufficient to give confidence to the Producer-Investors that would otherwise be swayed to lay off workers. An alternate strategy would be to temporarily absorb the laid-off workers in a temporary productive capacity, as our first Keynesian President, Franklin Roosevelt, did with the Works Progress Administration (WPA) and the Civilian Conservation Corps (CCC) the 1930s.

It is hard to accept that the optimal solution to this coordination failure should come from a government that capitalists would prefer to keep out of all other dimensions of their business. What we must understand, though, is that no one is arguing that government is the *best* entity to fix the coordination problem. Rather, it is the *only* entity with the credibility to pull off the coordination in this most peculiar and rare of times.

Once the market gets so far off kilter that a major intervention is required, we see the market can have some surprising bedfellows. It would be better if we identify tools to prevent the coordination failures in the first place, create diagnoses and better models that predict trouble before it arrives, and institutionalize the mechanisms that can circumvent market failures before they arise.

The remaining chapters look at the various factors and players that give rise to coordination failures, and the sometimes criminal, or at least unethical behaviors and self-interest that can generate millions for some but can cost the rest of us billions or trillions. We will also discuss the ways in which we can solve some of the market imperfections that give root to our greatest fears and worst economic panics.

As we share the story, we will try to focus on the factors that give rise to the problems, and the solutions that can give us some relief. The goal is to create an awareness of a healthy economy sometimes prone to a sneeze. If we recognize what is coming down the pike and we can face the challenge without overreacting and with a balanced response, we can tame the animal nature of the market. Of course, this requires a shared and rational outlook for our economy, and it requires an ability to put an economic virus into accurate perspective. In a complex economy it is true that many things can happen. The science tells us that. But, the art is to be able to focus on what is important and relevant, and to not let the virus spread unnecessarily.

I am assuming a certain level of detached interest on the part of the reader who is a spectator for now but a participant in our collective financial future. This detached interest is much easier if enough of our colleagues act the same way, and fewer try to profit from our attempt to do the right thing. All that is perhaps too much to expect. So, a well-educated government that is in the best position to protect us from ourselves will have to exercise economic leadership at critical times. Even the media can play an important role in keeping all the relevant factors in front of us without hyping those that can only distract us or make things worse. We must ask as much of our media, opinion makers, and leaders as we do our Economic Commanders in Chief.

Regardless of who is offering our economic leadership, it is important to acknowledge that complex economic interactions and coordinations will not suffer well from dogmatic or politically self-serving solutions. Just as a tax cut cannot possibly improve the economy in every imaginable state, complex and unique problems will typically require multifaceted and coordinated solutions.

Part II

Creation of the Consumer-Investor

The increasingly complex interactions between new market participants cast into disarray the economic model that the modern free market system had replaced. An emerging and economically significant middle class began to look for ways to receive a return on its investment. This simple innovation caused unimaginable problems and opportunities. And it required new economic institutions to cope with the new economic reality.

The next part describes these complications and their implications on financial markets and the economy.

4
The Anatomy of a Train Wreck

Let us next draw some parallels between the past and the present. The similarities between the Roaring Twenties and the 1990s are striking. Perhaps most striking is the dramatically increased pattern of stock market participation by the average Consumer-Investor.

Recall that consumer investment was the best game in town for the surpluses and wealth of the emerging middle class. These Consumer-Investors were different from those that came before them. The previous Producer-Investors typically chose to invest in an industry in which they knew – their own. But, the emerging middle class, with a hole burning in their pockets, needed some forum for investment that would return more than the 1% or so offered on savings.

Since time immemorial, Consumer-Investors could always invest in their home. And housing investment had the added benefit that it too tied the investment directly to production – of housing services. This has always been an economically significant form of investment – but it can only take you so far. Once everything has been done to our home that might make it more comfortable and a good investment, other investment opportunities must be found.

We could, of course, become Producer-Investors, but what do we know about production? Instead, we invest in the ownership of enterprises that are run by producers who do know something about production. As a consequence, the excess surpluses one earns as a middle class worker become increasingly channeled into the stock market. And as the Gross Domestic Product (GDP) of a nation grew, the Consumer-Investor workers earned larger surpluses to invest.

Today we all find ourselves to be Consumer-Investor traders. Defined contribution retirement plans that require you to specify the particular investment instruments have the same effect of fueling the demand for investment instruments. We will get to that later.

Investing on margin

The shear volume of surplus wealth created in the Roaring Twenties well outstripped the creation of new productive enterprises. As a consequence, this wealth was channeled into financial markets, with many more dollars chasing the few available investment vehicles. Banks too stepped in to help. Confident that the past is the best predictor of the future, lenders allowed the average (naïve) Consumer-Investor to borrow 50 cents of each dollar invested. The reasoning behind this was that investment values increase rather than decrease so it is safe to let Consumer-Investors borrow more when the economy seemed so certain.

This one-to-one leverage is paltry compared to the thirty-to-one leverage of modern hedge funds, or the even more dramatic zero-money-down lending common in the sub-prime mortgage industry in the 2000s.

These "margin" accounts that permitted Consumer-Investors to front only a fraction of their investment value allowed them to chase a limited number of investment vehicles with even more investment dollars. As with every instance of demand exceeding supply, the price (or the value of stocks and exchanges) rose dramatically. These price rises bore little relation to the return to investment from actual production, and instead reflected too much money chasing too few buying opportunities. As stock prices rose, but with earnings held constant, the effective return for new Consumer-Investors declined.

As a consequence of so much new money chasing so few investment opportunities, in the eight short years from 1921 to 1929, the United States stock market increased almost eight fold. This represented an average annual increase of about 40%, much greater than the single digit increase in the productive capacity of the economy. It became obvious to some (the smart money) that such increases were not sustainable, and something had to give. However, since future consumer-investment was based almost entirely on past success, few, if any, engaged in the enterprise of bringing the market down to earth – yet.

Stock valuation

Before we continue, let's discuss for a moment the correct level of valuation of a stock in the market. It is simpler to see this if we assume for the time being that an industry or enterprise is producing a constant flow of earnings, for the foreseeable future.

Ultimately, profits are reflected in earnings – the profit of a firm as measured by revenue minus costs, taxes, and so forth. Consumer-Investor stockholders are (roughly) entitled to their share of earnings each year. Of course, these earnings could be reinvested into the firm to realize even greater returns later. Let us assume for now, though, that these earnings are distributed among Consumer-Investor shareholder-owners. If a purchase of a 100 dollar stock yields a 5 dollar annual payment, this is equivalent to a 5% interest payment had they instead put their money in a savings account.

Another way of looking at this is to compare the price of the stock to its annual earnings – in this case $100/$5, or 20. In other words, the stock will pay for itself in earnings in 20 years. This is the familiar price/earnings (P/E) ratio often quoted when one discusses stocks. I think it is easier, though, to consider its reciprocal. The earnings/price ratio (simply the reciprocal of the P/E ratio) gives you a measure of the percent return you will accrue each year. In this case, the E/P ratio is 5%, which would be very attractive to a Consumer-Investor if the best they could earn in a bank account in the 1920s was a percent or two.

If the earnings/price ratio was favorable, when compared to the next best alternative, Consumer-Investors would continue to bid up the price P of the stock until the E/P ratio falls. The stock price will stop rising once the E/P ratio is in line with their next best alternative. If there were few or no good alternatives, the corresponding price/earnings ratio could rise substantially, to levels of 40:1, 100:1, or perhaps more.

The E/P ratio should roughly track alternative returns in the economy. For instance, if the prevailing interest rate in the economy is 5%, an E/P of 0.05, or a P/E of 20 on low risk stocks is appropriate. These P/E ratios are typically in the range of 15–25, but may spike to 40 or more during a speculative bubble.

Complicating matters is the expectation that earnings may actually grow in the future. Of course, it is unreasonable for Consumer-Investors to expect perpetual growth. However, it is reasonable to expect earnings for a promising new enterprise to grow at double-digit rates – so long as Consumer-Investors keep on consuming. Let us postulate a growth rate of a relatively modest 12%, perhaps because of consumers' willingness to pay more for a good product, improvements in technology decreased costs, and production was expanding to keep pace with increased consumer demand. A 12% growth in the earnings rate would double the annual earnings in just six years and, all else equal, also double the stock price because of the doubled earnings. As a consequence, an alternative measure calculates the price relative to earnings growth.

What if a Consumer-Investor's expected P/E ratio fell from a highly speculative and overvalued 100:1 ratio to a much more reasonable 10:1? Well, the value of the stock falls by 90%, which is what occurred to some stocks after the Crash of 1929. The speculative bubble popped, and many Consumer-Investors received only 10 cents on the dollar, or worse.

I say "or worse" because the Consumer-Investor also owed the banker in the process. Remember that 50 cents of every dollar invested was often borrowed on margin from banks or lenders who were very willing to front to the Consumer-Investor some of these investment dollars. We will discuss margin accounts in just a moment. In short, though, if a Consumer-Investor put up 100 dollars for a stock, of which 50 dollars were borrowed, and this stock fell in value to 10 dollars, the Consumer-Investor has lost all of his or her 50 dollar investment, and also owes the bank another 40 dollars. It is not hard to understand why so much middle class wealth was wiped out – with the Consumer-Investor owing the bank to boot. Imagine what effect that would have on consumer spending. A major depression was almost unavoidable.

Taken in isolation and one assumption at a time, none of this irrational exuberance appears inappropriate or excessive. If past success was the best indicator of future success, and if continued growth of valuations kept this pyramid scheme going, the Consumer-Investor, in isolation, appeared quite rational. And this good news caught on, until it seemed that almost every consumer became a Consumer-Investor.

It's a wonderful life

One of my favorite movies to illustrate the impending train wreck is *It's a Wonderful Life*. Imagine these well-intentioned local bankers "helping out" the local Consumer-Investors to realize their housing investment dreams. Careful and conservative bankers representing the interests of careful and conservative Consumer-Investors were the hens to the "smart money" trader-foxes in the proverbial hen house.

There is always "smart money." These are the sophisticated traders that know the market trends before they are broadcast to the rest of us. They are able to buy before prices rise, and sell before prices fall. They can profit from any market movement, and they invariably gain from those market movements. Today as often as not, these smart traders are "hedge funds" (much more on that later), and they manage to capitalize by figuring out trends, or sometimes even creating trends, before the rest of us do.

Remember that prices are determined by the transactions between a willing buyer and a willing seller. Even a dramatically declining market, like the one on Black Tuesday, October 24, 1929, requires an equal number of buyers and sellers. So, there are always Consumer-Investors and Trader-Investors who think they can capitalize on any market movement. And usually the "smart money" Trader-Investors are on the winning side of the transactions. Some made a killing when the market went up, and made a killing when the market went down.

Can these sudden and profound wealth effects somehow affect consumption so dramatically to induce a depression? A chosen few were making a killing – no matter which way the market went. But, these are the tiny minority whose wealth expanded dramatically, and whose consumption, perhaps, expanded marginally. While we might expect a few members of "smart money" to consume more, this dramatically expanded middle class of Consumer-Investors were suffering a lot, and consuming much less.

If consumption represents 70% of the total spending in the economy, and if we experience spectacular growth today when consumption rises by only perhaps 4%, imagine the consequences of millions of Consumer-Investors who lost almost everything they had, and were chased by banks holding margin account IOUs for their remaining assets. Dramatically depressed consumption and a depression were inevitable.

There are a lot of links in this chain that translated an albeit dramatic paper loss in the stock market to the creation of a major and prolonged depression. We have already discussed how the separation of Consumer-Investors and Producer-Investors could create the coordination failure that induces a depression. The more helpful question to ask is what we could have done to prevent this calamitous sequence of events. The answer is – not much.

Are we rational?

Our financial system is based on rationality. Careful and calculating investors pore over financial statements and business plans, and make educated bets on the profitability of the company. If the price of the share is low compared to the earnings accruing to each share outstanding, investors buy the stock until the increasing price they must offer usurps any bargain to be had. Such analyzes based on the fundamental value of the firm and its stock do not change quickly. The competitive climate, overall demand for their product, and their cost structure should slowly evolve to influence the stock price.

The analysis used in these finance models is completely rational. Unfortunately, human beings are not. While the rational investor should make investment decisions with the detachment of a green-shaded accountant, the market is decidedly human. The best analogy is that a rational trader is interacting with a market that is bipolar. Some days the market is in a good and optimistic mood, and stock market prices rise accordingly. On other days, the market is upset, depressed, and pessimistic, and stock market prices fall, regardless of the fact that the fundamentals of the market have gone unchanged. The rational trader makes a handsome profit by buying stocks from the pessimistic and depressed trader, and selling the stock back when the trader is happy and optimistic.

Sometimes, the market can get downright giddy and can rise dramatically, even in a day. For instance, the New York Stock Exchange has risen 5% in a single day 52 times since 1928. However, slightly more often, the market has been very upset, and has shed 5% in a single day 61 times since 1928. Unfortunately, the bipolar tendencies are not symmetric. Panicky lows outnumber exuberant highs.

Perhaps the market thrives on such drama. It is said by some who suffer from bipolar disorder that they'd prefer the highs and lows compared to the even moods created through medication. Certainly the "smart money" short-term trader who has learned how to make money in any market mood actually profits from the volatility. I will argue later that they may even fuel volatility to create profit opportunities for themselves.

Economic theory can actually explain the desperation that can set in from severe stock market losses. It is not unreasonable to assume that a thousand dollars would be more significant to a poor person than a millionaire. Let's assume you started with 500,000 dollars and I offered you a wager to flip a coin, double or nothing. Certainly if you won the bet and became an instant millionaire and I offered to give you an additional 1,000 dollars, you would take the 1,000 dollars but would not value it so dearly. On the other hand, if you lost the bet and everything you had, and I again offered you 1,000 dollars, you would certainly value the 1,000 dollars gift much more highly. How we value an extra dollar depends on how many we have.

We could do the same experiment with any equal gain or loss. Changes in wealth will always be significant if you have less. From this we can conclude that the pain from a loss (and hence perhaps the desperation to avoid the pain) is always more intense than the glee from a gain. It is precisely this intensity of loss that creates the very human emotional response to losses in the market. When such losses occur, people get desperate and try to cut their losses by liquidating their investment, perhaps even at fire sale prices. This is when the smart money steps in and takes away any further potential pain, for a fee.

As the data confirms, the market is almost as likely to go up as it is to go down. A rational long-term strategy would be to hold an investment until the market bounces back. But the knowledge that the market will bounce back seems fleeting when you are worried and scared that you may lose more. And this emotional response by a good number of Consumer-Investors in the red causes further selling and price drops, reassuring the Consumer-Investor that selling, indeed, appears to be the right thing. Downside emotions trump rationality. These emotions may not stop there. For some, the very loss can induce even greater investments in an attempt to salvage the loss, resulting in good money following bad.

Emotional trading also works to create irrational exuberance. When the market rises high, everybody wants a piece of the action, and wants on the bandwagon. These Johnny-come-lately investors push the value of the market up even further until the price rises substantially more than that dictated by market fundamentals.

There is plenty of evidence to support the emotional trader hypothesis. We must only observe the behavior of gamblers. Without a doubt, gambling is always a losing proposition on average over time. Even the most generous casino-style gambles return only 97 cents for every dollar invested (or gambled?). The three cents is the cut that ensures the gambling house will always make out fine in the long run. Lotteries have even worse odds, with only 60% to 80% returned to the purchasers of tickets. Gambling trades on hope rather than rationality. Many lottery buyers believe they are ahead, or not nearly so far behind, as the data would suggest. However, lose they do.

This example is not to say that the stock market is a gamble. Indeed, the stock market gains on average over time, unlike the built-in loss from most forms of gambling. Instead, the example demonstrates that the stock market can tap the same emotional response that causes some to lose all they have in gambling binges.

Is it safe out there?

Is there a way to protect ourselves from our own animal spirits? Let's get back to fundamentals, and at the same time understand what makes a winning baseball team.

Baseball is a game of statistics. Lately the game has become the science of statistics, with one of the most winning teams in the last few years demonstrating a mastery of this science. The game is unique in that a season is 162 games long, at least 1,458 innings long, and representing many more than 4,374 at-bats. These are large numbers, meaning that the game is dictated not by the long shot big play but rather by the huge gains to be had if our odds for success can be improved even a small amount in each of those 4,374 at-bats. This explains why a batting average is measured to the third decimal point. A team that collectively strikes out 70 times out of each 100 at-bats is a significantly better batting team than one that strikes out 72 times out of every 100 at-bats. Small improvements totaled over thousands of opportunities yields significant advantages.

The Boston Red Sox have created a science out of the accurate measurement and calculation of baseball fundamentals. Evaluation of players is based on their traditional measures of performance but also on more subtle measures such as their contribution to the success of others. Baseball managers understand the odds and make decisions based on these odds. While the statistics may not work out so well in any given game, the approach is shown to be sound over many games.

This focus on fundamental values is also the basis for rational investment. In the long run, it is fair to assume that over-valued markets and under-valued markets will both converge to the appropriate valuation over time. How long such overshooting or undershooting will take is an open question. Your success is improved though if you hold a sufficiently large number of stocks a sufficiently long time.

Fundamentals analysis determines the underlying profitability (in terms of earnings per share – EPS) and calculates the price of the equity in relation to the earnings per share (price/earnings ratio P/E). The stock's annual earning compared to the price is reasonable if it yields a return at least equal to the return on a safe investment, plus the increment to the return that would compensate an investor for the relative risk of the investment. Fundamentals investors buy stocks that are under-priced based on this approach, and sell stocks that become overpriced.

This approach can be modified to take into account the expected growth of earnings over time, or can compare a stock in a particular sector with other similar sector stocks to see if it is undervalued or overvalued in terms of the price/earnings ratio, compared with other stocks in the sector. Adhering to this strategy will produce better than average returns over time if the trader can avoid the impulses that arise as the market fluctuates as a response to emotional investing.

The science of risk and return is quite well developed. Economists and financiers can compare the return of a stock with the variations in its price that is not attributed to general market risk. A high-risk security must command a high return. If a stock has a return higher than that justified by its risk, its price will rise. A type of analysis called the

Capital Asset Pricing Model (CAPM, pronounced cap-em) can be used to determine the appropriate return for a given level of risk. Any excess return is called "alpha," and is a signal to investors "seeking alpha" or searching for perhaps risky assets that remain under-priced.

Of course, another strategy is to instead make investment decisions based on the trends in the marketplace, fueled by market emotion and sentiment rather than the underlying fundamental profitability of publicly traded companies. This alternate approach, called technical analysis, looks for price trends. An underlying premise of the theory is that stocks tend to revert to a normal trading range over time. If a stock remains higher than a historical price for a certain period of time, one can argue that it will likely decline toward a lower long run value, rather than increasing further.

Alternately, a stock beaten down for a significant period in time is more likely to rise toward its traditional value. This trading scheme explicitly creates rules to take advantage of the behaviors observed when herd mentalities drive the marketplace. While such an approach no doubt works sometimes, it is unlikely that it will work all the time. And it assumes, perhaps even requires, that emotional market sentiment is the driving force for investment opportunities.

Some of these Johnny-come-lately investment strategies are fueled by the margin accounts we mentioned earlier. In the next chapter, we will see how margin trading can back a trader into a hole, and force Consumer-Investors to lock in their losses as lenders protect themselves.

5

Get Your Money for Nothing and Your Kicks for Free

Financial markets have become much more volatile of late because of one looming and growing factor – debt. More specifically, the debt that is used to finance Consumer-Investor securities purchases has created fantastic profits and spectacular failures. And the fantastic debt tapped by hedge funds, sometimes 30 times their own equity investment, ups the ante even more. This debt gone wrong taps into one of our most basic human instincts – the fear of loss.

A margin account is a valuable financial instrument that merely extends to the market a commonly used financial tool. When you buy a house, a bank is willing to lend you 80 cents or more on the dollar, knowing that your house is good collateral for the loan. If things go badly (but not too badly), the lender can always sell your home to recover the money they lent you – so long as the price of your home has not dropped more than 20% since the purchase.

This investment is nicely collateralized because housing prices almost never drop. As a matter of fact, 2007 was the first year exhibiting a drop in the price of United States housing since the Great Depression. Peril in the US housing market quickly spread to the United Kingdom, and spun off around the world. Nonetheless, banks typically consider mortgage lending relatively safe. We will look at the phenomenon of mortgages, collateral, and housing price changes later. In the meantime, let us apply this same principle to the stock market.

A margin account is simply a mortgage on a different type of property. If you buy 100 dollars of stock and let the brokerage house use that stock as collateral for a loan, you can borrow another 100 dollars to buy additional stock. Your initial cash investment of 100 dollars plus the collateralized loan of 100 dollars permits you to buy 200 dollars of stock. This is quite attractive because a 10% increase in the value of the stock will now net you 20 dollars, all from the initial cash investment of 100 dollars. In effect, the return on your initial investment is now double – 20% rather than 10%.

Of course, the brokerage firm does not lend you the money for nothing. But, so long as the rate of return on the stock is higher than the interest rate on the borrowed money, the investor is still ahead. Indeed, as the price of the stock rises, the value of the collateral rises, and you can purchase even more stock.

Regulations prevent this innovation from getting out of hand. Of course, if you could buy a house with little or no money down, the bank assumes almost all the risk. But, while house prices consistently rise, stocks fall almost as often as they rise. This imposes dangerous risk on brokers or others that would lend you money to buy stocks.

Worse yet, with nothing at risk yourself, you are more likely to behave irresponsibly. Bankers, insurers, and regulatory agencies well understand the problem of moral hazard. This is the unfortunate response of human decision making when someone else has to cover the downside risk. By regulating the amount of stock collateral one can use to buy additional stock, regulators ensure that investors are risking their own investment.

The most obvious risk is leverage risk. In the two weeks ending October 19, 1987, the stock market fell by more than a third. If you had 100 dollars invested, you would have lost 34 dollars. However, if you had 100 dollars of your own money invested and 100 dollars borrowed, you would have lost 67 dollars. Your equity has been cut by two-thirds. If you had borrowed 200 dollars on the basis of your 100 dollars of collateral, you would have lost everything.

Leverage risk can have profound effects in very short periods of time. Of course, these effects can also be positive. A 33% rise in the market would allow you to double your investment if your initial equity was 100 dollars and your margin purchase was another 200 dollars. Unfortunately, looking back over 80 years of data for large daily market swings, there has been one plunge in excess of 20%, but no daily rise of that magnitude.

Enter the regulators

The Federal Reserve and other central banks, the Securities and Exchange Commission, the US Treasury, and bourses worldwide agree that we must be protected from ourselves by limiting the initial marginable amount to 50% for most stocks. In effect, at least half of the equity must be your own. This is known in the United States as Regulation T. However, the Federal Reserve relaxes the equity requirement following your initial purchase. If it did not, and the stock you purchased immediately declined, you would have violated the regulation.

Subsequently, the brokerage houses subsequently require you to maintain a much lower share of equity. This "maintenance requirement" is typically around 30% for stocks, but varies depending on the inherent risk of other types of securities. This means that investors can lose about half of their investment before they run up against a "margin call."

Margins permit much greater amounts of cash to be sloshing around the market. A greater supply of cash chasing a fixed number of stocks will increase stock prices. In turn, these higher stock prices create additional collateral and act as a basis for additional margin loans. There is even more cash chasing the same number of stocks, driving up prices still further. You may recognize this as a classic positive feedback mechanism. It drove the market in the Roaring Twenties to new heights, and is responsible for some of the speculative bubble in the 1990s.

Let's look at a rather stark example. We make a 200 dollars purchase, 100 dollars with cash and 100 dollars on margin. The stock doubles to 400 dollars, meaning we now have 300 dollars of equity and 100 dollars borrowed. We can use this as an opportunity to borrow another 200 dollars on margin while still meeting Regulation T, resulting in a portfolio value of 600 dollars, 300 dollars in equity and 300 dollars on margin. Next the stock halves to its original value. This will completely wipe out all our equity, even though the stock is at the same price it was when we invested 100 dollars in cash. Worse yet, we owe interest on the margin loan.

As you can see, margins can be risky. Even if you don't invest on margin, you are still affected by the practice if your investments, too, are caught up in a speculative bubble.

The example shows that margins can fuel market growth as more money chases the same number of stocks. Can margins also fuel a market decline?

The phenomenon of margin calls depressing the market is very real. Consider your investment in a mutual fund that has been rising steadily over time. With each increase, you can take out another margin loan to expand your portfolio. Your equity continually rises as does your margin borrowing. Of course you know that part of this growth is fueled solely by the increased liquidity that increasing margin borrowing provides. Everything is going fine – so far.

It is considered healthy for markets to occasionally go through a "correction." You can think of this correction as a return to reality, bringing stock prices more in line with the fundamental values they may have overshot. Some argue that this occasional rest will allow the market to regroup, to subsequently rise still further.

As markets correct, it is difficult to time just when to get out on top, and when to get back in before the market begins to rise again. And we all know that stocks are best viewed as a long run investment. So you try to "ride it out." The depths of the falls hurt, especially given the leverage risk described earlier. When the market comes back, this pain will show itself to be temporary.

This all too common scenario becomes dangerous once the market or fund drops a bit too much. At that point, margin calls are issued, forcing investors to immediately sell stock at the market price. If Consumer-Investors do not sell sufficient stock to meet the house requirement, the brokerage house will sell the stock on their behalf to protect its margin loan.

This wave of selling in a declining market can cause a secondary fall. And the secondary fall can induce even more margin calls, causing the market to fall still further. Such margin-initiated secondary declines are becoming more and more common as margins begin to be used by less sophisticated investors.

A financial life cycle

Investors generally follow a financial life cycle. Such life cycle models recognize that a young person embarking upon a career often has negative financial capital because they are often saddled with student loans and do not yet have home equity. Of course, young people have a good bank of human capital, accumulated through education. Those early in the life cycle rent out their human capital and even augment it through work experience.

Young people rapidly gain experience, and their education has yet to depreciate significantly. At some point during their career, unless they engage in lifelong learning and keep up with innovations, human capital depreciation eventually out-swamps the appreciation from additional experience.

It would be ideal if we could sell our human capital rather than simply rent it out. Let's assume an employee and employer could contract for a lifetime of employment services, in exchange for a large signing bonus and an annual salary. This agreement would suffer from moral hazard. You are protected from downside risk because you received the payment in advance. You would no longer be concerned about investing in lifelong learning. Nor would you be willing to invest the time in free education because the effort still costs you your time and the education provides you with no additional return.

If you are prohibited from selling your lifetime human capital, your compensation is typically least when you are just embarking on your career, at the very time when a conversion of your human capital to financial capital would be most profitable for you. Salaries at first are barely sufficient to meet the needs of student loans, a young family, and housing costs. As a consequence, financial capital investment is small. However, the lifelong return to early financial investment is substantial because returns have a lifetime to do their compounding magic.

These young would-be investors cannot take advantage of early investment because they are liquidity constrained though. Imagine the returns if earnings from year forty of a career could be transferred to the first year, providing discretionary investment income in the first year of one's career.

Let's ignore inflation by assuming a real (inflation adjusted) return of about 7%. A 100,000 dollar transfer of income from career year 40 to year one and invested at the modest return of 7% would be worth approximately 1.6 million dollars by year 40. This calculation takes advantage of the "Rule of 72." This rule states that 72 divided by the growth rate gives the number of years it will take the activity to double. In this case, a 7% earnings growth rate, equivalent to 10% nominal growth, depreciated by a 3% inflation rate, will double our investment in about 10 years. Forty years of growth will increase our investment to 200,000 dollars by year ten, 400,000 dollars by year twenty, 800,000 dollars by year thirty, and 1,600,000 dollars by year forty. Unfortunately, young Consumer-Investors have the best opportunity to benefit from compounding at the point of their career that they are most capital constrained.

This example shows that the liquidity constraint of productive workers reduces lifetime earnings. Interestingly, some institutions such as signing bonuses or home purchase down payment allowances that arise in competitive labor markets at least partially offset this constraint. However, any institution that could relax this liquidity constraint will permit greater income over the entire life cycle. As our example shows, a year of income invested in year one is equivalent to 16 years of salary by year forty.

The encouragement of the use of margin accounts for young Consumer-Investors, that have the substantial investment horizon to ride out market fluctuations, can produce tangible benefits. Society also produces other incentives to create liquidity for young people. Student loans are deductible until their income rises too much, and the marginal tax rate is lower commensurate with their lower income. However, these incentives are unlikely to be sufficient to create the discretionary investment funds that could allow young people to take advantage of a lifetime of compounding interest.

Diversification

Before we leave this topic, let us for a moment discuss the role of a long investment time horizon in the diversification of investment risk. Financial planners suggest that one's share of investment in stocks should be 110 minus your age. According to this commonly applied formula, a twenty-year-old should hold 90% of their investment portfolio in stock, while a sixty-year-old should hold 50% in stock.

We can use a simple example to demonstrate this. Let's assume the return jumps by plus or minus one percentage point, with equal likelihood. Over a one-year period, the return could be a point higher or a point lower. Over two years, the return would be a point higher with a probability of one quarter, a point lower with a probability of one quarter, and the two jumps would cancel out with a probability of one half. This trend continues, resulting in a much more certain return on average as the average return is spread over many years.

Many financial planners take this example to conclude that longer planning horizons reduces risk. Let's assume there is a financial calamity, perhaps arising from aggressive margining as described earlier, that wipes out our entire investment. Such a calamity would do far less damage in the first year of one's career than in the last.

More correctly, younger investors can accommodate more risk because they have a longer time to recover from an investment gone bad. In addition, young people have a greater stock of a very certain asset, their human capital, when compared with one nearing retirement. As a consequence, young investors can balance their safe human capital asset with a riskier asset, while one nearing retirement should balance safer assets such as bonds with riskier assets such as stocks.

A life cycle of risk

One other factor that can frustrate financial capital accumulation by young people is their higher rate of time preference. Just like asset accumulation rates, the rate that people discount the future changes through the stages of their life. We all have seen the teenager's sense of immortality. This is because the exuberance of youth has yet to be tempered with the brushes of mortality that comes with age and experience. If one assumes that tomorrow will always be as today was, there is no reason to dwell on the future or to sacrifice today to provide for tomorrow.

This logic is one rationale for public education. Even if children could afford their own education, they would likely prefer to devote their resources to other pursuits. And yet we know they benefit from education (as do we), so we provide it to them. But, once individuals contemplate raising a family, they attain a point in their life at which they discount the future the least, and are willing to provide for the future at the greatest rate. Unfortunately, the very nature of family formation makes early career saving almost impossible. This phenomenon is illustrated in Figure 5.1.

The savings rate as a share of income starts low, peaks in middle age, and begins to decline as retirement nears. The actual level of savings and wealth increases steadily over the life cycle because the savings compound over their life cycle. As retirement begins, the rate of saving as a share of salary income falls to zero and yet the level of savings is at its peak. With optimal financial planning, a retiree can adjust consumption so that the level of savings falls to zero when an individual passes on. However, because we don't know when we will pass on, retirees will typically consume at a level that causes only modest decreases in wealth over time.

Much of what we discussed is premised on an equal number of people at each level of the life cycle and does not take into account economic growth. In the next chapter we look at global demographics, varying stages of economic growth, and the effects of global investment.

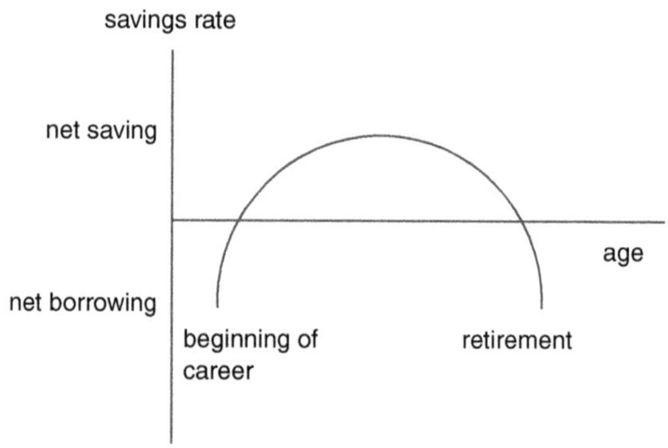

Figure 5.1 The pattern of savings over a life cycle

6
The World Threw a Party

Modern financial markets were a European Renaissance innovation. The merchants of Venice had been trading in various securities in the thirteenth century, and the Dutch East Indies Company began issuing stock in the seventeenth century. Indeed, the wealth from banking and trade allowed these Merchants of Venice, must notably the Medici family, to patronize the arts and sciences in the Renaissance. Soon thereafter, the Dutch created a market that resembles the modern stock exchange in many significant ways.

All these markets were designed to serve a few purposes that were critical for economic development. Markets allowed for more liquidity by providing forums to trade stock and, hence, reduce some of the risk of holding stock. This also permitted a lower cost of capital by providing Consumer-Investors with liquidity if they would like to change investments.

The industry of high finance did not develop until relatively recently. As the dominant economy in the twentieth century, it was natural that US markets were the most active, well developed, and innovative. The stock exchanges in the US collectively listed stocks valued at more than the next nine country's exchanges combined. The tools that created these large US exchanges are now easy to replicate elsewhere, and with the growth of commerce in Europe and Asia, other nation's exchanges have grown rapidly both in volume and sophistication. As a consequence, the traditional role of US markets as the center for global capital formation is no longer as significant.

This transformation and globalization of national exchanges reflects a pattern of economic growth that has great implications for the future of global economics. If we are to understand how the US economy became the predominant economy of the world, how Europe is increasingly assuming a leadership role, and what we might expect from emerging economic superpowers, we need to understand two phenomena. The first is the pattern of economic growth as a country develops. The second is the shift in world population and demographic patterns, and what this might portend by the middle of this century.

The modern cycle of economic growth

When the United States began as a nation, it did not languish for long in a protracted period of stagnant economic growth. It was the first nation formed as an economic premise, with life, liberty, and the pursuit of happiness at its base. To guarantee this premise, the US Constitution and its amendments enshrined property rights, and in doing so, enshrined the individual as the basic economic unit.

Of course, much of this emphasis on the propertied individual was a backlash from the British system of royalty and peerage that so frustrated early American settlers. But, by creating a strong set of property rights early on, the early revolutionaries also created a system that was perfectly suited for rapid economic growth.

The importance of well-enshrined property rights is absolutely essential for strong economic development, at least in the Western sense. Perhaps for some, the debate still rages regarding the ability of a capitalist system to thrive compared to a communist system. The capitalist system is based on private property, taking for granted that few would create new property unless they could keep the fruits of their development efforts.

The communist system instead is based on the notion of communal ownership of property, with the commune sharing the fruits of their collective effort. Unfortunately for the communist model, human nature seems better suited for production that remains with the individual, the family, or the small group. As the group gets larger, shirking becomes easier, and the immediate incentives of production for the common good seem to break down. As a consequence, it is relatively commonly accepted that development is most rapid when individual property rights are fully, or at least partially, protected.

Efficiency over equity

We should not confuse the efficiencies of creating rapid economic growth with the inequalities arising in a rapidly developing nation. An economist named Simon Kuznets observed that as income per capita initially rises with economic development, income inequalities also increase, to a point.[1] The intuition is that economic development does not occur evenly across the population. It is initially driven by entrepreneurs who own physical capital (machines, factories, etc.) and hire labor and other factors of production to produce more efficiently and in greater quantity than before.

This innovation of owners of physical capital dictating the path of economic development, combined with new forms of power, gave rise to the Industrial Revolution. This spurred first the dramatic expansion of the British Empire, and then the emergence of the United States as an economic superpower.

While we now attribute this system, now called capitalism, as the engine of economic development, it could not have succeeded without ownership of property. It is this right of entrepreneurs to keep the rewards of their ingenuity that conferred upon them great fortunes. And it is the neglect of the other critical component, the working class, which in turn created government and demanded some redistribution of the great rewards of a capitalist society.

As Kuznets notes,[2] the establishment of property rights, and the development of so much low hanging economic fruit once economic institutions are created, allows rapid economic expansion and growing economic inequality. This rapid economic growth for developing economies is typically double digit, ranging from 10% to 20% annually. Enlightened capitalists realize that some of these rewards need to return to the working class, that essential component of the economic engine.

The development cycle

As more wealth is created, and more join the working class, the growing urban population demanded a much stronger form of government to balance the growing power of industrialists. Modern government had as its base the citizen rather than the aristocracy, giving rise to a second revolution – the revolution of democracy.

Democracy, in combination with a stronger government, created the most effective tools for redressing income inequality. Taxation and education are the great levelers that are only possible once there is a sufficient wealth to redistribute. This secondary revolution of government permits further economic growth that allows a country to maintain double-digit expansion for a longer period of time.

Much of this rapid expansion comes through the unsustainable consumption of some finite resources. Developing nations working to join the family of developed nations will expand at the expense of the environment and perhaps without the same concern for worker health and safety.

As inequalities are redressed and a middle class emerges, citizens begin to appreciate and then demand environmental and health and safety standards. These interests are labeled luxury goods – we value them only once our basic needs are met. Environmental and other sensitivities are not the antithesis of economic development – rather they are its consequence. At the point where income has risen, inequalities have been redressed, and citizens have sufficient resources to take care of their basic needs, they begin demanding more free time and other environmental amenities.

When this occurs, economic development levels off to sustainable levels, and growth approximates the sum of population growth and the technological growth arising from new inventions, innovations, and processes. Real economic growth falls to a range of 2–4%, driven in equal measure by productivity improvements and net in-migration. Indeed, the role of in-migration becomes quite important because one of the consequences of greater affluence is a dramatically reduced rate of family formation. The pattern of growth is shown in Figure 6.1:

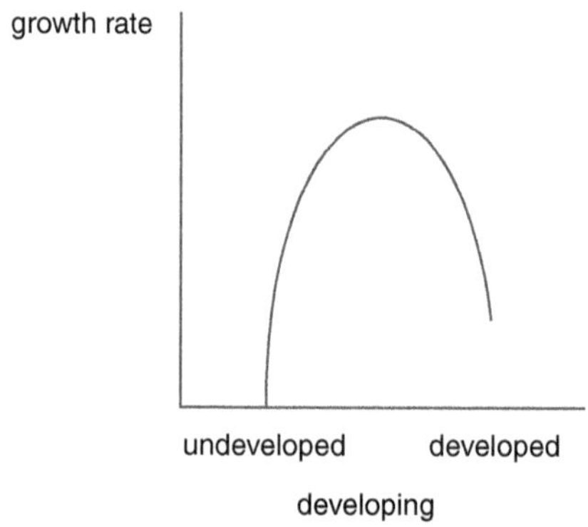

Figure 6.1 Growth rates at various stages of development

Brave new economic worlds

This process of spectacular early growth, followed by lower, but steady growth as the economy matures, is common in world economies. It is simply a corollary of the law of diminishing returns. The scale of an economic activity can increase easily at first, but subsequently becomes more difficult as good opportunities become fewer and farther between. The pattern observed everywhere demonstrates that the future of a well-developed nation rests almost solely with its ability to innovate economically.

Especially today when innovations can so easily be imitated, nations retain economic leadership only through constant invention and investment in education, research, and development of new products and technologies. In the next chapter we will discuss the false reliance of growth on financial innovation. In the meantime, let us explore the path of economic development worldwide as the lessons from the First Economic World are learned by the Second and Third Economic Worlds.

This notion of First, Second, and Third Worlds is a throwback to the Cold War. The First World was the set of capitalist countries aligned with the United States. The Second World was the family of countries aligned with the former Soviet Union, broadly labeled communist. The Third World consisted of nations unaligned with the other two. However, in an era when most of the Second World now practices the capitalist rather than the communist economic model, it is more instructive to view the world in economic terms. We can define the First Economic World (FEW) as those countries that have moved to the modest growth to the right-hand side of the Kuznets' Curve, with well-developed financial markets, the maintenance of property rights, and improving income distribution. The Second Economic World (SEW) consists of those nations experiencing rapid economic growth fueled by the establishment of property rights, fledgling, if economically immature, financial markets, and imitation of First World innovations. The Third Economic World (TEW) is still wrestling with the creation of trustworthy government, reliable and enforceable property rights, and the confidence of the First and Second Worlds in their eventual creation of markets. And all economics now wrestle with differing demographics.

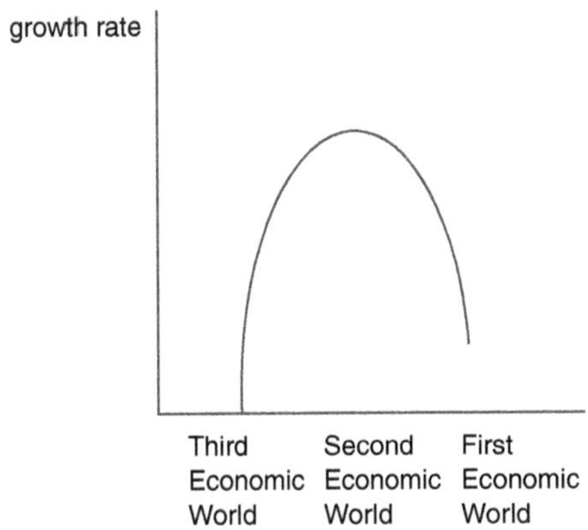

Figure 6.2 Economic growth in the First, Second, and Third Economic World

A changing demographic

In our analysis of global demographics, we can begin with a couple of observations. First, while Third Economic World development depends on the growth of a healthy and educated working class, they do not have sufficient wealth creation to provide for the needs of a growing population. At the same time, the First Economic World chooses slow or often negative domestic population growth, with net population growth usually arising through immigration from Second Economic World nations. It is this immigration from the Second to the First Economic World that hastens the ability of developing nations to imitate the economies of the developed nations, while at the same time allows the First Economic World to continue to grow even as they are beyond the peak of the Kuznets' Curve.

Let us ignore for now the movement of populations from the First to the Second Worlds. Let us also acknowledge that the Third Economic World cannot contribute to the growth of the global economy until they can establish the property rights and good government so necessary for economic development. Most all of the action then occurs in the relative growth of the population and the economies in the Second Economic World.

Let us look at population patterns arranged roughly along the lines of North America and Europe, Asia and South America, and Africa over the past couple of centuries. These divisions are roughly aligned along the lines of the First, Second, and Third Economic Worlds. We then look at the patterns that are likely to emerge over the next fifty years. In doing so, we will see we are at a tipping point in global economic power. This will have tremendous ramifications on the balance of political power that tends to follow economic power, the flow of global investment funds, and the valuation of global stock markets.

It will also have ramifications on the volatility of global economic markets, the level of booms, busts, and panics as new investors are brought into global financial markets. And it strains commodity markets as they fuel economies in the unsustainable stage of development. These subtleties will be discussed in later chapters.

Before we analyze the population projections, I am reminded of the prophecy of the eighteenth century economist Thomas Malthus. He started a panic by predicting that the geometric growth of population would outstrip the arithmetic growth of food supply by the middle of the nineteenth century.[3] While his dismal prophecy did not materialize because he failed to acknowledge the rate of change of family formation or the vast improvements in agricultural technologies, he nonetheless induced the populace to name economics "the dismal science." This label has stuck ever since, despite the jubilant and expressive personalities of economists.

The United Nations Population Division publishes perhaps the most generally accepted analysis of world population patterns.[4] In a recent report, they provided the following estimates of world populations since the beginning of the industrial revolutions of the First Economic Worlds (see Table 6.1).

The following Figure 6.3 starkly shows the dramatic and uneven growth between the First, Second, and Third Economic Worlds to the year 2150. It illustrates that population steadily grew in the First and Second Economic Worlds throughout the Industrial Revolution until 1950, while the population in Africa remained comparatively flat. However, in the post-World War II period, the populations in North

Table 6.1 World population (in millions) 1750–2150

Region	Year: 1750	1800	1850	1900	1950	1999	2050	2150
World	791	978	1,262	1,650	2,521	5,978	8,909	9,746
North America, Europe, Oceania	167	212	314	496	732	1,066	1,066	966
Asia, South and Central America	518	659	847	1,021	1,569	4,145	6,077	6,473
Africa	106	107	111	133	220	767	1,766	2,307

Source: As projected by the United Nations Population Division.

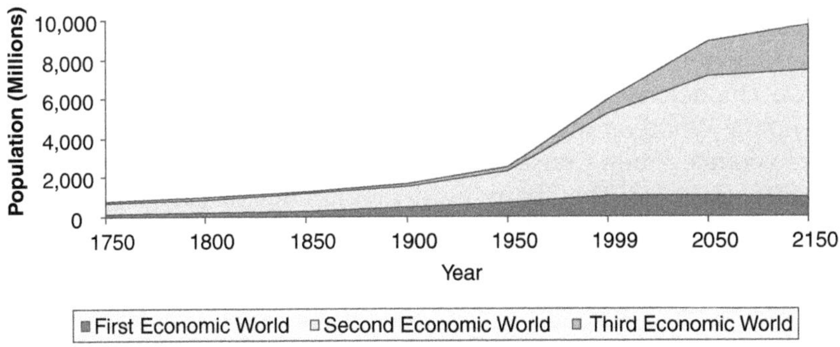

Figure 6.3 Population growth in three Economic Worlds

America and Europe fell flat, while the populations in the developing and undeveloped countries began to grow dramatically, especially in the Second Economic World. Beyond 2050, projections suggest that populations in the Second Economic World begins to flatten as they join the First Economic World, and advances in economic development allow the Third Economic World to assume the role of developing nations.

Convergence

Before we look at the role of demographics on this picture, we can immediately see important ramifications for global economies. Most dramatically, we see that the First and Second Economic Worlds are converging. The rapid economic development of Asia and Central/South America, and the spread of technologies from the FEW to the SEW nations mean that the world is dividing into just two categories by the year 2050.

These categories certainly include a dramatically enlarged family of developed nations by the middle of the century, constituting four fifths of the world's population. This family of developed nations will no longer be dominated by North America and Europe. This convergence means a full 85% of the population of the converged First Economic World will live in Asia, with China and India representing the two world's largest economies.

The wildcard will be the pace of development in the undeveloped world. Africa will develop either through technology transfer or through resource extraction, to fuel the production and consumption of the dramatically enlarged family of developed nations. This development future will, of course, require the nations to overcome the challenges of the creation of stable government and the establishment of property rights. Even in the absence of these innovations, commodity-based economies can be developed, as we see with oil extraction in Nigeria, but often potentially at terrible human cost as tremendous income inequalities arise.

Two characteristics will dictate the effects of the transformed First Economic World on world financial markets. The changing profile and risk tolerance of new Consumer-Investors will be treated in a subsequent chapter. However, the changing demographics of these nations will have profound effects on localized and global financial markets.

An aging demographic

The current First Economic World is aging. We will spend much more time on this later because the aging population will have profound effects on inflows and outflows in global financial markets. However, the nations and continents that are joining the First Economic World are young. Not unlike the talent fueling the United States and European economies, the young people in these emerging nations are rich in human capital. As these economies mature, they will follow the cross section of human capital found in developed countries. In the meantime though, the countries of India and China in particular will have a level of wealth concentrated more in the young adult cohorts than has ever been seen before.

There are a number of consequences of this wealth creation in a youthful class. The first is the effect on domestic politics. Never before have major economies or major countries been driven by the economic power of those under the age of forty. It is incumbent on governments to address the unique concerns of a demographic in their population that has very different needs than the other cohorts.

Issues of property, financial freedom, education, and mobility must be addressed. Political institutions must empower the youthful professionals, and recognize the need to provide the infrastructure and institutions that this class demands. Urbanization, safe streets, broadband Internet access, telecommunications, opportunities for economic advancement, and freedom of the press, are all values that are critical for these young professionals.

The second effect will be on property values. Once property rights are well established, young professionals will demand housing not unlike the expectation of young families in the FEW countries. We discussed earlier that financial capital formation is difficult for those in the first half of their adult life cycle. This is because most of their wealth is devoted to housing costs and consumption. While a large share of their wealth will dramatically raise local real estate values in China and India, this increase in housing demand creates secondary wealth for owners of existing property and for developers. This wealth in turn will make its way into global financial markets.

An urban and rural divide

The Table 6.2 shows the dramatic rate of urbanization, especially in the newly developed regions that shall be joining the First Economic World. This table is derived from the 2003 Revision of the World Urbanization Prospects, created by the Population Division of the United Nations.[5] For the first time in history, the total population of the developed and developing world recently became primarily urban.

Table 6.2 Urbanization and Global Populations (in millions) 1950–2030

Region	Year	1950	1975	2000	2003	2030
Northern America, Europe, Oceania – Urban		398	641	802	815	930
Asia, South and Central America – Urban		302	772	1760	1900	3266
Africa – Urban		33	103	295	329	748
North America, Europe, Oceania – Rural		334	300	273	270	203
Asia, South and Central America – Rural		1263	1948	2440	2467	2331
Africa – Rural		188	305	500	521	650

Source: As projected by the United Nations Population Division.

It is this urbanization that will translate into astronomically higher property values in Asia, Central and South America. With urbanization comes a much higher advantage for conveniently located housing, resulting in dramatically higher property values in urban centers compared to the rural alternatives.

Economic theory predicts that the wealth created from economic development will concentrate in those factors of production that are not easy to replicate. If we break factors into a number of classes based on their scarcity, we can group them in the following way. Raw resources such as land, hydrocarbon-based energy, and minerals are in fixed supply. These factors cannot be renewed, and are depleted over time. They command the highest price.

Educated workers and patented innovations take perhaps a generation to be replicated or imitated, but can be created, if given sufficient time. Their rewards may be high if there is a temporary shortage. These rewards rise and fall with economic booms and busts. However, immigration controls inhibit the flow of educated workers between countries, creating surpluses in some counties and shortages in others.

The least scarce is the management factor. Entrepreneurship can be created, and factories or industrial processes can be built quite easily. Because they are easily replicable, they earn only a modest competitive reward.

As a consequence, we can predict that global commodity prices will continue to be strong, land and housing prices will grow dramatically in fast growing economies, workers and young professionals educated in the regions and sectors experiencing high economic growth will earn rising salaries, and manufacturing will be mobile but within a highly competitive set of markets.

The countries in the best position to capitalize from the global economic transformation will be those rich in commodities and rich in the human capital necessary to fuel global economic growth. Secondary wealth will also be created in the regional real estate markets that contain the human capital necessary for the innovation economies.

The tables above also illustrate an aging of the FEW countries. We can predict a similar aging of the SEW countries joining this family of developed nations during the latter half of this century. Our next question to explore is the effect of an aging population on the rate of financial capital inflows.

Part III
An Emerging New World

The markets evolved, more or less, with the complications introduced following the Industrial Revolution. The First Economic World assumed the mantle of the economic superpowers, and the developing nations provided the FEW with the resources and the inexpensive manufacturing needed to fuel Western consumption. In a new, flat world though, innovation spreads rapidly, and a couple of very large countries in particular are beginning to transform the global economic landscape. We now delve into these emerging global shifts.

7
When I'm 64

When the United States Social Security system was first proposed, President Roosevelt could not imagine the dramatically transformed demographics just a few generations later. In 1935, the United States passed its first legislation offering social security payments to retirees who reach the age of 65. At that time, the life expectancy was only 63 years old. Today, those that reach retirement age are expected to live at least another two decades. And, a girl born today in Japan is likely to live to the next century. If this woman completes a graduate education by the age of 24 and retires at age of 62, she will live almost as long in retirement as she participated in the workforce.

If populations level off as predicted in the First Economic World, there may be only two workers for every retiree, and, in some sectors of the economy that require extensive education, there may be only one worker for every retiree. This mix will have dramatic implications for both the structure and performance of our economy, the level of capitalization in financial markets, the level of tolerance for risk in these markets, and the politics of the aged versus youth.

By the year 2050, the United Nations estimates that over 32% of the population in North America, Europe, and Oceania will be over 60 years old. The (by then) fully developed nations in Asia, and Central and South America, will have more than 23% of the population over the age of 60. In contrast, the aged will represent fewer than 11% of the Third Economic World population by the year 2050.

The other interesting phenomenon is the youth population changes. Just 17% of the population of North America, Europe, and Oceania will be under the age of 15 by 2050, while Asia and Central and South America youth will constitute 28% of their population. Only Africa shows a relatively large (and growing) youthful population.

Why does the rate of family formation differ?

These results are a simple consequence of economic theory. Economists categorize our preferences into three categories relative to our income. Decisions that rise in intensity at a relatively faster rate than our increase in income are called luxury goods. For instance, if your income doubles, the likelihood of your buying a luxury car or sending your children to private colleges more than doubles. Other decisions also increase proportionally faster. Our concern for the environment, democracy, a non-corrupt government, or laws to protect health and safety, all increase substantially with income.

Another class of purchases is the necessity good. These goods, services, or preferences also rise with income but not as rapidly as do luxury goods. Overall consumption rises, as does our demand for education in general, as income rises.

At a low level of income, our demand for economy cars rises with income. But, as income continues to rise, the necessity of an economy car is replaced by the luxury of a more comfortable car. The economy car has moved from a necessity to what economists call an inferior good as the country becomes increasingly affluent and actually demands less of such goods.

Using these labels, we see that family formation is a necessity good for very low-income countries in the undeveloped world, but becomes an inferior good as countries join the developed world. The net creation of social welfare as income rises obviates the need for children to provide income for the family and security for the aged.

Alternately, environmental protection is also a luxury good, valued much more highly as income rises and life expectancy increases. This of course makes sense as citizens realize longer life expectancy will mean that they must suffer the consequences of environmental degradation for longer.

We are bumping up against competing ideals though. It is obvious that the labor force is drawn primarily from those between the ages of 15 and 60. By the year 2050, the majority of the population will be in or nearing retirement or under the age of 15. With the extended demand for higher and graduate education, dramatic improvements in longevity, and with the desire for earlier retirements (both of which are luxury goods), many countries are finding there is only one person of working age for every two that are either retired or too young to work.

Ultimately, it is the working age bracket that produces the economic goods fueling the economy, and it is the retired class that commands much of the financial wealth fueling new capital formation. These two distinct groups create a conflict of two pies – the economic pie and the financial pie.

A tale of two pies

The economic pie represents the collection of goods and services we produce and consume. The financial pie represents the wealth which accrues as goods and services are produced, and the resulting financial return to Consumer-Investors.

Let us begin with the economic pie. If the minority of the population will produce goods for the entire population, the standard of living (as measured by the collection of goods we all consume) can be maintained in only two ways. We can continue to innovate technologically. Or we can rely on developing nations to provide the goods and services, at low prices, to the developed nations. This model by necessity requires "have" nations and "have-not" nations, which is not unlike the approach used by colonial powers to fuel their consumption from the resources and production of the colonies. This model works only so long as there are have-not nations to produce the low priced goods.

The economic pie is distinct from the financial pie. While the economic pie represents the goods and services we all consume, the financial pie is the wealth and profit accruing to the owners of the means of production. Historically, nations have thrived by expanding the economic pie. Perhaps for the first time though, we see economies built not on production but rather on manipulating the wealth that accrues when others produce. This changed emphasis is at the root of the financial meltdowns that we shall see can impinge on the economic pie.

Convergence once again

Developing nations are rapidly joining the developed nations, and income is leveling for much of the world's population. In 1999, just 18% of the world's population lived in the developed world. If Asia and Central and South America truly integrate into the First Economic World family by 2050, fully 80% of the world's population will live in the developed world. In a single century, we will have moved from a world in which one in five lived in the developed countries to only one in five who shall live in the undeveloped or developing countries.

There is still a great deal of development to be completed before countries like India and China fully integrate with the FEW. These economies are driven by a large newly urbanized portion that can benefit from education and economic opportunities. If, perhaps, only one in ten people in these countries currently benefit from their roaring economies, this low ratio may not stand for long. At a 10% annual growth rate realized in these nations, two in ten will be part of the new economies in seven years, and six in ten will be part of the new economies in perhaps a generation. These countries only need a generation of strong growth to create First Economic World opportunities for a majority of their citizens.

One could challenge the assumption that strong growth could continue in these countries for a generation. After all, their growth is fueled primarily because they are still developing and can provide cheap goods to the developed nations. If they, too, are developed, their goods will no longer be so cheap. However, until the vast majority of their population is part of their new economies, they have a built-in developing population. At the same time they have a growing middle class that provide the new wealth to demand the products of the developing portion of their nations.

Recall the law of diminishing returns, which states that at some point, it becomes increasingly difficult to make economic gains. These diminishing returns begin to set in once resources become scarce. If these economies are fueled on cheap labor, scarcity will not set in until the rural populations are close to fully integrated to levels found in the developed nations. At 82% urbanization in the developed nations and only 53% urbanization in the developing nations, there remains plenty of room to continue to fuel the rapid growth in these nations.

The challenge will be to provide the infrastructure necessary so as to not frustrate economic growth. This is a challenge that the governments of China and India understand, more or less. Vast resources are devoted to infrastructure improvements in these nations. However, each country takes a slightly different approach. India does so by taxing the growing middle class and the new economic activities. This rate of infrastructure capital formation is politically charged because it is directly borne by those that are generating the wealth, and have economic and political clout that is moving the nation forward.

A second approach has been adopted by the Chinese government. By maintaining relatively tight control over the domestic economy and the currency, their government can set an exchange rate that is just a little weaker than free markets would determine. This small tax on exports and imports alike has allowed their central bank to produce the largest foreign exchange surplus ever known in the history of the world – amounting to about two trillion US dollars, and growing by billions of dollars daily. These vast sums allow the Chinese the funds to invest in the infrastructure that has contributed to past, and will contribute to future, economic growth.

An enlarged FEW and a dwindling TEW

As these countries reach the end of the road in capacity to grow at such a fast pace, the newly enlarged First Economic World will need to turn to the remaining developing and undeveloped nations for sustained growth. As we mentioned before, growth is much easier, and the point of diminishing returns much more distant, when only one in five live in a developed nation rather than the predicted four in five.

A number of challenges will impede further expansion and economic growth in Africa. As we have discussed, this will require creation of substantial physical, political, legal, and educational infrastructures that currently do not exist.

There has been little investment in the physical infrastructure of road and transportation mechanisms, a manufacturing base, and telecommunications that are necessary for economic development in the Third Economic World. Such investment is difficult to mount given the political instabilities that riddle many African nations. The political institutions cannot thrive until there is the rule of law that will maintain integrity in the political process. And an appreciation for the importance of these innovations will not be forthcoming until the population is offered the education that will induce them to demand these innovations. There is multi-generational work to be done in these areas, but the fate of these countries, and the rest of the world, depends on this important work.

Once the world is mostly developed, there will be great pressure to fuel additional growth through other means. It is this avenue we explore next, and in a later chapter.

Scarce factors of production

We have been exploring the creation of goods, services, and wealth that take advantage of vast untapped labor and human capital resources. There are other resources that we can tap. The scarcest of these are the fixed resources of land, minerals, and hydrocarbon resources. Other commodities such as agricultural products are less scarce, but require water, which may be the next truly scarce resource. The commodity pinch will be treated later.

Perhaps the most abundant resource will be entrepreneurial capital. With the tools of business and management, and the global reach of modern corporations, we are able to create entrepreneurship seemingly at will. Like human capital, entrepreneurship only requires a sufficiently educated (or teachable) class of people.

The remaining form of capital is financial capital. This capital is derived from the savings of the Consumer-Investor class, and by the reinvested earnings of the companies they own. The investments give the Consumer-Investor the right to the wealth created by public corporations that issue shares. Even the wealth accruing to private owners of the fixed factors of production like land and minerals must either be spent or reinvested into other productive enterprises. Either way, most profits, and labor earnings in excess of consumption wind up in the financial markets.

As more financial capital is awash in the financial marketplace, Consumer-Investors bid up what they are willing to pay to secure a share of future earnings. This share price compared to earnings (Price/Earnings ratio) is a measure of the amount of capital chasing a fixed number of stocks, and rises with the collective optimism in the marketplace.

As the share of retirees increases in the developed economies, there will be a decrease in the flow of new wealth into financial markets. This is because a prudent retirement strategy is to spend the returns from investment each year, keeping the stock of investment constant. Retiring Consumer-Investors no longer re-inject all of their earnings into the market, and no longer invest the excess of their labor income over consumption into the market. In other words, if we move from an economy in which four people worked for every retiree to an economy in which two people worked for every retiree, new investment from the working class is halved.

Some have predicted a perilous market decline as the baby boomers begin to retire. We know that we will eventually reach a new steady state ratio of workers to retirees. In the meantime, we will have to cope with a large bubble of retirees as a consequence of the baby boom immediately following World War II. All else equal, this bubble of boomers would depress the market. Over time though as this bubble passes away, a more regular ratio of workers to retirees will establish itself, and the market would "come back" to a long-term value.

However, there is a significant factor that will mitigate or perhaps even reverse this prediction of perils in the stock market. The retirees will continue to consume, and this consumption will continue to fuel demand for production in the emerging economies. The resulting healthy demand for commodities and the new wealth and urbanization in these emerging markets, most notably India and China, will likely be sufficient to make up for the loss of new investment from retirees. The baby boom has timed things quite perfectly – retiring just as emerging markets begin to take off.

There will also be a baby boom in these emerging markets. Their population explosions that occurred in the latter half of the twentieth century, were reduced somewhat with the onset of the twenty-first century, and are expected to drop off beginning in 2050.

These countries will experience an increase in retirements over the next couple of decades, in synchronization with the baby boom retirements, and will see another decline in the latter half of the century. It is that second wave of retirements that may be more problematic. The pyramid of new Consumer-Investors and wealth producers in the emerging markets that will likely keep global financial markets strong for the first half of this century will disappear in the latter half of the century. Even if the population of Africa can be positioned to be the emerging markets of the latter half of the century, their numbers are not sufficiently large to continue to fuel global demand.

Thomas Malthus prophesized the exasperating economic reality that all good things must someday come to an end. I will discuss a wildcard that may prolong economic growth even if this dismal prophecy holds true in the latter half of the century. In the meantime though, we should celebrate this fortunate coincidence that is replacing one baby boom with another.

Modern medicine – a boon and a bane

Before I close this chapter, let's take a moment to explore the role of modern medicine on these results. I mentioned earlier that a girl born in Japan today is more likely than not to live to the next century. This dramatic expansion in life expectancy is taking an increasing toll on the gross domestic product of developed nations.

Prolonged longevity also creates a prolonged retirement class that will have its own effect on extended consumption and on reduced new inflows into financial markets. Perhaps the most significant problem, though, will be the eventual necessity to draw more laborers into the workforce to support the consumption of a greater number of retirees.

Perhaps technology will come to the rescue, and we will discuss this possibility in turn. However, a more likely outcome will be increased pressure for delayed retirement. Already in Europe and the United States, the policy debate has been converging on an expectation that the official retirement age will increase and indeed as is scheduled to increase to 67. A modest increase in the retirement age to perhaps seventy years old will have a very strong influence on the number of older workers relative to the number of retirees.

This debate in the United States is motivated by a different but not dissimilar phenomenon. President Franklin Roosevelt created Social Security as a fiscal response to the Great Depression. By offering a government-sponsored pension to every man that reaches the age of 65, when the life expectancy was only 63, Roosevelt hoped to inject some spending into the economy to benefit a class that was indeed suffering.

The Social Security tax also provided a new revenue source from the populace, while simultaneously creating the perception that the Consumer-Investors will themselves someday benefit from this innovation. Meanwhile the government was able create some badly needed revenue from which it could provide additional fiscal stimuli in the depths of the Depression. This of course is a good, albeit Machiavellian, reason to have the Social Security tax accrue to general revenue, with benefits paid from general revenue, rather than the social security accounts (lock boxes) that are now discussed.

US style Social Security has thrived ever since. To now, it has produced more revenue than it has paid out each year, and the government has been free to spend this bonus revenue. So long as there are more replacement workers than retirees, this pyramid-style scheme remains solvent. However, the reduced rate of family formation in the FEW nations is creating solvency problems. If there is a threat of insolvency sometime in the not too distant future, we will need to raise the Social Security tax now to create even greater current revenue.

While the United States adopted Social Security as a model of a publicly facilitated "pay as you go" system, Canada and many of the other FEW countries adopted a different philosophy. In these countries, the government facilitates Social Insurance. The philosophy is a system of state infrastructure to create healthy children, educated young adults, productive workers, and the ability to retire with dignity. This system requires a much higher level of state investment in the productivity of the workforce.

Like so many "financial innovations," it is apparent that the strength of Social Security, Social Insurance, and even the financial markets in general, is fueled by the constant need for new Consumer-Investors. We can create these new Consumer-Investors domestically through family formation, and when that fails, we can discover new Consumer-Investors in emerging markets. When these opportunities run dry, we will need to rely more on good old-fashioned innovation. This is the topic for our next chapter.

8
Progress Marches On

It is almost a miracle. The pace of innovation and change would be staggering to contemplate, if we didn't happen to find ourselves smack dab in the middle of it.

At this time, it is helpful to discern between an innovation and a revolution. I define an innovation as an improvement in the processes that benefits the current cohort of economic participants. For instance, a medical innovation provides us with better care or cheaper services, but does not much affect those that don't have access to high quality medical care. In contrast, a revolution dramatically affects not only those current market participants (some even adversely), but also expands the degree to which new participants can join the economic fold. Let's look at some of the past revolutions.

Talkin' about a revolution

Perhaps twelve thousand years ago, we experienced an agrarian revolution. Society has not been the same since. It freed humans from having to follow migrating animals and made possible more permanent structures and settlements. It also created the opportunity for specialization because one person could then produce enough food for many. With that specialization came markets to trade surpluses, the written word, culture, and formalized religion. Beyond the niceties and comforts of life, much of what we now value remains at its essence the qualities we first developed as a consequence of agriculture.

Then five thousand years ago, the now non-migrating agriculturally-based peasants with time to spare and food aplenty, began to experiment and soon mastered metalworking. The Bronze Age created a revolution in technology, tools, art, and culture. This was followed by the Iron Age, Copper Age and by more sophisticated tool making. But, while the first experiences with metalworking were likely revolutionary, subsequent innovations were more evolutionary.

The next revolution did not occur for another six millennia. About six hundred years ago, the printing press, attributed to Gutenberg but already in common use in China and Korea, created a democratization of ideas. Before then, the clergy monopolized both the literate class and the dissemination of ideas. With the printing press, ideas could be brought directly to the citizens, opening up a whole world to those who could not have otherwise fully participated in the old world. In turn, this revolutionized religion, allowed for creation of the individual beyond the control of the church and created a more independent marketplace for ideas.

The Industrial Revolution took off in the nineteenth century, followed by a second wave in the 20th century. While the roots of this revolution remain controversial, many attribute it to the invention of the steam engine by the Scotsman James Watt. By creating a power source that was both moveable and powerful, humans were at once freed from power generation and took industry to where the people were. As we have discussed, this revolution affected not only our ability to produce in much greater quantities at much lower cost, but liberated millions from the fields, created a working class from a peasant class, and gave rise to a middle class, education, and government. As with the other revolutions, this revolution dramatically expanded market participation.

A number of innovations continued to fuel this revolution. The next transforming revolution did not occur until transportation became safe and affordable. By the early 1800s, railroads were transporting people to the factories of England and goods to market. In 1869, the Transcontinental Railroad was completed in the United States, and Canada soon followed with its last spike driven in 1885. The revolution in transportation opened up huge tracts of land for settlement and created a breed of individuals and bountiful agricultural lands that would fuel the rapid development of North America and, with it, the FEW.

The creation of the automobile, and especially the mass-produced automobile in 1908, followed by trucks and a modern road system, allowed for further penetration of the modern economy by the people. In combination with trains, ships, and then planes, the transportation revolution spread the First Economic World model around the globe. Since then, robotics has improved the quantity and quality of manufacturing and has further reduced the number of people needed to manufacture the goods we consume. This de-emphasis of manufacturing allowed tens of millions of people to devote their human capital to the service industry.

Other innovations have arisen that many would call revolutionary. Indeed, the term revolutionary can be found on 62,300,000 (and counting) web pages recorded by Google. Even a new cat food has been labeled revolutionary. Disregarding overuse of the word, we can still make a case for a few more true revolutions.

There has been a revolution in electronics, which has allowed the broad dissemination of ideas not unlike the consequences of the printing press. The invention of modern computing is bringing literacy to emerging markets and undeveloped countries, with such efficacy that some of these countries can best the First Economic World at its own information technology game. To find Internet access in a village in India or Africa fits our definition of a revolution.

And the revolution in medicine is allowing our retirees to live longer than ever imagined, and is curing diseases like malaria that still kills more than three in ten children in some areas of Africa. An innovation as simple as an anti-malarial coated net for sleeping is expected to eventually save hundreds of millions of people. In our test, this innovation is indeed revolutionary.

Revolutions du jour

One interesting aspect of the plethora of revolutions is not only their transforming power, but also their increased frequency. We have moved from revolutions every few millennia to revolutions every few centuries, and now to revolutions every few decades. We have come to take on faith the forward march of progress and change. Indeed we find that our economy takes as a matter of faith the assumption that we will be able to advance constantly because some new idea, new population, new energy source, or new opportunity will come along that will fuel further growth. It is a natural conclusion to draw. After all, we have seen nothing else.

It is important to remember though, that this constant march of change, innovation, and wealth is merely an empirical conclusion. By that I mean that our conclusions rely not on some fundamental principle governing the world but rather on past data.

The data suggested to an economist named Joseph Schumpeter that innovation and entrepreneurship occurs in waves. One of these waves had a very long multigenerational cycle, one cycled over a generation, one lasted perhaps a decade, and one came and went every few years.[1]

When these waves worked together, their effects reinforced each other, upward or downward. When they were out of sync, they could cancel each other out, creating periods of innovation stability. However, beyond some hand-waving, Schumpeter could not produce a plausible theory for why these waves occurred. Nonetheless, his theory did seem to coincide with the observation that the economy grows and innovates in fits and starts.

Revolution and innovation are important for two reasons. They permit us to expand the size of the economic pie both by increasing the number of participants and by increasing the level of production through improvements in efficiency. Both are necessary to maintain our pyramid of progress and ensure the next generation is at least as well off as the last.

It would be a little scary, though, to pin our hopes on the continued march of progress, revolution and innovation. For one reason, while the pace of revolution has certainly accelerated, revolution needs a hinterland. By this I mean there must be a significantly large group of people that can be absorbed into the new economy the revolution will provide. As these revolutions absorb a greater share of the world's population, significant revolutionary advances become impossible – short of discovering new intelligent life in our solar system. We are beginning to hit the wall of diminishing returns to the dispersion of the new economy. When this occurs, revolutions become mere innovations.

Second, it is hard to imagine how a new innovation or revolution can continue to be truly transforming. That is not to say it cannot exist. After all, every revolution occurred because someone did not accept the status quo. While there is still a lot of capacity to spread the new economies to the Third Economic World, once that is completed it is hard to imagine what could be next. Education could become marginally more efficient, but the system of education has remained remarkably intact for millennia. Until there is a method to implant knowledge without the good old-fashioned hard work of students, it is dangerous to assure we will perpetually expand our capacity to absorb human capital.

Our methods to develop and process land resources are already so cheap in relation to the value they create that it seems unlikely that huge gains can be had there. Certainly our physical capital, in the form of factories and machines, will continue to improve. Already though the share of the workforce devoted to manufacturing has dropped precipitously as more robots and automated processes replace labor.

The service industry can also become more efficient. We have probably reached our capacity to absorb services like entertainment, banking and insurance, financial services, or even haircuts.

It is unlikely that the world will become a significantly better place if we have another ten television channels or if we can choose between thirty movies at the local theater rather than just twenty.

Third, we have a definitional problem. Revolution is measured by the spurts we see in the gross domestic product (GDP). These distinct jumps in GDP arise because we can somehow measure a discrete increase in the amount of "stuff" we produce and consume. Our next revolution may be in the creation of more free time rather than in the creation of more stuff, and may then go unreflected in our charts of economic progress.

More affluent societies are now looking with some envy at the slower and more relaxed pace of life in the lesser-developed world. The United Nations has been producing quality of life measures that take us beyond measuring progress based solely on wealth creation, and alternatively measuring progress in education, free time, health, safety, and the other things craved by an affluent society. However, until there a greater common understanding of the importance of alternative measures of well being, we will likely continue to focus on the most measurable one – GDP per capita. And certainly the SEW and TEW nations that aspire for affluence will continue to measure their progress in terms of wealth creation.

The fallacy of growth

What can we expect for growth in the future? Growth is ultimately generated in four ways. Nominal growth occurs because prices rise, causing the dollar value of all our stuff to rise at approximately the same rate. We set that growth aside though, because it doesn't represent an expansion of the economic pie. Real growth occurs only in three ways. First, we can have more factors of production, perhaps most significantly more labor. We expect real growth to keep up with population growth to ensure that the amount of "stuff" per capita does not decline. Second, we can have the improvements in technologies described above that allow us to produce more with less. This adds to growth. Finally, when more foreign countries buy from us than we buy from them, our products are more highly valued, and that generates growth.

The danger is in trying to maintain growth for growth's sake. While population may rise, other fixed factors of production are in decline. For instance, rising oil prices will necessarily stunt the growth of oil importing nations. To try to maintain normal growth when available resources are declining is impossible.

Consumer-Investors come to expect maintained growth though. Growth should decline because First Economic World nations must import more. Growth should also decline if resources become pinched, or if we simply decide we have enough wealth to afford to work less and enjoy ourselves more. To maintain growth for growth's sake will escalate commodity prices still further, put a strain on economic policy, and will ultimately fail. To not maintain growth for growth's sake will be a political failure, unless the Consumer-Investor is educated in the complexities of a modern economy.

One revolution that could dramatically affect us all and spur yet another round of dramatic growth is a revolution in cheap and affordable energy. Harnessing the power of the sun, through solar power, wind power, or even replicating the sun through fusion, will free up a large share of the workforce and resources, and would likely touch every corner of the planet. We are approaching the point at which wind power or solar power is only a little more costly than its non-sustainable, hydrocarbon resource-intensive alternatives.

With some more innovations, we can attain a smooth transition to an alternative energy world without causing a downward fall in economic prosperity. And with an equal dose of good fortune, we may be able to harness nuclear fusion, the process that fuels the sun and could provide for abundant energy for a very long future. The world has been looking for such a solution since the 1950s, and yet that solution seems more distant now than it did then.

A laborless society?

What are the ramifications if we could move to a world in which everybody has their basic needs met without the great use of labor? It seems likely that our next economic innovations will be not in producing more stuff, but rather in providing more leisure. Recall, though, that financial markets are fueled by the reinvestment of profits to produce more goods and services that, in turn, generate more profits.

If we reach a point when FEW nations are close to satiated on production, our next financial innovation might be in the buying back of our time rather than in the purchasing of more goods and services. If we move next to a 32-hour working week and then a 24 hour or 20 hour week, and still can produce what we want to consume, clever investment can only provide for us even further reductions in labor supplied. It may be the case that we create a world which is dramatically differentiated by those that have significant leisure and those that have to work a 40 hour week. These will be our new "haves" and "have nots."

Such an era will certainly be a renaissance for the Consumer-Investor. Investment will always be an opportunity to claim a share of the next innovation. Without economic growth in both the supply and the demand for goods and services, there cannot be a growing market. Remember Say's Law which states that supply creates its own demand? A subtlety assumed and often missed in Say's Law is that the supply produced must also be desired. The premise of Say's Law is that production creates income for workers and other factor owners, and this income then creates demand for products. But there must still be intrinsic interest in the product produced.

I would not underestimate the creativity in ensuring that the goods produced can develop viable markets. And nor could one possibly imagine the new ideas and innovations of the future. Finally, we live in a consumer society, and there is always a latent demand for something new, novel, or exclusive. There would always be a market, in the Say's Law sense, if people consumed for the sake of consumption. Indeed, it is this very quality that some may claim is the excess of First Economic World consumption. If there is value in consumption for consumption's sake, and if we find ways to do this in a sustainable manner, it may be the case that the First Economic World will continue to grow. The affluent nations may retain their status of exporting the culture of Western consumption to emerging nations that crave the values of the FEW.

Meanwhile, the owners of these same factors of production that cannot be created anew will command a greater share of economic wealth. It is this stark reality that we turn to next.

9
Fill 'Er Up

We stated earlier that market prices are determined by both demand and scarcity. In this chapter we will explore the determinants of consumer and producer demand, and show how this demand affects commodities differently. Let's begin with the nature of a demand curve, and differentiate between the demand by an individual and the demand for an entire market.

A demand curve is simply a line on a graph that describes the relationship between the quantity of a commodity, good, or service, and its price. By convention, the quantity of a good demanded is placed on the horizontal axis, but is ultimately a function of the price of the good measured along the vertical axis. Because a higher price should almost always result in a lower quantity of demand for the good, a demand curve should show a negative relationship between price and quantity demanded (see Figure 9.1).

Individuals will demand a good based on their intrinsic enjoyment, the consumption and price of comparable goods, and their income. We have already learned that income can affect demand depending on the nature of the good. Demand for some consumption goods rises rapidly as income rises. These are labeled luxury goods. Other goods, called necessities, rise only moderately as income rises. And demand for some goods, most closely associated with the consumption patterns of low income and not high income Consumer-Investors, actually fall as income rises. As a consequence, we can expect demand to expand for necessities and luxuries as per capita income rises worldwide.

The price of comparable goods also affects demand because as the price of a similar good rises, we will find greater value in our alternate good. For instance, as the price of tea rises, the level of demand for coffee also rises, as people discouraged by the price of tea choose to consume coffee instead. We call these goods or services substitutes because

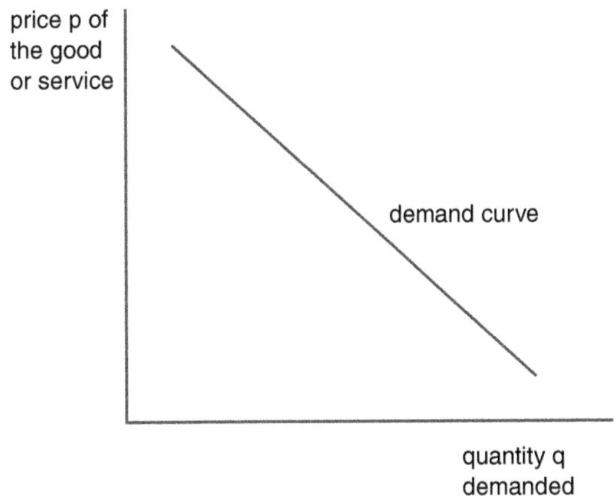

Figure 9.1 A graph of a demand curve

our demand rises as its substitute becomes less affordable. On the other hand, demand for coffee or tea will rise if the price of cream and sugar fall. The decline in the price of goods that complement our enjoyment of coffee or tea will enhance our consumption.

Our intrinsic enjoyment for a good or service also depends on such factors as age, gender, education, and culture. An aging population may consume more health care services, and a retiree may have more time to travel, enjoy entertainment, and take advantage of investor services and insurance. Likewise, an emerging nation with many young people investing in their own human capital will demand greater amounts of education, while an emerging middle class will demand new homes, and perhaps more fuel for minivans and home heating. Even weather can affect demand. Cold weather raises fuel oil usage and the demand for substitute heating technologies like heat pumps or natural gas furnaces.

Commodities that are used as a factor of production of goods or services are likewise sensitive to the overall demand for the good produced, the price of factors that can be substituted in the production process, and changes in technologies that may require less intensive use of the commodity.

Let's get technical

Commodity speculators take these factors into account in the long run. They can model the changes in demand as a consequence of changes in the price of substitutes and complements, per capita income, changing demographic patterns, and changes in population. It is most convenient for them to describe the percent change in the quantity demanded of a commodity for a 1% change in factors or events that influence demand. This could include the price of complements or substitutes, income, population, and so forth.

A good or commodity is considered cross-price or income inelastic if its demand is proportionally insensitive or unresponsive to a one percent change in other prices or income. Alternately, a commodity, good, or service is labeled elastic if it yields a greater percentage change in demand for a percentage change in these influences.

A good is considered (own-price) inelastic if the quantity demanded is insensitive to its own price. For instance, most people will not cut down on their dosage of a prescription drug if the price of the drug rises, unless of course there are plenty of alternative drugs they could consume instead.

As you can imagine, producers would like to somehow make your demand as inelastic as possible so you will not consume significantly less if they raise their price. Producers can use advertising, create brand loyalty, or buy out competitors to reduce Consumer-Investors' alternatives and make their product more inelastic. We shall use the notion of elasticity a little later on.

These descriptions of individual demand curves also apply to market demand. The overall demand in the marketplace is simply the sum of individual demands. For instance, as the cross-section of the population doubles, so should the level of market demand.

The supply side

However, we have quite literally only told half the story. The price of a commodity, good, or service depends on the interplay between both demand and supply. This is easy to see. Something in high demand may not necessarily be profitable to produce if there are a lot of substitutes, or if there are a lot of competitors who can also produce the good. So let us now turn to the supply side.

Just as a demand curve compares the price of a commodity, good, or service with the quantity demanded, the supply curve shows the amount of a good or service provided for various prices offered. A supply curve will slope upward because a higher offered price will induce more producers to supply more to the marketplace. Where the demand and supply curves cross determines the quantity bought and sold, and its price (see Figure 9.2).

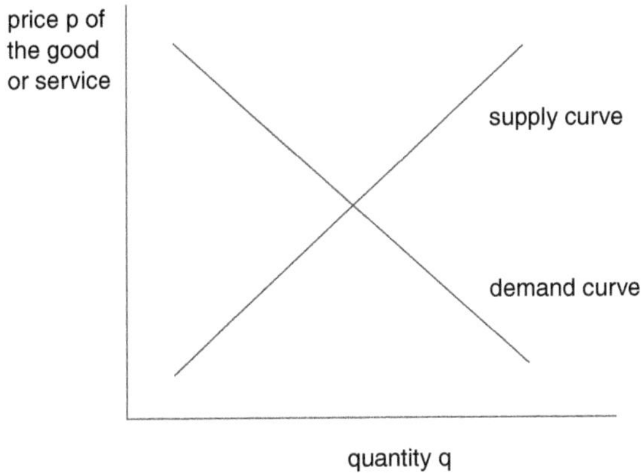

Figure 9.2 Supply and demand curves

Factors of production

A commodity, good, or service is created by combining earth capital (land, minerals, oil, etc.), physical capital (machines, factories, etc.), human capital (workers and employees), and entrepreneurial capital (the managers that put all the forms of capital together to produce the good). The process that combines these factors of production is called technology, and improvements in technology permits the same level of production with less of one or more factors, thereby decreasing costs.

If improvements in technology can reduce the price of a good, increases in the cost of any factor will increase its price. However, producers will adjust their combination of factors, if possible, to use less of the relatively expensive factor of production, and more of the inexpensive factors. We frequently observe this tradeoff when we compare the use of labor in First and Second Economic World economies.

I illustrate this with my story of building a walled room in Indonesia. I described the job to a local builder and agreed to a price. I was surprised and impressed when he took three long days to build the interior wall, brick by brick, and make the door, one laminated strip of wood at a time. To him, finished materials were dear, and his time was worth little. That same wall and door would be completed in a day in a developed country, framed with pre-cut lumber, covered with drywall, and finished with a pre-hung door. The choice of technologies and the combination of factors differ because the cost of labor is low in Indonesia, while the cost of labor is high in the FEW countries. And because labor costs are high, the job is completed much quicker and substantially fewer workers are employed in construction, for the same level of building.

The quantity supplied of a factor, good, or service can also be expressed as it relates to the price a producer can charge for it. If the quantity supplied can easily be increased by simply purchasing or renting more factors of production, and if these factors are plentiful, the supply is labeled elastic. Another way to view this is to notice that even a slight increase in the price offered for the product can result in a large increase in the quantity supplied, as more producers easily employ more factors of production.

On the other hand, if it is very difficult to expand supply because of some constraint in a factor of production, the product is considered inelastic. We see this particularly in the crude oil market, especially in the short run. A spike in expected demand for fuel oil can only be met with the oil in storage or in the proverbial pipeline. This limited supply of oil will go to the highest bidder, so prices can rise dramatically for a relatively modest increase in demand.

In the long run, defined as the period of time the oil industry can fully adjust to the higher prices, we will see an expansion in production and exploration, and a much more modest long-run rise in price. A product that cannot quickly adjust will be inelastic in the short run. A product that is fixed, like the number of seats for popular play or football game, is inelastic, the supply curve is almost vertical, and the price can be very high.

We now have the tools to see the fallacy of a reduction in fuel taxes to offer relief from high fuel prices, as proposed by some politicians of late. If gasoline is in fixed supply, its price is determined by demand. A lowering of the tax rate will simply divert this reduction directly to producers, resulting in higher profits by the same amount of the tax reduction.

The recognition of elastic and inelastic products also has some bearing on world financial markets as demographics change, population grows, and nations move through the various stages of development.

Black gold, Texas tea

Oil is an interesting and increasingly relevant example. It is in fixed supply, having been produced during the Paleozoic Era perhaps three hundred million years ago. Leafy plants, prehistoric forests, and algae were prolific creators of carbohydrates from the high levels of atmospheric carbon dioxide content and abundant sunlight. As plants and algae died, they sank to the bottom of swamps and oceans, and were subsequently covered by soils and sand that were compressed into rock. The combination of heat and pressure converted these decomposed carbohydrates into hydrocarbons, in different combinations depending on the particular combination of degraded material, heat, depth, and pressure.

It has been estimated that humankind have used about one trillion barrels of oil, and have about one trillion barrels of conventional oil left. Of course, the estimate of remaining reserves depends on both the price we are willing to pay (which will ultimately be bound by the cost of the next best alternative, to be described later), and the success of new technologies to extract the remaining oil. In any event, it is estimated that conventional reserves will last for another 40 years at current consumption levels.

Proven economical reserves have expanded dramatically with higher oil prices, with Venezuela holding vast quantities of buried oil sands, and Canada holding a similar amount of heavier tar sands that are easier to recover because they lie just below the surface. These fixed but abundant supplies of oil are each larger than the world's proven remaining conventional oil reserves.

Estimates of available oil lasting another 40 years for conventional sources, and a further 80 years after that for oil sands does not take into account the rapidly growing population of Consumer-Investors, especially in the demand from emerging markets that are growing rapidly. The SEW country's are increasing usage of commodities, especially oil, and still have a couple of generations to go before they become fully developed and imitate the consumption patterns of the FEW.

Given that the emerging markets are four times the size of the First Economic World now and projected to be six times the size of the existing developed nations once they fully integrate into the First Economic World two generations from now, it is fair to conclude that commodity demand, especially oil demand, will continue to accelerate until SEW population growth levels off in 2050.

In the meantime, these emerging nations, in the midst of their own industrial revolutions, are much more concentrated in the manufacturing necessary to fuel their newly discovered consumption. These manufacturing based economies use commodities more intensively. At some point, they will pass the manufacturing gauntlet over to the next set of emerging nations in the TEW countries. This subsequent growth cannot be as substantial in world terms because by then 80% of the world's population will be in developed nations.

Escalating commodity prices

We have seen in the last few years a dramatic growth of commodity prices for those commodities that are in fixed supply. Other commodities such as agricultural products will also continue to increase in price especially as arable land becomes scarcer, and urbanization competes with agriculture for the next scarce resource – water. The competition for this important resource may be alleviated if we can succeed in creating salt tolerant crops suitable for human consumption, or if we can produce an abundant energy source that can allow us to extract fresh water from salt water affordably and abundantly.

Critical in these conclusions is the role of backstop technologies. As mentioned earlier, the price of oil will depend on the creation of technologies that can replace oil. Any such technology will have to be transportable, sustainable, clean, and replicable.

The fallacy of the hydrogen economy

One important backstop technology will be solar power, from the energy impinging directly on solar panels, or the power of the sun to set up global temperature differentials that creates the wind and the ocean currents. Currently solar technology costs about four dollars per installed watt of energy. When this price can be reduced to a dollar per watt, solar power will pay for itself in about three years of sunlight. Some estimate that the technology can be driven down even further.[1] At that point, electricity would be cheap enough to offer a viable alternative to hydrocarbons.

Energy storage and transportability remain problematic. But hydrogen may offer a solution. Actually, hydrogen is not an energy source at all. There are no significant sources of natural hydrogen because it is the lightest of all elements. Any store of hydrogen would have long ago been lost to the buoyancy of gases in the atmosphere. Hydrogen, instead, is an energy storage mechanism. Other energy sources, such as solar, wind, or perhaps someday fusion, can be used to electrolyze water to create hydrogen and oxygen. Hydrogen can then be transported in pipelines with relatively low loss, can power fuel cells to create a portable electric supply for cars, and can supplant oil and natural gas in flame-related technologies.

The advantages in using existing networks to transport hydrogen, and the reasonable efficiency of fuel cells to power our cars must be balanced against the disadvantage of energy losses in the electrolysis of water. In the final analysis, hydrogen will be a supportive technology rather than a technology that will somehow play a transforming role in our modern economies.

Similarly, corn-based ethanol is not a viable energy alternative, given its high-energy input requirements for a given unit of ethanol energy produced. A national drive to substitute ethanol for a small share of the gasoline consumed in the United States has driven up agricultural land prices and hence the cost of all crops worldwide. However, a more likely candidate for ethanol production with a much better energy balance is cellulosic ethanol, derived from the biodegradation of switch grass and waste wood. Again, the scale required to make a sizeable dent on national or global energy usage is a formidable obstacle.

These alternative energy sources will be judged against the market for the Earth. The Clean Air Act Amendments of 1990 created markets for those pollutants that damage the environment. While creating a market for pollutants seems antithetical to the protection of the environment, such a commoditization of pollution and effluent for the first time provides a market incentive to reduce pollution. Traditional polluters were given a quota to pollute, and could not exceed the quota without buying additional pollution rights from another producer.

A firm wanting to exceed its quota (at a market-determined price for each unit of effluent) is made aware of the price of this previously unpriced factor of production. On the other hand, a clean producer that is below its quota has excess pollution credits to sell and it realizes it can still profit by becoming even cleaner. Either way, there is an incentive to reduce pollution because the negative externality of pollution is now priced. As society develops an additional taste for cleaner air, the quotas can be tightened, the market prices will rise to recognize this scarcity, and there will be even greater incentives to clean the air still further.

This methodology for pricing polluting discharges is also used by some nations for the emission of the global warming gas carbon dioxide.

Finally, there have been claims that we are only a decade or two away from replicating on Earth the fusion that fuels the sun. However, these claims have been touted for decades, and are unlikely to be the backstop technology that will replace oil.

What does this mean for world financial markets?

As you recall, profits to factors of production (labeled rents by economists) flow to the factors based both on their overall demand and their scarcity. We have seen that worldwide demand for many factors of production will increase as the vast majority of the world's population moves from developing to developed nation status. We see already that India and China, representing 40% of the world's population, are already commanding a sizeable share of global commodities. This is occurring even before the consumption of commodities by their Consumer-Investors has reached the levels of the most developed nation. The vast majority of these nations have yet to join the Consumer-Investor middle class. Until these nations have a fully developed and fully dispersed middle class, and until we develop backstop technologies that are sustainable and permit us to be weaned off of scarce commodity resources, we can expect commodity demand to be strong. Indeed, we cannot imagine anything else.

Before we close, let's observe that scarce commodities have been used as a store of value throughout history. For instance, many still turn to gold as a reliable store of value when we have faith in other forms of money. In a diversified and sophisticated economy such as ours, it is unlikely that a scarce resource that also serves other purposes would be primarily devoted to a store of value for a significantly large segment of the market. There may be a role to play for gold, at times, and at the margin of investment, but its inability to contribute to the growth of the economic pie limits its value. We will return to this theme next.

10
Gold, Oil, and Dollars, and the Decline of an Economic Superpower

Where have all the dollars gone?

We discussed earlier why the convergence of the First Economic World and the Second Economic World will have inevitable effects on the upward spiral of prices on fixed resources of all sorts, like gold and oil, and a reappraisal of the value of sustainable agricultural products that require arable land and water.

How will these factors affect the value of the US dollar, and when will it end?

The US dollar was a store of value, primarily based on the pre-eminent grip the US economy held in the global economy. The dollar has been well maintained by a sophisticated Federal Reserve System and its counterparts in the Group of Eight (G8) nations of the United States, Canada, Japan, Russia, the United Kingdom, France, Germany, and Italy. Historically, the dollar has acted as a good store of value. It is reasonably difficult to counterfeit, at least partly because it is not issued in very large denominations. The US legal system is also sufficiently sophisticated to punish transgressors that would attempt to debase the currency. And, like all superior forms of money, it can readily be converted to consumption of just about any type, anywhere.

Some of these factors are equally well replicated by other currencies, like the Euro. A US economy that is mismanaged also removes some of the luster from the US dollar. Ironically, as the US dollar loses its luster, the Canadian Loonie polishes up nicely. Canada seems to weather economic storms better than the United States. Perhaps one significant reason is that their Federal Reserve equivalent, the Bank of Canada, and the Canadian government work in a more concerted way to conduct economic policy. Also, in the current crisis of the US dollar, assets have fled to commodities, mostly gold and oil, both of which Canada has in abundance.

One reason that keeps the Canadian currency strong is its consistency in maintaining an even or improving federal debt. As a matter of policy, and in ways that we describe later, the Canadian government targeted a very consistent inflation rate to create a predictable budget climate. A consistent federal debt also allows them to better predict and manage investment as the government does not need to compete with private investment for the financial resources of Consumer-Investors.

Of course, it does not hurt to sit on vast stores of oil, diamonds, gold, copper, and other commodities. Nonetheless, a government and a central bank working in concert with a set of economic goals that remain consistent from administration to administration is a strength that provides a good business climate.

How the US deficit stacks up

One measure of the budget deficit is its size in comparison to the overall gross domestic product. According to this measure, the Euro and the US dollar may face continued pressure. At nearly 70% of the annual gross domestic product, the US deficit is now more than twice that of the 75-year low point during the Carter Administration and at its highest level since World War II. European deficits are not far behind, even though they are somewhat constrained as a condition of membership to the European Monetary Union.

A burgeoning federal debt is problematic not just because our spending today incurs a huge liability on our successors tomorrow, but also because maintenance of the debt competes with domestic investment funds. Interest on the debt must be paid, and whatever is left can be used to ensure domestic economies remain competitive in the future. It also burdens current federal spending and causes debt service that dwarfs any other form of federal spending. Finally, it increases a nation's dependence on foreign nations as it must rely on the reinvestment of excess dollars other nations earn to support its growing debt.

As investors become concerned about the ability of the FEW economies to remain strong and keep inflation under control, there is increasing skepticism that the US dollar can hold its store of value. This fear is also somewhat self-fulfilling for a nation so dependent on foreign oil. Just as we discussed an addict is easy to tax, speculators realize they can drive up the price of oil, at least in the short run.

A wild ride

If worldwide oil is priced in dollars, the United States is triple whammied. As global Consumer-Investors shy away from the dollar and into assets like oil that will likely hold value better, it drives up the dollar price of oil, while simultaneously driving down the value of the dollar. Oil producers must demand even higher prices for their oil because it is denominated in a currency declining in value. Finally, most FEW countries are dependent on oil imports. A declining US dollar worsens the balance of trade, forcing the United States to pay more to import oil at a higher price, thereby worsening its trade deficit, and pushing its dollar down still further.

At some point this spiral will stabilize. Things may have to get worse, though, before they level off. It seems unlikely that the US dollar will ever again attain the status it once had, given the convergence of the First Economic World and the Second Economic World, and the ascendancy of the Euro. The US dollar will likely remain but one of a handful of world currencies for the foreseeable future.

What are the forces that will allow this spiral to level off? Already we are seeing a strong improvement in US competitiveness because of a depreciated dollar. Just a couple of years ago, the United States held perhaps five of the top twenty cost effective industrial locations among a hundred comparable sites in the First Economic World.[1] With the beleaguered US dollar, American locations dominate all but two of the top fifty sites worldwide. The US exports have already begun to turn around and this tendency of increased US competitiveness is likely to accelerate in the future.

The magnification effect

Economists have theorized the existence of a magnification effect that allows countries to reap disproportionately large benefits when the underpinnings of their economies become highly prized. For these reasons, we see a tremendous strengthening of positions of the commodities-rich countries and a dramatic weakening of the economies and currencies of the commodity poor.

The currencies of commodity-rich nations, especially those endowed with the scarcest commodities in demand, will show disproportionate increases in their terms of trade. This will create a challenge for their central banks to control the inflation caused by economic overheating. Nations able to coordinate their monetary and fiscal policies can divert some of this wealth from inflation-induced spikes in consumption to long-term economic growth built on a foundation of infrastructure improvements.

The twin deficits

Perhaps the biggest concern is the vulnerability created by the Twin Deficits. The value of the US dollar is derived from both demand for dollars to buy US goods and services, and to invest in US stocks and bonds. If the United States runs a trade deficit, it is sending US dollars abroad to purchase goods and services around the world faster than its global partners are sending the dollars back to buy US goods and services. These trade partners have to do something with their excess dollars, so they instead invest in US capital goods.

The Balance of Payments is simply the sum of its Trade Account and its Capital Account. A flexible, or floating, exchange rate will adjust to keep this current account balanced at zero, meaning a trade deficit must be balanced with a capital surplus. In other words, a trade deficit translates into an inflow of investment, to buy its stocks, companies and real estate, and the bonds that allow the US federal debt to grow. In essence, a trade deficit creates the backflow of capital to fuel a federal budget deficit. This is why some speak of the "twin deficits" in the United States and elsewhere.

This worsening trade deficit and growing federal debt occurred back in 1987, for reasons similar to those experienced today. The trade deficit was worsening because oil prices were high and the United States was losing its competitiveness in manufacturing. Meanwhile, on the strength of fuel-efficient auto production for a resource poor island nation, Japan was thriving. They had to do something with their excess dollars, at any cost, and they were willing to buy US treasury bonds for lack of many other good opportunities. The US treasury was relieved the Japanese were buying US bonds because this allowed the treasury to sell enough bonds to fuel the rising budget deficits in the wake of a Cold War arms race and Star Wars.

On one unfortunate day, Japanese investors decided not to participate in the weekly Treasury auction. This created shockwaves in US investment markets, and forced bond interest rates to rise to renew Japan's interest. This further choked off the investment the United States so desperately needed to re-attain global competitiveness. If the US Treasury did not raise interest rates, capital inflows would diminish, the Current Account would go in the red, and the US dollar would plunge. In an environment when the United States became dependent on continued repatriation of dollars, it lost control of its own interest rate policy, and hence the main tool of domestic monetary policy.

More recently, an increasing oil dependency, a federal debt that has grown dramatically because of the two longest and most costly wars this country has ever fought, and a failure to monitor financial markets that became too clever by one half, has cost the United States a fair degree of control of its own economic future.

While the United States will never be a world leader in the fixed commodities so in demand as the First Economic World and the Second Economic World converge, there are certain franchises and brands it can still promote. The US ingenuity and innovation are its scarce factors of production. Because of this, there has always been a certain cachet to the US dollar and our international posture can still improve its brand. In the past, the value of the franchise was very much because people believed in the vibrancy of the United States of America. This vibrancy can be re-established, as we will envision in the next chapter. Finally, throughout the peaks and troughs of the post-war era, the U.S. has always retained its luster in one important dimension so tied to the psyche of the nation. It is a nation of creative entrepreneurs always curious about how to produce a better mousetrap.

This vibrancy is the American spirit. When one wants to invest in inventiveness and research and development, the possibility to invest in the United States can never be far from one's mind. Add to that the still-strong consumer climate, and American industries that take American culture to every corner of the world. One can remain optimistic, or at least hopeful, that there shall still be cachet for the US dollar, while a strong Euro representing a coherent and strong Europe, and an increasingly assertive Renminbi reflecting China's economic ascendancy produces strong competition for the US dollar.

A liberation in monetary policy

In some sense, the emerging reality of a weaker US dollar is monetarily liberating. We shall also see that the US central bank, the Federal Reserve, has more influence in the value of the US dollar than any other entity. The added pressure to maintain a consistent global store of value could not help but complicate discussions at the Federal Reserve. Also, the strength of the US dollar is ingrained in the national psyche, as if it was somehow the measure of the country. A nation that defines its place so uniquely in the world equates a strong dollar to a strong nation.

On the other hand, trade oriented nations have, at times, welcomed a weak currency because they recognized this will translate into improved international competitiveness, exports, trade, and jobs. Some countries have even gone so far as to attempt to weaken or devalue their currency as a viable economic policy. True, such a strategy inevitably means rising import prices and some inflation as a consequence. Even this cloud has a silver lining, though. The higher prices for imports cause a substitution away from imported goods, when possible, and the creation of new domestic industries.

To come to the realization that a weakening US dollar can become a national asset will require a new acceptance that the United States is becoming a participant in global economics rather than the leader of global economics. Like the aging athlete that learns how to play smart rather than play fast, the United States can attain a new and more sustainable posture in global markets that will be the basis for a rationalized but still strong and steady era of economic growth.

A new recognition of a nation as an international participant will also have some ramifications on our international political identity. A dramatically stronger and more assertive China, Russia, Europe, and India, might help hasten the inevitable transition to the new global landscape.

Part IV
Banks and Central Banking

Innovations in production, consumption, and investment dramatically changed the nature of the banking industry. This industry quickly discovered that it, in effect, could create money. With this realization came the need to regulate money creation, which in turn created central banking.

As nations became increasingly sophisticated in central banking, governments realized that this can be an important tool for economic growth. We now realize that a nation's central bank is indeed the most potent economic entity. With that potency comes a responsibility, and opportunities for political mischief. We next describe what central banks can and cannot do to influence economic well-being. First we describe why we should care.

11
Too Clever by One Half

The past ten years will most surely go down as the most financially troubled since the Great Depression. And, unlike most other eras of financial suffering, much of the pain was brought about by chicanery.

The FEW nations have replaced the goal of expanding the economic pie with an obsession to expand the financial pie. Leaders in the financial markets have become too clever – by one half. They have become inventive, with good old-fashioned hard work replaced by financial cleverness. By using every possible tool at their disposal, they made hard-nosed financial decisions, and were surprised when the Consumer-Investors, so dependent on their new-fangled financial products, became hard nosed too, willing to walk away from mortgages, for instance. The losses from the recent credit crunch amount to, by some estimates, a staggering trillion dollars and counting. All the while, many middle-men got rich without much effort and with no risk. And the public was left holding the bag.

The three Cs

There was a time when banking and finances were local. Our bankers were drawn from Frank Capra's *It's a Wonderful Life*. They attended our Rotary International meetings, met with our local Jaycee chapter, prudently invested our money, and lent us money in return when we wanted to buy the house next door to them. There were three Cs that governed these transactions – Character, Collateral and Credit. And bankers were willing to sacrifice a bit on the first two if a borrower had oodles of the last characteristic. In turn, we would not let George Bailey down, and his rate of foreclosure was staggeringly low, despite the fact that property values grew only slowly for decades.

Mortgages have been securitized for a long time. The long Federal Housing Administration (FHA) form many US homebuyers have filled out was designed to make commodities out of homes. If a house met certain criteria and the buyer qualified, investors could take comfort that the collateral was good and the credit was fine. This was the point when the first C dropped off from consideration, and in stepped the credit agencies.

After all, character is only of local importance. A faceless investor a thousand miles away is not concerned about whether someone is a local teacher, or has never missed a tithe at church, even while they are putting their kids through college or paying for sets of braces. These mortgages that met the underwriting requirements would be "sold" to a Wall Street finance house and packaged with many like mortgages and mortgagees across the country. The business that was the mainstay of local banking and local credit was now a sexy new Wall Street mortgage-backed security, and the local banker was reduced to a commissioned sales executive, not unlike the used-car dealer down the street.

The next C to drop was collateral. These mortgage-backed securities were in great demand, as were any investment opportunity for a growing class of Consumer-Investors. Real estate was hopping, and indeed had not fallen in value in any year since the Great Depression. This had the character of a pyramid scheme – real estate was a fine investment so long as more and more new people look for housing all the time. In the generations before wealthier Consumer-Investors developed a preference for smaller families, we could always count on increasing housing demand with increasing population. In a world of steadily (and sometimes dramatically) increasing housing prices, even collateral became less important. The standard 80% loan with 20% down was soon replaced with a 100% loan, or sometimes more. Collateral was just not an issue.

The final shoe to drop in the Credit Crisis was the loss of good credit as a criterion. Local mortgage brokers processed mortgage applications for a fee (and no risk), so if you told them you were credit worthy and with a good income, then that was fine with them. They took the commission and sold these NINJA loans (No Income, No Job or Assets to verify) to packagers on Wall Street. These packagers, also for a fee (and no risk), created mortgage-backed securities that were sold to their best institutional customers and Consumer-Investors.

The Consumer-Investors are a careful lot, and were not going to take a Wall Street finance house's word on the integrity of these new instruments. So the investment houses asked bond raters to give their stamp of approval, again for a fee (and no risk), on these instruments. Now we have a nice investment instrument, which the bond raters stamped as good quality, with a high rate of return, low risk, and a (hopefully) steady flow of returns. In passing these mortgages through so many intermediaries, no one knew what the mortgagees were told, or for that matter, what they told the brokers.

We know now that some new homeowners were not told about the rapidly escalating interest rates once the initial and attractive "teaser" rate expired. And even if they did understand this, they had no other options and if worst comes to worse, they could always sell the property for a handsome profit, repay the loan, and have enough left over for a nice down payment to do it again. This perfect pyramid scheme, with everybody profiting, worked well so long as housing prices continue to climb. These housing prices would continue to climb so long as credit was abundant and enough people wanted to take advantage of this scheme. But, what happened when this scam became oversold?

The Paul Revere of the mortgage market

The jig was up in the summer of 2007. Actually, some feared that this was too good to be true much earlier, especially a renowned Federal Reserve Board of Governors economist, Professor Edward Gramlich, who was also a noted urban and real estate economist. As far back as the year 2000,[1] Gramlich tried to convince his Federal Reserve colleagues about the impending "sub-prime loan" crisis. He saw this crisis as threatening the twin dreams of homeownership and the acquisition and maintenance of wealth by Consumer-Investors. But, few listened, instead choosing to focus on the strong improvements in the rate of homeownership, and the increases in consumption arising from the perceived wealth of those that owned homes.

One does not need much trouble to truly shake the housing market. The expenses of a vacant home are is high because interest payments and taxes still come due, pipes freeze, vandals break windows, roofs leak, and the lawn becomes unruly. A homeowner responsible enough to want to sell the home when payments become unbearable must sometimes sell at any cost or face foreclosure or worse.

Alternately, a bank that forecloses can lose an additional 25,000 dollars or more each year if the home goes unsold. When the number of homes for sale exceeds the number of people looking for a home, prices can fall to desperation levels. And this depresses the wealth not only of those trying to sell, but also of everyone who owns a home and finds the valuation of their primary store of wealth has fallen.

Once this perfect storm became apparent, reporters and analysts figured out what Prof. Gramlich knew all along; this depressing effect on housing prices could force hundreds of thousands out of their homes. But, worse yet, all homeowners would feel a little poorer as housing prices dropped, and they would scale back consumption. Or perhaps, they would forego that home equity loan they were contemplating in order to buy a new car, do some home improvements, or whatever else they could imagine.

Because home equity loans are more likely to be used to purchase domestic products like construction, college expenses, and the like, a small downward tick in this sort of consumption in a consumer society can have far reaching effects. These effects added to the hundreds of billions of dollars of lost wealth by Consumer-Investors who had purchased these dodgy mortgage-backed sub-prime securities.

A conservative estimate of the value of the US housing stock is fifteen trillion dollars. That is fifteen thousand billion dollars, or fifteen million million dollars. An equally conservative estimate of the drop of housing values as a consequence of the sub-prime meltdown is 10%. This constitutes a loss in wealth of 1.5 trillion dollars, in addition to the multi hundreds of billions of dollars in losses and write-downs from the big banks and investment houses alone.

While a loss of this magnitude might only represent 10% of a fifteen trillion dollar US economy, it is sizeable enough to threaten a recession, and jolt world financial markets. Add to that a UK mortgage industry that replicated the U.S. sub-prime innovations, most notably through Northern Rock, and we have a two-continent meltdown that rapidly spread. The inter-connectedness of world markets caused secondary declines in the US financial markets that continue to ripple around the world. The power of these ripples is the subject of another chapter. Suffice to say, we are all in this together.

Generation X'ers know

How did we ever get ourselves into such a position? Just ask a Generation X'er. These post-baby boom individuals, born between 1964 and 1980, came of age post-Watergate. They casually observed the consumption excesses of the 1980s and the financial crises of the 1990s. They saw Chrysler bailed out, the Savings and Loan crisis of the 1980s, the convictions of market manipulators Ivan Boesky and Michael Milken, and the scandals at Enron and WorldCom. Gen X'ers do not trust institutions to the same extent as their parents and do not share the same outrage when scandals occur. Indeed, they often expect no better of society.

The recent scandals and financial meltdowns do not surprise the Gen X'ers. The cynicism of our society has shifted our emphasis not on wealth through production, but rather wealth through financial cleverness. New financial instruments, new financial techniques, and new wealth without new production are the order of the day. But, while these new instruments do little to expand the size of the economic pie, they have well succeeded in creating an environment in which clever people instead compete for a bigger slice of the existing economic pie.

Baking or cutting the economic pie

Economists divide economic activity into two categories. One is an effort that improves economic efficiency, allowing us to get more by putting in less. Such innovations are always good because we can always make the world a "better" place by distributing this new production. Invention and technological improvements are so desirable because our efforts in these ways allow us to improve our lot. Economists do not feel we are in a position to determine who should get this bonus bounty, but we trust that whoever does will value it. And so, expansion of the economic pie is invariably a worthy enterprise in the world of economists.

On the other hand, efforts designed to expand one's slice of a fixed economic pie at the expense of the slices going to others is not an economic improvement. We recognize that such efforts to gain in a zero sum game may be politically desirable at times. For instance, redistributive taxation is designed to do just that – to take from one group and give to another. These are attempts to profit from the Robin Hood principle by taking from those that value it less, to give to those that value it a lot. But, valuable resources should never be employed solely to capture another's share of the economic pie.

Unfortunately, we have created a cynical culture in which expanding one's share at the expense of another is now considered acceptable. Perhaps it is this cynicism, borne from the get-rich-quick schemes that wind one in prison, or worse yet the public trials that seem to more often than not end in acquittal, that has produced a mentality in which one tries to "catch as catch can." In an anonymous world when we are no longer judged by our character, why not get ahead at the expense of others?

The Enron meltdown

Perhaps the most blatant example of "too clever by one half" was the Enron meltdown. While thousands lost their lifetime retirement savings, and perhaps a few people went to jail, this series of unethical actions most problematically confirmed what many were already thinking: some corporations care less about people and more about getting rich. We wonder if they ask first what is good for the bottom line and then, possibly, if it is good and ethical, rather than the other way around. Of course, Enron is a one in a million exception, but it did a lot to define corporate irresponsibility in the public's mind.

Enron was a firm that started off as a small trader in natural gas futures. In this capacity traders can, for a fee, take the risk away from future contracts between buyers and sellers of a commodity. By guaranteeing future contract prices, buyers and sellers can get on with their main business of supplying and using a commodity. In this case, the commodity was natural gas, but other cases include corn, oil, coffee beans, or whatever one can imagine. Buyers are willing to engage in this transaction because they abhor risk and would be willing to pay now to gain some price certainty later. Both sides of the transaction are willing to pay to shed the risk of changes in commodity prices, and Enron was willing to take on that risk, for a fee.

A company like Enron can do this by trying to anticipate the market. There were thousands of clever people employed by Enron to help figure out how to better predict, and hence profit from, the market. But, as an intermediary, buying from many and selling to many, Enron soon discovered that they can withhold some of the commodity in order to drive prices up.

For instance, Enron stood accused of taking advantage of California energy deregulation by buying energy in California at the going rate of 250 dollars per megawatt hour, and selling it almost immediately to a buyer in the Pacific Northwest for 1,200 dollars per megawatt hour. They were also accused of shutting down electricity generation plants at critical peak times. In California alone, it was estimated that Enron defrauded the State of billions of dollars through manipulated shortages. Californian homeowners paid hundreds of dollars more in electric fees solely because of clever, and illegal, market manipulations.

Executives at Enron were eventually convicted of shady dealings, perpetrated not primarily on the public, but on the investment community. In addition to the losses to an unsuspecting public, Enron went bankrupt owing almost 32 billion dollars, and leaving 21,000 people without jobs. It also brought down one of the top accounting firms worldwide, generating billions more in losses and lost employment. But, while the schemes cost citizens billions of dollars and rattled the confidence of investors and the public alike, the fines and jail terms bore no relationship to the public costs. Total fines amount to a penny or two on the dollar of damage done, and actual time spent in jail for all the principals will likely total a couple of dozen years.

These scandals and the subsequent lack of judicial deterrence have created a level of cynicism that seems reinforced every few years. Of course, it would be impossible to effectively deter such massive crimes upon the unsuspecting public. Only greater transparency and greater regulation will rid us of our cynicism. However, the regulatory burden that results will be borne primarily not by the rogue corporations or individuals, but by innocent Consumer-Investors and the 99.9% of businesses that run ethical and legal operations.

Sarbanes-Oxley

As a consequence of the Enron and the WorldCom scandals, the US Congress and the worldwide accounting industry have provided greater regulation, primarily in the form of the Sarbanes-Oxley Act of 2002 and its international counterparts. Also known as the Public Company Accounting Reform and Investor Protection Act, this law requires a chief executive of a publicly traded company to personally vouch for the accuracy of the information provided on an accounting statement. In doing so, it takes away the defense that chief executive officers had no idea what creative accounting mischief was occurring under their nose.

Cost estimates for this greater level of accountability and transparency range from over 2% of revenue for smaller publicly traded firms, to about 1% for the nation's largest firms. These costs will be minor if indeed the Act can re-establish confidence and trust in the financial reporting of publicly traded firms.

The three Is

Both Enron and the Sub-Prime Crisis point to three problems that frustrate financial markets. Markets rely on integrity, information, and incentives.

Financial markets are in some sense self policing. While there are laws and institutions designed to regulate the markets, they are miniscule in staff power and resources in comparison to the millions of corporations and trillions of dollars they regulate. At best, they can go after only the biggest or most public fish, in the hopes that the public humiliation sets a sufficient example for others.

The problem is that someone contemplating the risk will compare the deterrence and the probability of getting caught with the often immense reward of fraudulent or unethical behavior. It would be impossible to deter even nearly the amount of the damage inflicted. And securities fraud of all sorts is very difficult to prove. Those initiating such a fraud are necessarily secretive, as are their co-conspirators. These are clever people who will cover their tracks well. With insufficient deterrence in comparison to the damage caused, and with low probability of detection, it seems likely that the vast majority of illegal and unethical behavior goes undetected. All such behavior tears at the integrity of the market and undermines returns for honest Consumer-Investors.

As discussed earlier, securities pricing depends critically on the accuracy of information. With the current compensation schemes of corporate executives, most of which is tied, rightly so, to the performance of the corporation, there is a terrible urge to accentuate the positives in the financial statement summaries, and bury the negatives in obscure accounting footnotes. There is a principle among accountants that all the interesting stuff occurs in these footnotes. So a company may be meeting the letter of the law in providing the public with the relevant information, but it may not be making that information sufficiently easy to comprehend. If a tree falls in the forest, does it make a sound?

Finally, markets assume the incentives are in the right place for good economic decision-making. We could see from the sub-prime induced Credit Crunch that breakdowns occurred because of layers of middlemen sequentially obfuscating information while still receiving their commission. There was no risk associated with their reward.

Recall the problem of moral hazard. This occurs when one makes a different decision than would otherwise be optimal were they to absorb the costs of their decision-making. In the end, someone will pay for the returns received by each middleman, and will absorb all the risk that will only be discovered too late. That someone is ultimately the Consumer-Investor who has been told repeatedly that the price of a security accurately incorporates all available information.

There is a principle in economics called Gresham's Law. Simply put, it says that bad money drives out good. Named after a fourteenth-century financier, the law is interpreted to imply that when we cannot distinguish between the good and the bad, there is an incentive to put more bad assets into the marketplace, thereby driving out the good assets that cannot afford to be mixed in with the bad. If a few bad securities pollute financial markets, and this makes us suspect of all securities, market prices will be depressed and the cost of raising capital then rises.

Recall our discussion of market failures and our mention of externalities. Perhaps the greatest tragedy of financial wheeling and dealing without the associated creation of a larger economic pie is that the resulting cynicism drives some from the marketplace. It took us a generation to renew the faith in the banking system after the spectacular failures in the Great Depression. By the actions of a few that impose such great costs on the many, the market breaks down. This negative externality must be priced to the full extent of the costs imposed. Given the difficulty in detecting when the externality is occurring, the appropriate price is likely a large multiple of the damages imposed by each transgression. The courts are willing to impose treble damages for the convicted, but even treble damages are unlikely to compensate for the low probability of getting caught. And these damages take into account only the direct and easily ascertainable costs, but cannot account for the costs of increased cynicism and mistrust in the marketplace.

What can we do to lend greater confidence to the market and to weed out cynicism of our institutions? For one thing, we must ensure that those receiving the rewards are also bearing their share of the risk. This problem certainly became apparent in the sub-prime led Credit Crunch. We may want to revisit corporate executive compensation schemes, too. If the majority of compensation is in the form of stock options, executives can earn astronomical sums when times are good but still receive a very generous base pay when times are bad. In effect, executives benefit from upside risk but are not penalized from downside risk. The Consumer-Investor receives a lower return on the upside because executives then take their cut, but the Consumer-Investor is left holding the whole bag when times are bad. Assumption of risk to sharpen one's decision-making of course requires assumption of risk even when things are bad. To do otherwise creates externalities, a perverse system of incentives, and increased market cynicism. And none of these are healthy if we want to create an efficient financial market.

12
Who's Minding the Store?

Coordinated monetary policy has typically been borne out of financial calamity. Regardless of the motivation, monetary authorities have emerged as the single most effective economic players in most all of the FEW and SEW nations.

Monetary unions and authorities go back to colonial days, sometimes as a response to colonial policies. In New England, four states in Colonial America formed a union that set the example for a common currency in the United States. And in Latin America, a group of countries formed their own currency union to buck the control and influence of their European colonial powers.

By wresting control over the creation of money from the colonial powers, these states and countries could develop monetary policies that met their economic needs. While all the subtleties of monetary policy were then unknown, they recognized that markets needed confidence in the currency. Money creation ought to be performed with a level of prudence that prevented the inflations seen when too much of a currency was minted. Money should also be plentiful enough so that transactions can take place. If money is like the oil that keeps the economic machine from seizing up, some responsible entity has to appropriately replenish the oil-can. This is the purview of treasuries and bourses, central banks, and, in the United States, the Federal Reserve.

All Fed up

The Federal Reserve ("Fed") has an illustrious history and has attained the status of the premier economic watchdog in the United States, with central banks playing identical roles abroad. Enacted in 1913 as a response to a financial panic in 1907 when stock values were almost halved, the Federal Reserve Act of 1913 was designed with two goals in mind. The first was to wrestle control of national finances from Wall Street. The second was to ensure that a national economic entity acts to maintain confidence in the monetary and banking system. There had been a number of bank panics and recessions over the 50 years preceding the creation of the "Fed," and many clamored for greater governmental oversight of banks and the currency.

There were diverse interests represented in the debate over the Federal Reserve Banks. Wall Street had an obvious interest, while the agrarian base of the country had a growing concern over economic stewardship and currency reliability. The compromises resulted in a Fed that performed two roles – to act as the bank to bankers, and to help manage the currency and financial markets, through some clever techniques we will discuss. It will become clear that the Fed can accomplish a lot but, at times, its power is limited to rhetoric.

Monetary unions and coordinated policies – an international perspective

> The economic health of every country is a proper matter of concern to all its neighbors, near and far.
>
> Franklin Roosevelt at the opening of Bretton Woods

The Bretton Woods Conference of 1944 arose from the post-World War II realization that international economic cooperation is necessary. Adopting the name of the New Hampshire location where the group first met, the conference had the goal of combining the economic development interests of the two victors in World War II. The United States promoted the goal of free trade, while Britain elucidated the Keynesian objectives of full employment and steady economic growth.

From the conference came a spirit of international cooperation, the formation of an International Monetary Fund to help create global monetary stability, and discussions to ensure exchange rate stability.

Economic cooperation was motivated to avoid the increasing tendency to form trading factions and blocs, at the expense of free trade. Only by providing for a system that would benefit all would the increasing economic factionalization be avoided. This cooperation would also speed reconstruction, and be at least partially credited with sewing the seeds of the post-World War II economic prosperity.

Early in the creation of a European Economic Union, the member countries recognized the value of a common currency. Such a currency would ease trade, reduce uncertainties arising from relative exchange rate movements between the member countries, and help control prices. Statutes to establish the European Economic Community and a system of central banks began the process for community monetary coordination. Always sensitive to the need to ensure some autonomy in member country's economic policy, the European Monetary Union (EMU) and central banks confined their attention to the maintenance of price stability within the union. As a side benefit, the EMU authority would manage foreign reserves for the member countries and facilitate payment clearance, just as the Fed performs in the United States. The European Central Bank also helps coordinate policies of its member central banks, and assists in maintaining a stable financial system.

Roles of the Fed

As the United States economy grew and banks and commerce spread geographically, it became increasingly complicated to clear the checks written from one bank but deposited to another. In addition, it became more difficult to oversee the banking system. The Fed can respond to these two functions simultaneously by acting as the bank for bankers. By establishing twelve regional banks for bankers, distributed across the country, banks could more conveniently go to one place to receive cash for checks they have taken in but drawn from another bank. This national clearing-house for inter-bank checks would also allow the Fed to monitor banks.

The next innovation was the fractional reserve system. Economic folklore helps us to understand this most important tool of monetary control, by describing the business of the early goldsmiths of Europe. These goldsmiths kept large stocks of gold, and obviously needed to keep the gold secure. So secure were their facilities that other owners of gold asked the goldsmiths to hold the gold for them. In return, the goldsmith would issue an IOU stating that the slip of paper represented perhaps one ounce of gold. This paper representation of gold subsequently could be traded for goods and services, and thus acted as a monetary system under a de facto gold standard.

Under that system, who would know if a goldsmith produced a few extra IOUs? And that is just what they did. They found they could print up these extra IOUs, lend them to (hopefully creditworthy) borrowers, and, in essence, create a banking system. This system of issuing more IOUs than there was actual gold in the vault was safe so long as all the holders of IOUs did not come to the bank simultaneously to claim their gold. And this system worked, until one notorious day when a major borrower of IOUs (and a member of the royal family) announced he had no intention of repaying the loans. All of a sudden, the holders of the IOUs received from the Prince "ran to the bank" to collect their gold. We simultaneously had the first bank run and the first bankruptcy.

To guard against that, we now regulate how many such IOUs a bank can create. With innovations like the Federal Deposit Insurance Corporation protection of our deposits, this share of obligations held in cash or gold need not be large. For instance, so long as we don't expect more than one in twenty to come to a bank in a given period and demand all their cash, we could get by allowing banks to issue IOUs, in the form of loans, worth twenty times the amount of cash in the vault. In a modern economy, this would probably be adequate because so few transactions are denominated in cash, with the banks and customers relying primarily on checks and electronic fund transfers.

However, the banking industry is regulated more tightly yet. The Fed requires banks to hold approximately 10% of their checking account liabilities to customers in the form of cash. The other 90% of a bank's assets are held primarily in loans and mortgages it has extended. These loans create new money, above and beyond the original cash it holds. This expansion of money well beyond the initial deposit is known as the "deposit expansion multiplayer.

Even 10% of a modern bank's assets is a huge sum. The Fed steps in here too, offering to hold these mandatory reserves on behalf of the banks in its region. By having stacks of cash in its vaults, representing the mandatory reserves from each of its member banks, the Fed can now easily reconcile a check drawn on one bank but deposited at another. The Fed can simply take the amount of cash from one bank's pile and put it in the other bank's stack. Of course, nowadays this is simply done with entries in a huge computer ledger, but the idea remains the same.

Banks would obviously prefer these mandatory reserves to be as small as possible. It turns out that a bank can create 100 dollars of accounts for every 10 dollars of cash. This is because they ultimately must hold only 10% of their assets in the form of cash. However, if the Fed permitted a bank to have only 5% of their accounts in the form of cash, they could create a 100 dollars of accounts for every 5 dollars of cash, and could make twice as many loans for a given initial deposit. If they make their money by lending out money, their profits could rise as their capacity to make loans increases. They would then also threaten the security of the banking system and the ability of the central bank to control the money supply.

In fact, such innovations as federal deposit insurance help prevent bank panics and bank runs. The real goal of a system of mandatory reserves is simply to regulate the amount of checking account balances that can be created through new loans. Because checking accounts are included in our most common measure of the money supply, M1, a central bank can effectively determine the supply of money and purchasing power circulating around in the economy by tinkering with this ratio of cash to bank deposits.

While this method we call fractional reserves is very powerful, it is almost too powerful. There are two other ways in which a central bank can affect the money supply that are far more commonly employed. But, before we describe them, let's spend a moment discussing why central banks are interested in affecting the money supply in the first place.

Oil for the machine

Think of the money supply as the oil that lubricates the economy. Too little money means that the economic engine is not well lubricated and does not spin freely. Transactions that ought to occur cannot occur because there is not enough cash to support the payments. If there is not enough money to support transactions, some will have to discount their transactions, causing prices to fall, and deflation. While falling prices sounds attractive, a deflation is problematic.

For instance, we only have to look at the grave concern nationally as housing prices fall just a little bit. Homeowners feel poorer if their housing prices fall, threatening their consumption. This causes existing mortgages and loans to become less collateralized, making bankers nervous. Falling prices also can cause a declining stock market, creating a double whammy for Consumer-Investors.

On the other hand, too much money is unnecessary, and, even more problematically, causes too much money to chase too few goods, causing prices to rise and inflation. Businesses abhor inflation because it makes contracting and planning difficult and riskier. Those on fixed income dislike inflation because it erodes their buying power and consequently reduces overall consumption.

Control of the money supply and hence the level of inflation is an inexact science. We cannot risk pushing ourselves into a deflation, so we usually aim at inflation just a couple of points above zero percent. It is one of a central bank's goals to keep inflation just right – not too low, and certainly not too high.

A central bank also looks at other things in its effort to optimize the inflation rate. They know that too much economic activity, beyond the capacity of the economy, will also drive up prices. If demand for the products firms produce outstrips their supply, the only way they can cope in the short run is to ask for higher prices to keep up with demand. Something similar happens for workers. If growth in the demand for our employer's product means that we must work harder, faster, and longer, we will demand a higher wage, which will also translate into higher product prices down the line. So not only must a central bank try to manage inflation through the money supply, but they must also try to aim at just the right level of economic activity that is not too hot and not too cold.

Before we get to the difficulties involved with these twin goals of inflation and economic activity, let us return to the two common tools the central bank can use to influence the money supply. They have discovered that changing the cash reserve requirement is like swatting a flea with a cannon. It is just too cumbersome, too powerful, and too difficult to implement too often. There are more subtle and clever tools at their disposal.

A steady hand on the throttle

In the United States, the fine-tuning of the money supply is done by a subset of the Board of Governors of the Fed called the Federal Open Market Committee (FOMC). The FOMC is chaired by the chairman of the Fed, now Ben Bernanke after the retirement of Alan Greenspan. The FOMC routinely meets eight times each year, and sometimes more if necessary. They set out broad monetary goals and then have their staff use a tool called open market operations to implement these goals on a daily basis. Let's see how that works.

The Fed is reputed to have the most sophisticated and elaborate economic model found anywhere. An economic model is a mathematical abstraction of the entire economy, and takes in data to predict economic trends. If the model tells them that the economy is running too hot, they will try to cool down the economy. And if the model suggests the economy is running a little tepid, they will try to heat it up.

In the first case of a hot economy, the Fed would like to rein it in through "tight monetary policy." They would like to contract the money supply to discourage transactions and thus slow down economic growth. The Fed can do this because of their control over banks. If they can discourage banks from lending, businesses cannot expand, and growth is slowed.

Now here is where the fractional cash reserves system and the "bank for bankers" comes in quite handy. To reduce the money supply, the

Fed can simply take cash out of the piles of its member banks, forcing the banks to not renew some loans that have expired and perhaps delay new loans for a while. The Fed must give the banks something in return for the lost cash though, and they do by selling them treasury bonds. The Fed gives up the bonds, and gets the cash, and the economy is cooled through loan contraction.

You might ask what happens if the banks don't want to give up the cash. The Fed is not selling bonds to profit. Rather, they sell bonds to realize economic objectives. So, in the words of Mario Puzo's *The Godfather*, the Fed can always offer the banks a deal they cannot refuse. They could even sell bonds to customers of the banks, to the same effect. The Fed gives the customers the bonds, the customers give the Fed a check, and the Fed clears the check by taking cash out of the stacks belonging to member banks. This then forces commercial banks to contract lending.

To expand, or loosen, the money supply and expand economic activity, we simply do the reverse. The Fed can buy bonds back from banks or its customers, and in doing so, put cash back into the banks' stacks. The banks can't afford to hold too much cash (above the 10% reserve requirement) because that would be an idle asset not working to make profits for the bank. So banks will try to lend that money out, and in the process expand the money supply and encourage growth and spending.

The Fed does a bit of these open market operations just about every business day to be sure they have the cash reserves and the money supply just where they want them. Few Consumer-Investors monitor the Fed's open market operations, or the size of the money supply, so these daily actions are not very apparent and do not get much press. The effects are relatively slow too because, to be effective, the Fed must wait for the lending operations of the banks to do their part.

One more arrow in their quiver

There is one more tool though that gets a lot of attention, and has the ability to shake markets – around the world. It is the Fed's control of what is called the "discount window." When we hear about the Fed setting a key interest rate, that's what we're talking about.

To see how this works, and sometimes doesn't work, we need to remember that the Fed is the bank for banks. If the cash reserves of commercial banks get a little too low, the Fed will offer them a short-term loan to prop up their reserves. Everybody gets a little overextended once in a while, even a commercial bank. But, the bank would not remain in the Fed's good graces if it did this all the time. The bank tries to create a bit of a cushion of reserves above what they are required to hold just to be sure they don't wear out their friendship with the Fed. Banks don't want to keep much of these excess reserves because they want to lend out as much as possible – after all, that is how they make money. They don't want to keep too little in excess reserves because they would run the risk of wearing thin their relationship with the Fed. And a bank doesn't want to offend the Fed.

Once in a while the Fed wants banks to lend aggressively, and again they can make an offer the banks can't refuse. They can encourage the banks to reduce these excess reserves by offering to lend banks some cash at an attractive interest rate. Banks will borrow to prop up their reserves, and this will allow them to lend out perhaps ten times more than they borrow in cash from the Fed, again as a consequence of the fractional reserve system. Alternately, if they want to discourage bank lending, they can say to the member banks "we'll bail you out if you get caught short, but it's gonna hurt." They do so by raising the interest rate offered at the discount window to member banks.

A common misunderstanding

This process is deceptively simple but remarkably misunderstood. The Fed and the press certainly make great fanfare over their setting of the discount rate. It is commonly misunderstood to imply that the Fed somehow sets the market interest rate, or at least strongly influences all sorts of interest rates. Rather, most all the rates that matter to us as Consumer-Investors are determined by the banks and by the supply and demand for loanable funds, neither of which the Fed can directly control.

Actually, the Fed can create a climate for more loanable funds by encouraging the banks to lend more, and vice-versa. It is true that the greater cash or liquidity the Fed can create for member banks will encourage the banks to provide for more funds to lend, and this greater supply of loans brings the price of loans, the interest rate, down. But, a 1 percentage point, or 100 basis point, decline in the discount rate may have a larger or smaller effect in the interest rates we all see as Consumer-Investors, depending on a lot of other factors.

To see the rub, let's imagine that the economy is in a bit of a panic and the Fed announces that to quell our fears of a recession, it is going to lower its interest rate. You can take a horse to water but you can't make it drink. What if the banks say that creating more money for them to lend out is all fine and dandy, but all this talk about a recession makes them rethink whether more lending is wise? Perhaps this is not the time to extend new loans, even though the Fed has increased liquidity available. In this case, the Fed's policy may not be effective. The Fed can usually be effective in discouraging loans by forcibly reducing cash reserves. They can be less effective in encouraging banks to lend money out.

Pushing a piece of string

This asymmetry, in which the Fed can nicely contract the economy by pulling on the monetary string, but cannot as easily expand the economy by pushing on the string, requires the Fed to use one more trick up its sleeve. It is the power of rhetoric. Recall that monetary policy can be ineffective if we simply cannot induce the banks to lend. Some of this may be the banks' doing, perhaps because of a change in lending policy when the economy seems a little shaky.

Some of this may also be driven by the Consumer-Investor who looks at all the talk of a recession and says, "I think I will put off purchasing that car, or that home if there is a threat of housing price falls." If the Fed cannot easily push the string because of bank or Consumer-Investor pessimism, it may have to resort to the bully pulpit to convince us that we must keep spending. The value of the bully pulpit cannot be underestimated, as we will learn later. But, in the meantime, we see that the Fed's job can be tough indeed.

Enter the credit crunch of 2007

Let's look for a moment at policy paralysis. The Fed has the most sophisticated models, and employs some of the brightest economists on the planet so that they can understand the economy and anticipate its every twist and turn. They know the world is watching, as we will describe later. So, the stakes are high. And they feel the pressure.

Sometimes there is a lot to manage though, and there may be competing objectives and too many masters to serve. The Credit Crunch crisis is a case in point. As a consequence of the many factors we have already described, oil prices shot up in 2007, having doubled twice, in inflation adjusted terms, in just ten years. With oil price rises often come agricultural price rises because the technologies used in agriculture and in transporting food are energy, mostly hydrocarbon, intensive. When oil prices rise substantially, food prices rise as well, and inflation rises as a consequence.

Sometimes prices rise and we have to live with that. Rising oil prices will inevitably mean wealth is moved from the oil dependent economies to the oil rich economies. This results in a permanent rise in prices, and we cannot put that genie back in bottle. If we do not accept the higher inflation, and instead try to cool down the economy to rid ourselves of the higher prices, we risk slowing down the economy inappropriately.

Fed chairmen are sensitive to inflation. Former chairman Paul Volcker had the unfortunate task of overseeing the double-digit inflation of the 1970s and early 1980s. A Fed may have to wrestle with the prospect of upsetting everybody because of inflation, or upset a few people an awful lot because they were laid off from work as a consequence of tight monetary policy. Either alternative is a deal with the devil. As a consequence, when a Fed is confronted with both talk of a recession and with inflation, it may freeze. This dreaded no-man's land of a stagnant economy and inflation is called stagflation, and manages to upset just about everybody.

Any of these policies of tightening or loosening the money supply take some time to work their way through the economy. The art of the Fed is to try to anticipate where the economy will go and guide the trajectory. A lot of foresight is required. It also takes a long time to correct a misstep. As a consequence, Fed policy is a careful act, sometimes choosing to do nothing at all rather than something wrong.

The problem is that, at times, the public clamors for action. They need to be reassured that the Fed is watching carefully and has everything under control. If something unexpected happens, it fuels pressure from the public that the Fed was not watching close enough or acting quickly enough. When the public believes the Fed is asleep at the wheel, they get very concerned, and they act, usually by delaying consumption. In an economy in which consumption represents about 70% of economic activity, any irrational change in consumption patterns can be most problematic.

Policy paralysis – a deer in the headlights

We can identify at least one more challenge that can delay timely central bank intervention. Stagflation, a relatively rare phenomenon of simultaneous inflation and high unemployment, puts central banks in a dilemma. To resolve one challenge will worsen the other. The stagflation of the late 1970s and the policy paralysis following the Credit Crunch of 2007 required the US central bank to make a Faustian bargain. The Fed could slow the already declining economy still further to reduce spending and hence reduce the pressure on prices to rise. Or the Fed could stimulate the economy to ward off the recession, but would then increase spending, prices, and inflation.

The anti-inflationary policy of slowing the economy will significantly hurt the small number whose jobs are threatened. The anti-recessionary policy would help those threatened with unemployment but would then hurt all those who must face rising prices. The choice is to hurt a few a lot, or to hurt a lot a little. Neither proposition is attractive. If the principle is "first, do no harm," then the central bank found itself doing nothing. This is the safe strategy given the difficulty in re-establishing control in an economy suffering from the stagflations we saw worldwide in the 1970s.

The Supreme Court of Monetary Policy

Imagine feeling all these pressures while at the same time being buffeted by political forces. While central banks are not completely immune to political pressures, their chairmen and members cannot be fired. For instance, in the United States, members of the Board of Governors are given 14-year terms, and are appointed by the President and confirmed by the Senate. As a consequence, they are relatively immune to administrations that they are sure to outlive. This is not to say that administrations and Congress do not try to exert as much pressure as possible to have a strong economy. Political appeals are relatively ineffective as the Board has every incentive to maintain a strong economy in the long run, if not also in the short run as politicians might prefer. Of course, with politicians, sometimes the Fed is asked "what have you done for me lately?"

Before we close, let me point out one final problem. Sometimes we can have too much of a good thing. The analogy I use is that it might be nice to have a cow in my office. I'd have fresh milk and cream for my coffee every day, and actually cows make pretty good company. However, five cows in my office would be too much of a good thing. Too much good interest rate news can be the same way. If the Fed recognizes that its main tool is the lowering of the discount rate, or its associated Federal Funds rate that banks lend to each other to prop up their cash reserves, what happens when the rate goes to 3%, then 2%, then 1%? At some point it cannot go any lower without paying borrowers to take their money.

When the interest rate has been forced too low and Producer-Investors are still not willing to borrow, the economy finds itself in a liquidity trap. Once interest rates fall too low, Consumer-Investors see little incentive to deposit their money in banks, and the source of credit funds dries up. Keynes knew this to be a problem even 80 years ago. It is another reason why Keynesians believe monetary policy will not always be effective, especially if the economy is in really bad shape and we are at our wit's end with monetary policy.

We have seen that the Fed can have an especially powerful influence on loanable funds, especially in the contractionary direction. Later we will see that their rhetoric is also powerful, and is the voice that echoes around the world. The next chapter shows they do not have to do all the heavy lifting. There are important economic principles at work that can help the Fed realize its economic goals.

13
Who Spiked the Punchbowl?

Economic policy is often a confidence game, with the strength of moral persuasion arising from the monetary authority's power to influence economic investment and consumption. Can a central bank actually fine-tune its way out of a recession?

We believe it can, or at least we want to believe so.

Central banks actually have a few instruments to back up their rhetoric. They can use the instrument of changes in reserve requirements, which is so blunt it is almost never changed. They can put more cash in the hands of banks and Consumer-Investors by buying bonds from us at favorable terms. Or they can lower the rate it charges for banks to borrow to prop up excess reserves, who in turn lend out some of the excess to stimulate investment and consumption.

As we have seen, these various tools can be effective in theory, and even effective in practice, more or less. The linkage between a monetary policy shift and the size or growth of the economic pie is a little shaky sometimes.

Let us begin with a description of the circumstances when a central bank can effectively spur the economy. We will use the example of the Federal Reserve, although all central banks follow the same practices.

Recall the linkages that must simultaneously work to be effective. First, the Fed can sell bonds to put some cash into the reserves of banks. This is not too difficult to accomplish because the Fed can choose to sell these bonds at whatever price it wants and can always make us an offer we can't refuse. Alternatively, the Fed can offer banks a low interest rate to borrow cash to prop up their reserves. In doing so, the banks can then lend out these excess reserves to create more loans, perhaps even ten times the loans as the cash the bank originally borrowed.

This technique of using excess cash reserves to create multiple loans is the principle of the fractional reserve system. But, like any market, what happens next depends on supply and demand. Sure, the banks can increase their supply of loanable funds, but that does not mean they will be willing to lend this money out or that Consumer-Investors or Producer-Investors will want to borrow.

Just as the Fed can encourage the banks to sell their bonds or borrow from the Fed by making us offers we can't refuse, banks must also be willing to lend money out. If the market is hungry for new investment and there is optimism and opportunity in the air, the climate might be right for some new lending. Naturally, lenders will want to have a sense that the investment will result in production in markets for which demand is strong. Certainly if the economy is rolling along nicely, healthy demand will not be a problem.

Unfortunately, banks have been characterized by their willingness to lend money out when we don't really need it, but not so willing to lend money out when we do. There are reasons why banks may not want to cooperate with the central bank when the market most needs a spur in investment. We most need to spur investment when growth is declining and inventories are increasing because of weak demand. Growing inventories and weakening demand are precisely the conditions that make bankers nervous. It is against their better judgment to cooperate with the Fed in these times when the Fed needs banks the most.

You can take a horse to water

Let's assume for the moment that the central bank can somehow induce banks to lend at these critical times when the economic train is teetering toward derailment. A central bank can spike the punchbowl, but can it make us drink? The essential ingredient for any such monetary policy is our willingness to go along with their plan. This requires us to offer our full faith and credit in the central bank's plan.

Our faith is challenged if a central bank tries to do too much. A central bank that lowers interest rate below about 2% finds itself contributing to its own irrelevancy. Under no circumstances can it give money away. As the solid line on the diagram in Figure 13.1 indicates, the US Federal Reserve has found itself dangerously close to giving money away. Banks, too, must be induced to drink. If the punchbowl is spiked too much but the economy is not intoxicating enough, the banks may refuse to borrow. This is the classic liquidity trap in which the Fed finds monetary control out of its grasp. And no governor of a central bank wants to supervise the order decline of the effectiveness of monetary policy.

The Consumer-Investor or the Producer-Investor will borrow for many of the same reasons the banks will lend. We believe we can produce greater wealth later by investing in productive capacity now. Consumer-Investors also have secondary motives to borrow, perhaps to consume now by capitalizing on their increased housing values through a home equity loan. The reasons for their borrowing are also related to their level of optimism. As the economy worsens, Consumer-Investors may be induced to borrow more to avoid getting behind in bills, cover margin calls on investments gone badly, and so on. It is these sorts of loans that make bankers most wary.

As a consequence, it is likely that the Fed can encourage investment and spending when there is a relative sense of buoyancy in the market. Let us next compare the overall level of consumer confidence with the policies of the Fed. The consumer sentiment survey has been maintained by the University of Michigan ever since the economic malaise following the Organization of Oil Exporting Countries (OPEC) oil crisis. Since then consumer confidence has varied widely, as the dashed line on Figure 13.1 demonstrates.

You can see by the dotted line that consumer confidence in the 1970s was low, primarily because of high inflation, interest rates, and the

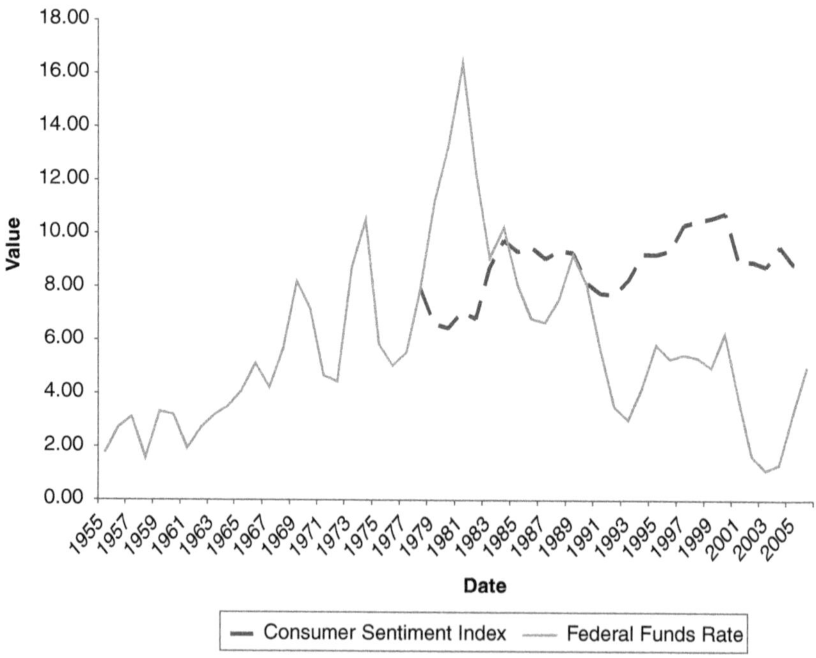

Figure 13.1 Federal funds rate and consumer sentiment, 1957 to present

Federal Funds rate. Consumer confidence began to improve over the 1980s, dipped during the first Bush administration and rose steadily until 2001.

Most interesting is the relationship between confidence and the federal funds rate. The federal funds rate drops after consumer confidence begins to decline. Once confidence troughs and begins to rise again, so does the Federal Funds rate.

In other words, Federal monetary policy tends to respond to the level of consumer confidence and the myriad factors that influence consumer confidence. This leads us to our essential point. The economic climate must be just right for Fed monetary policy to be effective. If the market begins to enter a cycle of pessimism, monetary policy effectiveness is reduced if banks or borrowers throttle back their lending and spending. Paraphrasing the words of the hockey star Wayne Gretzky, the Fed is most effective when it can skate to where the puck will be, not where it is.

This level of anticipation is difficult, especially if there is a concern over inflation. Recall a Fed that pushes an already strong economy instead risks its gains to be eroded by inflation. Fearful of pushing the economy too far that would subsequently require tight money to choke inflation off, the Fed tries to push just enough but not too much or too early. This concern creates a conservative bias that sometimes appears as "too little, too late".

With perfect hindsight, it is easy to predict what the Fed should have done after the fact. The creation of twenty-four hour cable news has created quite a sport of Fed-watching. Wednesday morning second-guessing of Fed decisions is commonplace and markets now routinely factor into their performance the actions they expect the Fed to take. Now if the Fed does not do what the market expects it to do, the collective level of discouragement can spell trouble. As the market now conspires with the Fed and the Fed with the market, the element of shock and awe has been lost.

Perhaps now the best analogy of the Fed is the conservative helmsman at the tiller of a big economic ship. Small and not unexpected corrections to square off against the approaching wave can keep the economy on track. Big corrections or late corrections will likely stall the tiller and will be relatively ineffective.

Fed-speak

In this period of hyper-Fed watching, the Fed has become increasingly important not in what it does, because that is now assumed to a great degree, but by what it says it will do. The Fed increasingly sets the tone for the economy, sending out messages that it stands prepared to act if a rogue wave appears.

It is this comfort that more than anything lends calm to the market. The Fed has been called upon to exercise its rhetoric more lately, calming fears that may start in Asia and spread to Europe. Even before US markets open, the Fed has found itself announcing that it stands by to provide whatever market liquidity is necessary. The Fed has assumed the role of the voice of reason and confidence.

The rhetoric of the Fed has changed too. At one time, they were renowned for their ability to speak volumes and yet say little. This newfound skill has come at a high cost. On December 5, 1996, then Fed chairman Alan Greenspan notoriously uttered the words "irrational exuberance," and created sensation and turmoil in the market that was very significant at that time. Markets worldwide fell by 3% or more. For a business press corps that hang on every obtuse word Chairman Greenspan spoke, this seemed like a direct signal that the Fed was concerned about excessive market valuation and may be prepared to do something about it.

The conventional wisdom at the time was that anything but the most oblique references would be too strong a signal for the market to grasp. Speaking in subtlety and code, the so-called Fed-speak, was considered a necessary ingredient for financial order. With a new Fed Reserve Chairman, Ben Bernanke, this Fed-Speak has been replaced by the "straight talk express." We seem destined to hear more frequent statements that the Fed stands ready to provide the market with as much liquidity as necessary to maintain market integrity. Our comfort no longer lies in what we wonder the Fed might be saying and instead has been replaced with firm intentions on the part of the Fed.

There is a saying among economists that we will tell you what will happen, or when it will happen, but never both. Not surprisingly given the number of economists associated with the Fed, statements now indicate what they will try to establish, but not necessarily when or how. It is the when and how that causes market frenzy as individuals try to capitalize on this indefinite news. The Fed gives its flavor of the market, saying it will maintain liquidity, create a tightening bias, keep inflation in check, and so forth to instead give guidance without particular details.

This evolving role of the Fed to comfort the market and reduce clouds of uncertainty has become their emerging role. In global markets that now require global-sized interventions, it is not clear that the Fed has the same horsepower as it once did. Rather, it acts as a signal to indicate to the domestic economy, world markets, and not least, foreign central banks, what it hopes to accomplish in an increasingly global and integrated financial marketplace.

A new game in town

The decreased effectiveness of any one nation's monetary policy and the emerging stealth and sophistication used by the Fed to demonstrate world financial leadership is simply a natural evolution of globalization. It is not so much that the Fed has lost hold of its power to control the economic destiny of the United States. It is more that the Fed realizes it has become a smaller fish because the sea has expanded. The European Central Bank and its counterpart in China now realize they have the sophistication and the clout to also turn markets. The People's Bank of China, with reserves in the trillions of dollars and with the power and authority to set exchange rates, may come to realize that it is the world's most significant and potent economic power.

The future of global economic stability may lie in the ability of central banks to act in concert. Until recently, the G8 nations met regularly to coordinate monetary policy. Much of these efforts were devoted to keeping the value of the US dollar within a reasonable range (or band). US dollar stability was necessary for healthy markets worldwide because so much of world consumption was then derived from the US economy.

With the growing consumption of the Second Economic World, the United States' role in world economic stability is reduced. There is less global concern about maintaining a strong US dollar, and the Euro and China's Renminbi are now touted as increasingly important world currencies. With the emergence of alternative currencies comes a certain luxury for the United States; no longer must the Fed be preoccupied with the effects of its monetary policy on world markets. As but one major currency in the world, the Fed may find a luxury in dealing with the global economy rather than dictating the global economy. This may be a luxury we can afford.

If it is the case that the Fed cannot always push on the string and stimulate the economy, is it possible though that the Fed is more effective in pulling on the string and choking off excess demand or irrational exuberance? This is the topic for our next discussion.

14
Who Stole the Punchbowl?

While the jury is out as to the reliability and effectiveness of loose monetary policy in all circumstances, there is one thing most all would agree – if the Fed wants to make the economy hurt, it can. Interest rates can only go so low, but they can go sky high. This asymmetry translates into a much greater ability for the Fed to slow, rather than bolster the economy.

Remember the reasons why tight monetary policy can fail? You can bring pessimists to a punchbowl, but you may not be able to make them drink. For all the problems that could frustrate the policymakers' best efforts to stimulate the economy, there are only opportunities on the flip side.

Tight monetary policy requires the Fed to soak up excess cash reserves of banks to limit their ability to lend the money out. This foregone lending reduces spending and hence future deposits, limiting subsequent rounds of lending to boot. Tight monetary policy also sucks up the cash liquidity as Consumer-Investors repay loans, further contracting the supply of loanable funds.

The Fed would commit to these strategies only in an environment in which they foresee too much demand and investment. While loose monetary policy can be likened to opening the tap for an economy wary of drinking, tight monetary policy taps off the supply of loanable funds for a thirsty group of Producer-Investors. Such a tightening cannot help but decrease the spending of Producer-Investors, permitting the Fed to reduce investment to just about any value it chooses.

The Fed relies on the banking industry as its vehicle for tighter monetary policy. It works by limiting the capacity of banks to make loans and create money. However, its power is not limitless. Like water finding its own level, alternative markets will form to fill a big void if bank credit dries up. Alternative institutions beyond the reach of the Fed can form that will raise loanable funds in different ways, as we saw with the now infamous sub-prime mortgage industry.

To what degree could the market work around a choked-off banking industry? Recall the frustration of the regulator. Any imposed policy will bring on a raft of innovations designed to skirt the policy. Mutual funds will form to pool savings and offer a combination of return and risk that spans the spectrum of investor preferences. Some funds will seek low return at low risk and will make available funds for mortgages. Others will seek high return at high risk and these funds will find their way into the venture capital market where more speculative projects seek funding. Middlemen will be employed, just as they are now, to match savers and borrowers, and rating agencies will develop underwriting practices so both sides understand the relative risks and rewards.

These alternative investment channels can sprout amazingly rapidly. Mutual funds arose very quickly as a reaction to the Depression era Regulation Q that prevented banks from paying market-determined interest rates on checking accounts. Forty years later, a zero interest checking account could not provide protection against the inflation that reared its ugly head in the 1970s. Venture capital burgeoned in the 1980s when more speculative ventures found they could not successfully raise capital through banks or through initial public offerings of new stock. And sub-prime loans quickly extracted a large part of the mortgage market just about as quickly as mortgage-backed securities created an investment opportunity. After the meltdown of sub-prime mortgages placed in jeopardy the entire mortgage-backed security market, collateralized debt instruments immediately appeared. Investors will find investees and every return and risk combination will eventually be satisfied, even if regulations are frustrated in the process.

The multi-headed beast

In response to regulation Q, one innovation in the 1970s was the creation of near banks. With capital formation by banks drying up as they were prevented from offering competitive interest rates, brokerage houses provided easy avenues for savings. We could open an account, invest in a money market mutual fund, and liquidate some of there money market accounts simply by writing a check against our account, just like a bank. Retail brokerage houses like Fidelity, E-trade, and Charles Schwab allow its customers direct deposit, electronic funds transfer, bill paying services, checking accounts, debit cards, and the other trappings of retail banks.

Even large one-stop retail chains like Wal-Mart offer near-bank features like low cost check cashing, electronic funds transfers, and money orders at rates more competitive than those found at traditional banks. By partnering with retail loan providers or trust banks, Wal-Mart is close to offering the range of services demanded by their clientele but outside of the auspices of bank regulators. Ironically, it is the banking industry that has prevented Wal-Mart from full-fledged membership in the banking fraternity for fear that it will dominate that industry just as it has dominated modern retailing.

Consumer-Investors can make tight monetary policy less effective. By reducing the amount of cash awash in the economy, Consumer-Investors are forced to re-evaluate how they use money. We use money in three ways. There is the precautionary motive in which households keep some cash on hand for emergencies; the transaction motive permits households to consume with their cash; and the speculative or investment motive. As the Fed drives up the prevailing interest rate, households can conserve their cash liquidity by reducing the amount of their assets they keep in cash for precautionary or transactions balances. For instance, as money becomes tight, a smaller amount of money may simply circulate more rapidly to support the same level of transactions. This increased "velocity" of money is one of the undoing responses of tight monetary policy.

While the market will sprout mechanisms to frustrate the Fed and match savers and borrowers with amazing speed and efficiency, there remains a role for monetary policy especially in the short run. For short bouts of tightening, monetary policy is effective when it can throttle back perhaps one or two percent of growth. Even then, it need only do part of the job, with the deposit expansion multiplier working in reverse to do the rest. One percent of a 15 trillion dollar economy is a mere 150 billion dollars, which can be attained by cutting back excess cash reserves by just 10 or 20 billion dollars. This is just a drop in the bucket for the well funded Fed.

The advantage of tight monetary policy is its speed and efficiency, especially in the short run before households can resort to alternatives. Tight monetary policy may hamper fiscal policy however. The Fed determines when tight monetary policy is warranted and, invariably, politicians do not agree. This tug-of-war of a Fed increasing interest rates to reduce spending, demand, and jobs, may be counteracted with politicians creating jobs and hence demand. The higher interest rates also raise the cost of government spending and the cost of new debt issued as the government must replace retiring debt.

Finally, an increase in interest rates and a reduction in economic growth can reduce tax revenue, requiring government to borrow still more at higher interest rates. And these high interest rates cause an influx of foreign investment, making the dollar more attractive (and more valuable), and reducing exports while increasing imports. Both effects rob the economy of jobs and reduce domestic tax revenue, but at the same time they work toward the Fed's goal of reducing domestic economic growth. This complex back-and-forth between one branch of the public sector and another somewhat increases policy uncertainty and can hamper its effectiveness. However, there is no antidote to short sharp shocks by a Fed determined to bring the economy back under control.

Economic policy gone wild – hyperinflation and hyperpain

There is a nightmare that I'm certain leaves every Fed chairman lying awake at night in a cold sweat. It is hyperinflation, an inflation so out of control that the economy has been uncoupled from its institutions.

Hyperinflation often begins well-meaning enough. A zealous government wants to create jobs for its citizens and tries to do more than it should. A bit of borrowing from the International Monetary Fund (IMF), some major infrastructure projects that already strain an overheated sector of the economy, and a belief in the necessity of bigger government, are the common ingredients that get the ball rolling. Perhaps in a different circumstance these ingredients would be precisely what are needed, but, in an undiversified and immature economy, they portend to disaster.

Remember Say's Law? It stated that production creates new jobs, which creates the income to purchase newly produced goods. So long as there is no mismatch between what is produced and what newly employed workers want, everything is fine.

What if the production is in a sector that nobody wants or nobody is willing to pay for? This production is not viewed as productive, resulting in new income chasing the same old goods and services that existed before the new spending. This new money chasing the same old goods causes prices to increase, and the cycle begins.

In a mature economy, increasing prices overall may act as a signal for new enterprises to develop and new goods to be produced. In a centrally planned economy that is already diverting production to the national interest or has little capacity to create more workers out of the existing population, something has got to give. Sometimes prices vent the economic steam. Examples include the massive production of armaments in 1930s Germany, large government expenditures in infrastructure in 1980s South America, and the fiscal mismanagement in the face of declining production in the 2000s Zimbabwe.

Each of these episodes arose because of a production-consumption mismatch. If production is in a sector not typically purchased by Consumer-Investors or if production is declining while the income of Consumer-Investors is maintained, demand for consumer goods and services exceed the supply, and prices rise. Often in desperation, a government will simply print more money to stabilize the purchasing power of Consumer-Investors. But, without more production in the goods and services Consumer-Investors purchase, prices rise further.

The stagflation innovation

The United States and Europe experienced a cycle of widespread inflation in the 1970s. Before the formation of the Organization of Petroleum Exporting Countries (OPEC), much of the world oil production was directed and dominated by large United States and European firms. As far back as 1949, Venezuela approached Iran, Iraq, Kuwait, and Saudi Arabia to organize an association of oil exporting states. Algeria, Qatar, Indonesia, Libya, and the United Arab Emirates joined the association in the 1960s.

Some of these members, irate over Western support for Israel's re-supply following the Yom Kippur War, retaliated by embargoing US bound oil in 1973. Oil prices per barrel rose from less than three dollars to twelve dollars in just a few months, and doubled again in the next eight years. New oil sources could not satisfy demand and the OPEC nations realized that constraining their rate of production of such a scarce resource could actually raise revenue. OPEC oil revenues actually tripled in the 1970s, while OPEC production was level or declining up to 1985.

Just as today, growing US trade deficits became the sign of the times. This growing diversion of wealth from oil dollars accumulated by OPEC countries began flowing back into investment in the United States and London financial markets. It was clear that something had to give. More and more wealth moving offshore meant that the US Consumer-Investor could not maintain the standard of living it had grown to expect. But, economic times were good otherwise, leading Consumer-Investors to demand indemnification from rising prices.

Some countries responded by printing and distributing more money. In the US, labor negotiated contracts at higher wages. These institutionalized Cost of Living Allowances raised wages and nominal purchasing power, just as more of the economic pie was being diverted to oil producing nations. More nominal wealth chasing fewer goods resulted in an enduring inflation that began to spin out of control.

If caught quickly enough, the inflation contagion could at once be absorbed and nipped in the bud. But by delaying the pain through purchasing power indemnification, the dull headache became a migraine. Eventually, people would need to be made poorer because a good chunk of wealth was forever diverted abroad. But, nobody wanted to be the one to pull the bandage off quickly.

It was under Fed Chairman Paul Volcker's watch that the US economy experienced this runaway inflation. The inflation rate peaked at 15% in 1980, a far cry from the 50% per month inflation used to define hyperinflation. It was sufficient, though, to have become a structural part of wage increases, and it made price planning for firms, interest rate determination for banks, and contracting for workers quite uncertain.

This inflationary spiral could only be solved with some tough medicine and tougher rhetoric. The medicine was tight money. This tight money, coupled with rising interest rates, and consumer and investor pessimism, forced the unemployment rate up from less than 5% just before the OPEC oil embargo to over 10% by 1982. Tight monetary policy was having its effect. With the income lost from those who are unemployed, and with workers fearing job retention more than cost of living protection, wage and price increases began to moderate and inflation came under control.

With steadier and more predictable prices, interest rates could drop, investment (especially construction) could resume, and employment could begin to grow. The inflationary spiral had been broken and the role of tight monetary policy was forever validated.

Ever since that experience, Fed chairmen have watched inflation like a rabbit watches a rattlesnake. No chairman (and there have only been two since) wants to repeat the experience of Paul Volcker. It is tough medicine, with doses much larger and for much longer if not prescribed early. But, we have discovered that the short-term pain of sluggish growth is sometimes worth it if it prevents a cycle of inflation for years and years that becomes institutionalized and tough to eradicate.

And in the process of understanding and fearing inflation, the United States created a growth industry of economists willing to wring inflation out of economies worldwide, through a painful dose of tight money and through a return to market forces that seem much more adept at aligning production with consumption.

15
Seems that We Have a Failure to Coordinate

When John Maynard Keynes recognized that Say's Law, supply creates its own demand, may not always work, he shocked his classical economist colleagues. The classical school was one of permanent equilibrium, unless of course some irrational animal spirits plunges us, presumably temporarily, into disequilibrium. Keynes was the first to create a consistent theory that explains how an economy can be in a persistently bad state of affairs.

Recall how Keynes broke the economy up into three sectors – Consumer-Investors, Producer-Investors, and Government. By investors, Keynes was referring to those that make decisions to build factories, new houses, and the like, usually from money borrowed from banks, or ultimately from Consumer-Investors. These are the Producer-Investors we spoke of earlier, rather than the Consumer-Investors who are determining how to invest their retirement accounts. We saw that monetary policy directly affects the rate at which these Producer-Investors can access capital and create jobs.

The entire weight of the world is not on the Producer-Investors, though. If they can hire one more, preferably unemployed, worker for a new investment project, that worker then has an income to consume. The products they would not otherwise have purchased will create demand for the services of another worker, and so on. This allows the income from this original job to ripple and reverberate around the economy. It turns out that one new job created will ultimately generate many more new jobs. A lot of factors influence just how many jobs will eventually be created, but the answer is typically more than the one original job and less than ten jobs in total.

The multiplier effect

The total number of jobs created as a consequence of the creation of one new job is called the multiplier. It allows us to get the economy back on track without having to do every bit of the heavy lifting ourselves. It is the power steering of the economic system. And it works incredibly efficiently – usually.

Central banks are the primary driver of the economy car. Others try to augment and contribute to economic growth, but no entity does so on a day-to-day basis, has the broadest interests, and holds the most expertise as a Central Bank. Fortunately, central banks merely have to affect excess bank reserves, which controls the loanable funds made available to Producer-Investors, which in turn generates the primary jobs and gives rise, through the multiplier, to many more jobs.

This process also works in reverse, as we have seen. Tight monetary policy can discourage investment, resulting in cancelled plans to build new plants and purchase equipment, causing reduced job creation from those that depended on the completion of the factory and those that depended on the income from the construction and factory workers.

Obviously, quite a chain of events must occur in turn for this to work. It requires the central bank's effort to translate into a change in interest rates for new investment, new investment to occur because of the change in interest rates, and new jobs to be generated in the domestic economy because of the change in investment, without resulting in a loss of jobs elsewhere. Such a plan, while usually successful, is also sufficiently complex to be prone to failure, at times.

Coordination failures

Let's look at possible failures in coordinating the necessary events, one by one.

As we noted earlier, a change in the incentives the central bank provides for the banks to lend out excess cash reserves depends on the belief by banks that they can profit from a change in their scale of lending. Even if the central bank is seeking an expansion, the banks may not want to liberalize their lending policies or lower their interest rates. In the recent credit crunch, banks burned by a lot of sub-prime borrowers became very conservative in their lending practices. A central bank could not make them drink.

The lending industry responds less to the character of borrowers and more to national policies of very large banks. When banks get their wagons in a circle, even good projects may be left out in the cold, regardless of what the central bank might be doing to loosen monetary policy. As a consequence, some very good projects could be put on hold, and the construction jobs the central bank anticipated simply do not materialize.

As an example, I live in a small community that was looking forward to the ground-breaking for a major new project that would generate many construction jobs, and then perhaps 1,500 high paying professional and support jobs. Financing was almost in place to break ground when the credit crunch hit. Despite the Fed's best efforts to loosen monetary policy, financing dried up as those willing to lend money began to have cold feet about a possible recession. All the Fed optimism in the world will not make bankers lend when they are nervous, even if the project is sound and the multiplier large.

The second coordination failure can occur if the investment from the domestic banking industry goes to support a project somewhere else. As the economy in the United States and Europe has gone from 70% manufacturing to less than 30% manufacturing, profitable outlets for capital intensive projects are often overseas. These projects may help bolster other economies but will do little to bolster the domestic economy.

The third failure is in the inability to create long-term jobs domestically as a consequence of the investment. There are entire pulp and paper or sawmills that can be run by just a handful of people where hundreds would have once been employed. The affluence of the First World Economies means that physical capital now employs a lot of relatively cheap machines, and few relatively expensive workers. This problem is compounded by the Social Security, pension, and medical benefits that they must pay on behalf of their workers but not for the machines that replace them. Even the construction industry itself, commissioned to build and outfit the factory, is amazingly capital intensive, relying on precast concrete, prefabricated buildings, and ready-to-assemble equipment.

Finally, when our Consumer-Investors are nervous, they may not be so inclined to reinject their hard-earned wages into new consumption. Recall that this phenomenon is called the paradox of thrift. Consumer-Investors might prefer to keep their money in a money market account or under their pillow rather than convert it to consumption or investment, and in turn fuel consumption and investment for those that would have been paid for the products they didn't buy.

Those that accept the Keynesian model, and most economists now do, are divided into two schools of thought. Both schools should be called Keynesians because the mechanisms each advocate were first proposed by Keynes. However, those that subscribe to the central bank-led economic policy are typically called Monetarists, leaving the remainder to claim the title of Keynesians.

We have a plan

The last chapters defined how monetary policy can be used to fine tune the economy to stimulate growth or prevent inflation. Not to be outdone, the Keynesians have a plan too.

Keynesians do not argue that theirs is the most elegant plan, or the least costly plan. Rather, they argue that theirs is the most reliable plan – the Chevy, rather than the Mercedes of plans. Their plan is direct – if you want investment, have the government build roads, bridges, schools, and economic infrastructure. If these investments are wise, then they too will generate first round jobs in the construction phase, and subsequent jobs in the flow of commerce that will result from these infrastructure improvements.

The beauty of this plan is that it is fast, if anything Congress or legislatures do can be called fast. It is also direct and certain. It is guaranteed to keep most of the first round spending and the improvements in efficiency within the domestic economy because politicians recognize the folly of investing taxpayer dollars to stimulate economies abroad.

There is a catch though. Just as Keynesians can easily criticize the Monetarists for the many ways monetary policy can fail, Monetarists strike back with a criticism of their own. The Keynesian plan will have to find workers to build their plants. If they simply divert workers from other construction and infrastructure projects, this program won't succeed. In defense of Keynesians anywhere, such "crowding out" of workers diverted to public construction creates a problem for new investment funding in private construction.

For either plan to work without the crowding out effect in the construction industry there must be a surplus of unemployed labor, with the appropriate skills, to rely upon. Of course, if we recall that Keynes unveiled his model during the Great Depression, we know that it was just this circumstance of significant unemployment and excess capacity that Keynes wanted to remedy.

Crowding out

There is also another crowding out effect that leaves the Keynesians open to criticism. While the Monetarists advocate increasing the supply of loanable funds through excess cash reserves and the money multiplier, the funds for Keynesian-style investment must either be borrowed or raised through taxes. If raised through taxes, income, and hence consumption, is depressed. If raised through government borrowing, the interest rate must rise, choking off private investment that is no longer profitable at the higher interest rates. How do we resolve this ugly quarrel?

Monetarist policy makes sense when there are no coordination failures, when the economy is humming along, and every link in the chain is willing to do its part, as is usually the case. Monetarism is powerful, inexpensive, effective, and because it relies primarily on the private sector, it is especially reliable in inducing economic contractions that might ward off excessive growth and induce inflation. Keynesian policy is likely more effective when the economy is on the ropes and the Fed has a hard time pushing a piece of string. It is direct, fast, and relatively certain. It also requires public investment to prime the pump, and we must have faith that government makes good infrastructure investments. In the long run though, the original projects will be forgotten if the pump is successfully primed and the economy begins to flow nicely again.

There is also a hybrid approach, which is not always politically palatable. We will spend more time later talking about the use of tax policy to stimulate spending and investment. For now, let us point out a hybrid Keynesian policy in which the government directly injects cash into the private sector. The government can make subsidies, grants, and loans available to private corporations so that they may build new plants, create new jobs, make new discoveries, and so on.

The advantages of this hybrid form of Keynesian policy are that the investment crowding out problem is negated, and private firms motivated by eventual profits (and hence taxes able to at least partially offset the government investment) are probably in a better position to recognize what society demands. The disadvantage is that the government is spending taxpayer money to target good investments. There is nothing that sharpens the senses more than investing your own hard earned money in projects, and we may rightfully be skeptical that bureaucrats have the expertise or incentives to do this as well as can be done in the private sector.

It may come as no surprise to hear that monetarism is most often associated with the US Republican Party and Britain's Conservative Party, while Keynesians are more likely to reside among Democrats and Labour. After all, monetarists rely on the private sector, and Keynesians believe in direct government-driven policies.

As an example, US President John F. Kennedy advocated a grand plan in the 1960s to ward off fears of a recession. He asked his policy advisors for a project that would require a substantial amount of government spending and that would yield lasting benefits for all of humankind. One of the plans that did not go forward was desalination of the earth's oceans. If the marine mammal organizations are upset now, imagine how they would have felt had Kennedy taken that advice. What did go forward was a plan to send a man to the moon and back within the decade. That spurt of Keynesian policy rebalanced the Cold War, spurred research and development from the hundreds of thousands of scientists and engineers trained by a vastly enhanced higher education sector, stimulated computing and robotics, and helped create Velcro and Tang.

Enter the foreign sector

This Keynesian multiplier that makes our policies so potent depends on an important caveat. We need the spending we inject into the economy to keep circulating around. There are a couple of leakages that are problematic. One is the tendency of people to keep their hard earned cash under their pillow, literally or metaphorically, and hence frustrate the circulation of spending that the multiplier relies upon. The other is to have their spending diverted abroad. This is a particular problem for the First Economic Worlds. Much of its consumption is purchased from the developing countries. This phenomenon is precisely what allows the developing countries to develop and the FEW to consume.

These leakages are good Keynesian or Monetary policy for the developing countries, but not so good for the First Economy Worlds, unless its imports come right back at us in the form of exports. So long as we run a trade deficit though, we know that the dollars do not come back in the form of purchases of our products, at least at the rate they leave.

For instance, tax rebates are often proposed under the guise of Keynesian policy. The next chapter describes the king of tax rebate policies. For now, let us consider a tax rebate that is given to all taxpayers, who are encouraged to go out and buy stuff to stimulate the local economy. If we went out and bought haircuts and medical procedures, and were sure the barbers and doctors also went out and bought haircuts and more procedures, this would be an effective policy. If instead we went out and bought big screen color television sets with this free money, the SEW manufacturers of big screens will receive a nice jolt from our Keynesian policy. That will also create a worsening trade surplus for us and leave them with more money to lend back to the FEW – which can help pay for the tax rebate. See the problem?

An economy on autopilot

What if all these stimuli during downturns could be done automatically? Indeed, there are some mechanisms that will do just that. They are called built-in or automatic stabilizers.

The principle is to inject cash into the economy when output falls or unemployment rises, and reduce the injections when output rises or unemployment falls. We can provide an automatic stabilizer if we can find a target that is correlated with these movements in output or unemployment. Of course, unemployment and applications for food stamps are directly (and negatively) correlated with output. As output falls and applications for unemployment insurance rises, these government disbursements will rise commensurately to help stabilize the economy.

If it is determined that the stimulation through this built-in stabilizer is insufficient, payments per worker could rise, or the duration that a worker can collect payments could rise. Simply raising payments may create the moral hazard problem we discussed earlier, as people find it more attractive to stay on unemployment insurance than accept a job. Payments that are sufficiently low to be unattractive but enough to allow subsistence strike the right balance and do not encourage sustained unemployment if a job offer becomes available.

We will spend more time on the tax system later. Notice that a progressive tax system is also a built-in stabilizer. As income rises, tax revenues rise more than proportionately, taking some spending out of the economy. Likewise, falling income reduces the average tax rate. The trick is to exercise sufficient fiscal discipline in legislatures and government to ensure that the high tax revenues in good times are saved for a rainy day. Governments should routinely be running surpluses in low unemployment periods, and reinjecting these surpluses, and running a deficit, in higher unemployment periods.

Such fiscal discipline also addresses the crowding out effect. If government restricts its injections to times of high unemployment, it does not face the prospect of competing for workers.

Policies that retrain unemployed workers are also built-in stabilizers, with the simultaneous benefits of discouraging idleness and encouraging investments in human capital. Education, in general, tends to be anti-cyclical, meaning that education activity and enrollments increase as the economy falters. The reason is that the opportunities sacrificed by going back to school are less significant when income falls and unemployment rises. This reduced "opportunity" cost reduces the effective cost of education. Business schools have long observed such changes in enrollment because of changes in the economy. It is simple economics. Perhaps we should better fund universities and be more generous with tuition aid at times when the economy weakens. We are then investing in the future at the very time businesses find it difficult to rationalize such investment.

However, our model of higher education is one that does not easily permit adjustment to the size of the higher education sector over the business cycle. Consequently, while education is an effective way to invest in the aggregate human capital of the economy, it is not so finely tunable to act as an effective automatic built-in stabilizer.

Some of these concepts on Consumer-Investor led injections will be treated separately later as they occupy a special place in the political economy discussion. First though, let's take one last stab at trying to reconcile the Keynesian world and the Classical world.

There is no doubt that the Classicists are correct in that markets will eventually reach an equilibrium, just as we will conclude later that the stock price financial markets will eventually find its correct value. There is also no doubt that markets can grope around for a long time, in a seemingly persistent and bad state of affairs. The Classical solution is to wait a little longer, while the Keynesians want to solve the problem now before people suffer any more.

The debate may be one of semantics. The long run prescriptions of the Classical school may take a long time indeed. In a Keynesian state of affairs, we may need to nudge the market from one persistent and bad state to another that is better. Ultimately, Keynesians are activists and Classicists are laissez-faire – or "just let it be."

16
The Timely Death of Supply Side Economics

It is good form in public debate to try to express the other point of view from the most favorable perspective. So I will try.

To now, we have prescribed an increase in aggregate spending to augment economic growth, through expansion in consumption, investment, or government spending. This is typically labeled aggregate demand management because it focuses on those that demand goods and services, to either consume, or to produce more goods and services in the future. What if instead we increase supply, creating more output for our given use of resources? The additional output would expand the economic pie, increase income, and through the increased income, increase domestic spending sufficient to purchase the additional supply. This notion, first advanced as policy by US President Ronald Reagan, has come to be known as Reaganomics most charitably, or Voodoo Economics less so.

We must differentiate between real and nominal changes in supply. A real change in supply occurs if there is a new technology or new production that permits the expansion of supply of goods and services in the market. This expansion occurs when we spur investment, perhaps through monetary policy, and its effect on interest rates, or through fiscal spending on infrastructure.

Let us differentiate this real growth in goods and services from the nominal growth that occurs when the economy is already fully employed. If such is the case, injecting greater wealth through fiscal spending or through windfall profits from resource sales will not ultimately increase production and will instead increase prices. It is this area of what economists call an inflationary gap that central banks try to steer clear.

The concept of supply side economics is clever – except this notion is already the very basis of the capitalist system. Supply siders developed a theory of expanding aggregate supply and then use Say's Law to ensure aggregate demand follows suit. However, Keynesian economics already assumes investment dollars will flow to a more productive enterprise, or to speculative investment that could someday produce a better mousetrap. By implying that there is insufficient investment in techniques that would expand productive capacity, supply side economics implicitly states that there must be a market failure.

Recall that the definition of a market failure is some sort of distortion that prevents the market from properly determining the correct level of output and prices. Distorted prices will distort the incentive to make the correct market decision. There are times when the level of investment may not be optimal. Monetary theory directly targets investment and can presumably scale investment to meet any reasonable target. If the problem is insufficient investment, a wide variety of instruments could be employed to stimulate investment, many of which would be probably significantly more effective than tax rebates, most of which will likely not end up in the investment sector.

Let's assume that the level of investment is correct. Could it be that investors would choose those projects that do not yield the highest economic benefits? If this were the case, some smarter investor would come in, make better decisions, make a larger profit, direct the new profit into other good investments, and eventually corner the market. The well-informed market is in the best position to analyze range of investment alternatives and decide accordingly.

It is possible that a society may not invest sufficiently to allow the economy to thrive in the long run. After all, an economy is presumably infinitely lived, but it is populated with mortals. If a retirement community built homes that would last only fifty years, would that be considered an inappropriate investment? The decisions of Consumer-Investors must be presumed to properly reflect their preference between present consumption and future consumption (savings), in the absence of a glaring market distortion.

Sustainable investment

Nobel prize-winning economist Robert Solow observed that the socially optimal rate of time preference is zero.[1] By this, he means any generation is as important as another. A public investment made for immediate reward rather than for eternity is distorted, in the Solow sense. However, Solow speaks of social investments, not private investment intended to meet the needs of a private mortal. If government believes private investment is too short-sighted, it may choose to explore policies to enhance long-term investment. This strategy may be politically risky. But let us assume for a moment that the goal of supply side economics is to do just that – to enhance long-term investment.

Government already creates incentives for long-term investment. For instance, deductibility of home mortgage interest in the United States makes ownership more attractive and expands investment in the single most important investment asset of most households. Likewise, borrowing by Producer-Investors is also typically tax deductible as one of the costs of production, effectively subsidizing investment costs. Supply siders must have something more in mind than these Keynesian solutions.

In the absence of a clear problem to solve, supply side advocates appealed to the Laffer curve. This curve, named after economist Arthur Laffer, is based on the simple observation that tax revenue will be zero if the tax rate is zero.[2] Likewise, if the tax rate is 100%, there is absolutely no incentive to produce, implying that production will again be zero, as will income. A 100% tax on zero income will likewise produce zero tax revenue, as Figure 16.1 illustrates.

Somewhere between 0% and 100% taxation is a sweet spot that will yield the maximum level of tax revenue. If our goal is to increase tax revenue, a tax rate higher than the rate corresponding to maximum revenue should be decreased, and a tax rate too low should be increased. The idea behind this is simple. If taxation is so high that it reduces economic activity, we could relax taxation and still generate more tax revenue if the increase in output is larger than the reduction in the tax rate.

One who takes only a convenient snippet of the last statement may hear that a reduction in taxation will increase tax revenue. Such selective hearing is attractive to one that will argue for reduced taxation in

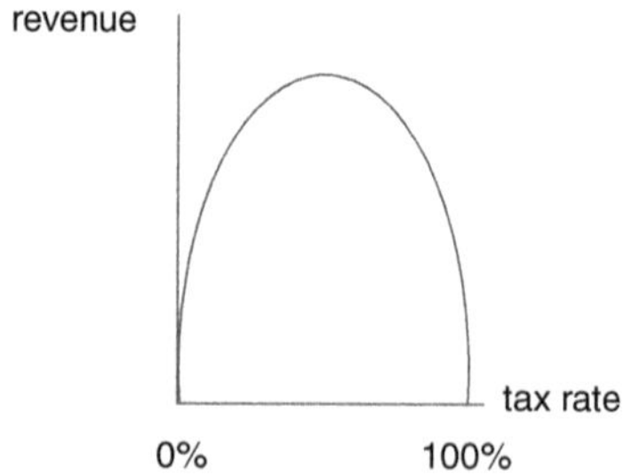

Figure 16.1 Tax revenue as a function of tax rate

any event. It is not unusual to hear some argue for reduced taxation when the economy is doing well, and argue again for reduced taxation when the economy falters. In effect, the tax reduction advocate is claiming the economy always resides on the far side of the Laffer Curve. They are concluding taxes are by definition too high, and must then conclude that Keynesian policy or government spending to support investment in infrastructure is never desirable.

It took some time to disprove these various prescriptions of supply side economics. Its main prescription is to reduce our personal taxes, under the argument that we would invest the reduction and make the economy more productive. It is not improbable that some of the tax reduction would translate into additional investment, and much of that investment would likely revalue the stock market. The amount of the tax reduction that actually translates into new plants, equipment, research and development, and other improvements in technologies is likely small.

It is ironic that supply side economics is still advocated by some "laissez-faire" proponents. If one advocates for "let it be" economics, while also advocating for supply side tax refunds, they are both Classical and Keynesian economists, as much as they would hate to admit it. They at once argue that markets always work but also that the free market-determined investment is somehow insufficient.

Reaganomics has come and gone, with the Wall Street Journal announcing its ultimate demise in 2003. Politicians who advocate on idealistic grounds for tax cuts or tax rebates no longer associate themselves with supply side economics. They are now more likely to appeal to the equally attractive belief that taxpayers can better determine how they want to spend their money better than can the government.

We return to this proposition later when we ponder how a stimulus package should be designed. If we put spending back in to the hands of households in times of insufficient consumption, will they invest in new roads, schools, and research and development? Or will they buy a big-screen television made in China? If they do the former, domestic output increases by a nice multiple of the stimulus. If they do the latter, the Gross Domestic Product of China will increase instead, and the domestic trade deficit will worsen.

Part V

Financial Failures

Never before have so many hundreds of millions of people directly or indirectly participated in something so complex that only thousands or tens of thousands truly understand. But participate in financial markets we must, if we are to plan for our own retirement. We shall next see how some have learned to profit from asymmetries in what they know and what the rest of us knows. Hopefully, we can glean from this analysis a way to create a more level playing field for markets that seem increasingly skewed.

17
The Higher You Go, the Farther You Fall

Stop me if you've heard this one. Coming out of the back door of a club and onto a dark alley, a fellow loses his keys. He continues to his car and starts looking around for his keys. A policeman ambles up and asks him what he is looking for. He tells the policeman he lost his keys in the alleyway. When asked by the policeman why then is he looking out on the street for them, he says, "this is where the light is."

The efficient market hypothesis is the beam of light for finance theorists. It states that the price of a stock should only incorporate the valuation of all its fundamentals, such as the expected discounted earnings per share, and the inherent risk of the pattern of the earnings per share. Put very simply, if the price of a security differs from its efficient price, arbitrage possibilities exist, meaning smart money can profit from the gap, and thereby cause the price to converge to its proper long run value. If capital can move in mind boggling amounts almost instantaneously, any deviation of the price from its long run value will allow the arbitrageur to sweep in, make a profit, and sweep out to the next arbitrage possibility almost immediately.

To see arbitrage in action, let's say on your way from the parking lot to the football stadium, you see scalpers selling tickets easily for a 1,000 dollars a ticket. Another block down you see scalpers struggling to sell tickets for 500 dollars. Assuming of course that scalping is legal, you have the clever idea of buying some tickets for 500 dollars, and reselling them for a 1,000. If you buy enough of them, you'll find the price a block down has risen to 750 dollars, and if you sell enough of them in the parking lot, you find that the price there has fallen to 750 dollars. The arbitrage possibilities have ended, you have made a handsome profit, and you continue on to the football game.

We discussed Enron's use of the arbitrage strategy earlier. A company formed by two brilliant University of Chicago mathematicians used this idea to take advantage of differences in foreign exchange prices that may only be fractions of a penny. If they could make these fractions and buy and sell hundreds of millions at a time, they can make millions of dollars per transaction. Billions of dollars of profit later, they were two successful arbitrageurs.

The efficient market hypothesis also would predict that few market transactions would take place. If all have the same information, and the stock price incorporates this information, the only reason to buy or sell a stock is because the security's risk profile no longer matches yours. If we add some noise to the equation, perhaps the security price will jump up and down randomly, but would not follow the trends up and the trends down we commonly see.

There is one problem though – the efficient market hypothesis cannot explain the speculative bubble.

Perhaps nor can Isaac Newton, widely considered to be the founder of classical physics and calculus. It has been popularly attributed to him to have uttered, "I can calculate the motions of heavenly bodies ... But, not the madness of people!," after he lost the equivalent of millions of dollars as a speculative bubble popped early in the eighteenth century.

Back around that time, economics, philosophy, and psychology were intertwined. When was the fork in the road that caused economics and finance to veer off into the world of mathematics and assumptions of rationality, and for psychology to continue on the path of trying to understand human decision making? After all, the roots of economics were firmly in the political philosopher's camp, using any tool at their disposal to try to create order out of the economy.

The separation occurred when economists tried to get a handle on a dilemma – if water was much more important than diamonds, why are we willing to pay so much for another diamond but so little for another glass of water? From the ensuing explorations, we realized that it is not the overall value of water or diamonds that affects our willingness to pay for some more of them. Rather, it is the valuation we place on having a bit more of something. I'm not willing to pay much for one more glass of water because I consumed a lot of water and I am not very thirsty. Actually, I'm probably not willing to pay much for another diamond either, but heck, that ruins my story.

The punch line is that we recognize people make decisions on "the margin." The relevant question is how much additional happiness will I get from an additional bit of consumption. This sounds strikingly like what you might have learned in a calculus class – things are measured, compared, and optimized based on rates of change of one variable relative to another. And calculus has remained the primary tool of economic theory ever since.

There's a new tool in town

The emphasis on scientific tools of analysis, such as calculus, also required us to adopt the scientific assumption that people behave rationally, or at least they appear to do so. And if we have the rationality of Spock from Star Trek, we will constantly be optimizing every decision. And psychology was unhelpful – for a while.

Our friend, John Maynard Keynes, provided one of the first formal models that departs from the Classical model and embraces some elements of psychology. Keynes recognized the importance of human autonomy in decision-making, and explored the consequences of the autonomous consumer and investor. In doing so, he recognized that households and firms may consider themselves in equilibrium even if the Classicists would not. In a Keynesian world, if perception is 90% of reality, then human perceptions can influence equilibrium.

Keynes is remarkable in the eloquence of the stories he tells. Even the most laissez-faire proponent is convinced, clamoring with us all for the central bank to intervene when the economy goes south. A new classical school called "rational expectations" attempts to push us back toward the classical world, but even these proponents likely have a conversion on the road to depression.

Irrational exuberance

Robert Schiller, the economist who gifted the term "irrational exuberance" to former Fed. Chairman Alan Greenspan, recently concluded that "prices change in substantial measure because the investing public en masse capriciously changes its mind."[1] It will likely be a long while before a finance model can capture all the psychology of market movements. In embracing the efficient market hypothesis and arbitrage, finance models assume traders are rational. Now, if we really want to understand financial market prices, we might want to better try to understand psychology rather than economic theory. So let's see what we don't know.

Market psychology

An economist named Nicholas Kaldor observed way back in 1934 that information delays can cause prices to gyrate and overshoot, much like we see in speculative bubbles.[2] His approach at least offers a more realistic pattern of price movements, but doesn't make much sense in today's world of instantaneous information beamed around the world. We will have to dig deeper.

Other researchers have used herd mentality to explain how bubbles and busts can occur. If investors buy securities when prices rise and sell as prices fall, markets can become volatile. In a last ditch attempt to preserve rationality, we can even conclude it is rational to "jump on the bandwagon" to profit from group think.

We can draw an example from formation flying. In the famous Diamond Formation Crash of 1982, four US Air Force Thunderbird aerobatic pilots flew into the ground. The reason was that only one of the pilots was flying the Diamond Formation maneuver. The other three pilots were simply following the leader by firmly affixing their wing to a fixed reference point on the leader's plane. When the leader flew into the ground because of insufficient control stick pressure in the loop, all flew into the ground. If highly trained military pilots can follow their leader to their own demise, it seems not unlikely that naïve Consumer-Investors can too.

Others have suggested that Consumer-Investors have overconfidence in their own private information, for some unexplained reason. Because of their overconfidence, investors see any market movements supporting their own conclusions as confirmation of their private information, and discount movements contrary to their own conclusions as somehow mistaken. This may be because people see patterns that they expect. If you believe a depiction of the Virgin Mary is just waiting to be revealed to you on a grilled cheese sandwich, someday it likely will. The "successful" confirmation of your intuition merely strengthens your self-confidence. If a number of people are looking for the same non-existent pattern, the stock price can seem to act accordingly. Gains won on the upswing of a speculative bubble can only breed further self confidence.

Extending this concept a little further, group think can result. You may discard your own opinion of a stock if it is at odds with others, even if you are correct. This is kind of like the Yogi Berra saying, "It's so crowded nobody comes here anymore."

Perhaps we can learn from gambling behavior to explain some stock market tendencies. If stocks move somewhat randomly, the analogy to roulette might be appropriate. At other times, a bid and bluff game like poker may be more appropriate, especially if there are some players entering and exiting the market to reinforce momentum in either direction.

While these anecdotes suggest that psychological models make a certain humanistic sense, through carefully designed experiments in decision-making, a new form of economics became an accepted course of study. This "behavioral economics" proved that humans very often make decisions inconsistent with economic theory, especially in complicated situations involving risk or decisions over time. Does this sound like a financial market?

People strive for order and simplicity, and probably don't pull out their slide rule to determine whether they ought to buy a cup of coffee. Instead, they develop certain "heuristics," or simple rules that seem to work alright most of the time, but save them the headaches of over analysis. We also tend to frame our problems in ways that reinforce our preconceptions as mentioned earlier.

Of course, regret is a very real emotion that drives a fair bit of human decision-making. We might regret the decision we made in investing in a particular stock, and ride that stock all the way down, in the human hope that it will somehow turn around and, in doing so, validate our original decision. A better response would be to ask ourselves if this stock would be the purchase we would make if we again had the cash. If the answer is no, the rational response is to sell. The all-too-frequent human response is to hold on.

How would a rational investor respond to an irrational market? Would it make sense to rush into a stock trading off its fundamental value when a rational investor knows the market will trend further away before it trends back? If the rational investor knows the market will overshoot the fundamental value on its way back, would the rational investor not want to buy low, and ride the stock up, timing a sale only when it begins to trade downward? Rational trading in an irrational world is an interesting question, with smart money likely holding many of the answers.

While it seems likely that these various factors do creep into the psychology of financial markets, economists are still loathe to accept behavioral economics as a mainstream branch of the discipline. Their resistance is understandable because, after all, economists are humans too. To accept such alternative explanations for their world would require them to discard the tools they have worked a lifetime to master. There is little room for advanced calculus in behavioral models. Such approaches do not lend themselves to elaborate equations and clever analyzes.

Of course, it would be unnerving for any of us to abandon our hard earned tools and skills. Economists would also have to abandon our perceived perch on top of the social sciences. I'm not sure we are quite ready to do so, but perhaps with some psychological therapy.

18
America Sneezes and the World Catches a Cold

One of the most far-reaching effects of globalization has been in the increasingly interdependency of national economies. These links are not new, but are much more extensive today. For instance, it has long been said in Canada that when America sneezes, Canada catches a cold. Separated by the longest undefended border in the world, and with 90% of the Canadian labor force residing within 100 miles of the border, it is not surprising that the economies of Canada and the United States are intertwined, and form the world's largest bilateral trading partners.

To be sure, this interrelationship has not always been so mutual. While the balance of trade between these partners had always been relatively even, Canada was more dependent on the United States than the United States was dependent on Canada. The United States provided a fair amount of the investment capital and expertise that accelerated Canadian economic development. Much of the big manufacturing in Canada came from US subsidiaries.

Canada, in turn, provided commodities to the United States, many of which the United States could have easily purchased elsewhere. The analogy is less one of the symbioses of equal partners, and rather one of Canadian dependence on the large US economy. As a consequence, when the US economy coughed, the Canadian economy choked.

Globalization has created many such intertwined economies all around the world and between the First Economic and Second Economic Worlds. These interrelationships have dramatically expanded our mutual dependencies, and have certainly created interdependencies that did not exist even a decade ago. Over the course of globalization, the United States has remained the dominant world economy, but that position has been challenged now by a united European Economic Union and by a rapidly growing economies in China and India that may surpass the US economy in sheer size within a decade.

Ironically enough, globalization has reduced the dependencies of some countries. Canada is not nearly as dependent on the United States economy as it once was. The Canadian economy may even be countercyclical with the US economy. Holding non-conventional oil reserves, in the form of tar sands, larger than the entire remaining stock of conventional reserves worldwide, Canada is oil rich whenever the price of oil is above 40 to 50 dollars a barrel. The higher the price of oil, the more Canada thrives, while at the same time the US economy suffers.

The US financial markets remain the most mature, well developed, and liquid markets in the world. And with the thirst of the United States as the largest market for consumption goods, the expanding US trade deficit still creates a good supply of US dollars abroad. These dollars have to come back home somehow, and they do through investments in US denominated stocks, corporate bonds, and government debt. As a consequence of the twin roles of high US consumption and high repatriated investment dollars, US markets remain the most important in the world, and will likely remain so until other major global markets attain full membership in the First Economic World.

In the meantime, so long as the United States retains its position as a global economic leader, the world's largest economy, the world's largest consumer market, and the nation of the most capitalized financial markets, it seems likely that the rest of the world will remain sensitive to the health of the US economy.

We are all now buffeted by global waves

The most recent innovation, though, is the degree to which US financial markets are now influenced by world markets. This is occurring for a couple of reasons. One is the increased maturity of other markets. With active markets now encircling the world, and of increasing sophistication, economic or financial news at any time of the day or night are immediately digested. The reactions of these markets are then mimicked as markets simultaneously open around the world, partly because all are feeding off the same information, but at different times, and partly because of the mutual interdependencies. The US markets are part of that global financial information-processing machine.

A second reason is that wealth is now created in the Second Economic Worlds, and this wealth finds its way into the well-developed US financial markets. Either way, foreign profitability now affects capital flows in US financial markets. This phenomenon is new and it seems destined to be permanent.

A final reason may simply be in the very nature of international capital flows seeking short-term reward. To see this, let's take a look at a theoretical consequence of international capital flows that respond to arbitrage opportunities. Although I wrote earlier that the financial world is likely driven by psychological forces rather than (solely) the passionless efficient market hypothesis, I am not quite ready to abandon arbitrage quite yet, even if its implication of efficient markets is a bit hard to swallow.

If you don't mind a bit of hard theory, let's explore what would happen if markets were truly efficient, with arbitrageurs buying undervalued or selling overvalued stocks until the fundamental stock price is re-established. Arbitrage opportunities will attract a lot of arbitrageurs if the price gap is large, thereby narrowing the gap substantially. The remaining gap will attract a few arbitrageurs, and so on, until the gap is gradually reduced to zero and the stock is priced accordingly.

This gradual reduction of the price gap would occur if, for instance, all traders discover simultaneously that a US recession is more likely to occur. In such a case, the price path will reduce any excessive valuation over time as shown in Figure 18.1.

This gradual arbitrage process will eventually get the market back to equilibrium, perhaps even rapidly given the instantaneous flow of information and rapid flow of capital these days.

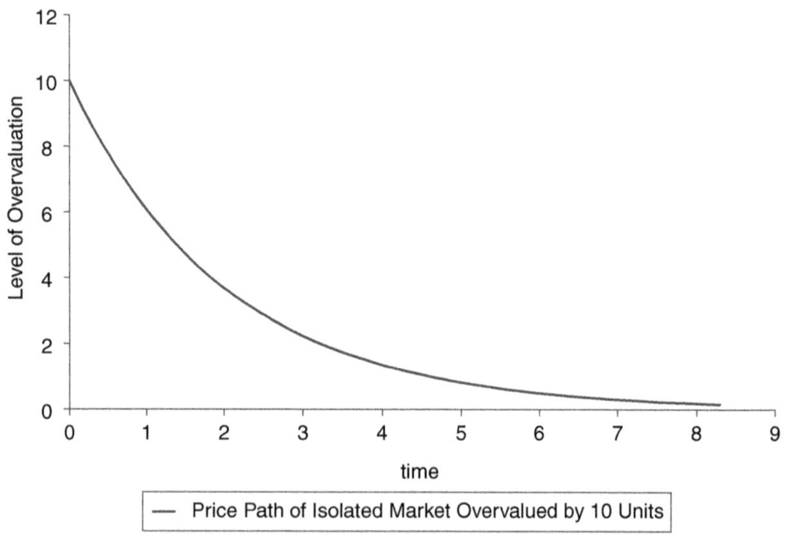

Figure 18.1 Convergence of a market to equilibrium over time

Now let's assume a couple of markets are doing the same thing at the same time, each reverting back to its proper value once the new information is incorporated. Let's just add one facet that has become increasingly significant in the past decade or so. Allow capital to flow from one international market to another, seeking the best returns. Once we allow arbitrage to do its thing and bring the price of each stock back to equilibrium, all the while responding to capital ping-ponging back and forth across the ocean, we find an amazingly complex pattern of adjustment, as shown in Figure 18.2.

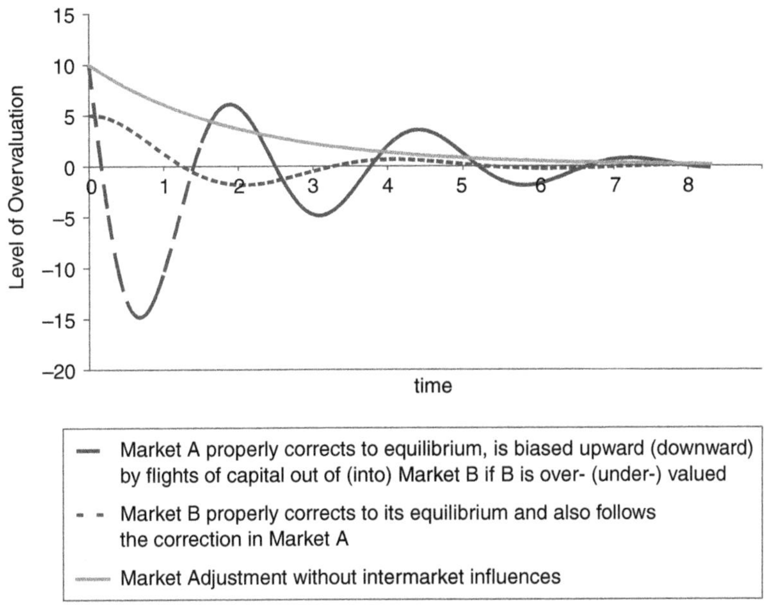

Figure 18.2 Oscillations of linked markets over time with capital flight

Compare the original path to equilibrium (the solid line) with the paths for each stock once inter-market capital flows occur. While the markets used to converge smoothly to equilibrium, they now seem to oscillate like a bucking bronco, primarily because of these large capital flows between markets. While the underlying mathematics that gives rise to these vibrations and oscillations is complicated, the result is astounding. Even rational efficient markets following a simple arbitrage process can overshoot their targets and behave just as we observe.

When things get out of hand, take a rest

One of the regulatory outcomes of the Crash of 1987 was the creation of regulations that stop all trades if the market oscillates too wildly. It was thought that halting trading when there is too much volatility can calm the market and allow traders to regroup around fundamentals rather than follow a herd mentality. Ironically enough, the analysis demonstrated here actually shows that speedier trading rather than artificial delays will get the market back to normal more quickly.

These results allow us to better understand the movements arising from the global effects of an Asian Contagion in February of 2007, the Credit Crunch over the summer of 2007, the panics of January 2008, and Great Crash II in October of 2008. Such corrections, defined as a drop of 15% off the market highs, seem to occur more often. Our results show that surprisingly large movements that can cause the market to overshoot may be more common now that international capital is very mobile.

19
Asleep at the Switch

Our central premise so far is one of enlightened capitalism. This notion recognizes the uncanny ability of self-interested individuals to make superior market decisions. This flow of resources to their most profitable employment is the "invisible hand" that has enamored economists since Adam Smith in 1776. If markets are so clever, why do we need regulation or government?

First, while a well functioning market may indeed be a beautiful thing in its ability to direct resources to their best uses, there are other ideals as well. Humans crave for some sense of equity, the beautiful and elusive quality that is always in the eyes of the beholder. For instance, well functioning markets would devote every last bit of wealth to one single owner of a single scarce factor of production if they happened to own a monopoly on that factor, all technologies depended on that factor, and if all other factors of production could be replicated at cost. As an example, if one person owned all the land in the world and if we all depended on land and the other factors it uniquely provides us, we would all become serfs and the land owner would accumulate all wealth. Of course, we have tried such a system of inequitable serfdom in our economic past with politically destabilizing results.

In a democracy, it is expected that those who benefit from the fruits of our economic system will spread the wealth. This is the underpinning of the tax system, which we shall leave for another chapter. Suffice to say that equity is a democratic value determined collectively by the citizens of governments overseeing free market systems.

The second rationale for government is in the protection of our property, as we've covered earlier. Without property rights there can be no ownership and without ownership, there can be no markets to exchange what we own. Ultimately, government then is the protector of the free market system insofar as they are willing to protect property rights. But, like equity, the beauty of protection of property is in the eye of the beholder. For instance, we see that the protection of intellectual property is one of the most contentious issues in the dialogue between the First Economic World and the Second Economic World. Inherent in the tension is a clash of cultures over whether an idea one has ought to be part of the public domain or be considered personal property.

The same countries that are now exerting such an influence on the world economic order have also contributed to shared human knowledge for millennia. Some of the oldest forms of sophisticated civilization have thrived with a notion of shared intellectual property. They naturally wonder why intellectual property should be regarded any differently simply because of a couple of centuries old policies of patent protection in some new upstart nations. On the other hand, there would be little incentive to create intellectual property if one knew their investment could be usurped by others. Here is where the free markets of the last two centuries clash with civilizations of the last two millennia. Major SEW countries like China and India foster a culture of shared innovation. Their economic system arose as a result of their culture, and as a consequence they accept a liberal sharing of intellectual property. Newer cultures like in the United States had constitutions developed since the Industrial revolution. These legal systems then arose with free markets in mind, and enshrine the notion of the protection of individual and property rights.

The third rationale is in the correction of markets when markets don't work as well as they should or could. We began these discussions with some classic categories of what economists call "market failures." These failures arise when some entities are able to exert significant market power, when information is not perfect, when the production or consumption of one factor or good somehow affects other goods not part of the original transaction, or when an activity cannot be credibly provided by the private sector because it is difficult or undesirable to restrict access. The latter goods are known as "public goods."

There are very few careful analyzes that guide us in determining just the right level of government intervention. One alternative is in government regulation rather than government competition. Government as regulator works on the premise that the focus of profit maximization is an important ideal. Government should then simply act as an overseer, correcting the market when imperfections arise, and standing out of the way when markets are functioning well and doing their thing. Even the model of government as regulator creates some problems, though.

Sometimes only government can help

Let us begin by recalling the unique role for government in its provision of public goods. A public good is one in which additional consumption of the good costs a producer nothing and the producer can do nothing to exclude the consumer. Regulation often falls into this category. While it is costly to monitor and prosecute financial market abuse, everyone benefits. Privatizing the regulatory function would create various market failures, in principal-agent problems, or in an inability to have all those who benefit pay a fee.

There was a movement afoot during the 1980s to impose the "fee for service" model to the provision of some of these "public goods" to unburden the tax system. The moment we do that, we must necessarily exclude those who benefit from regulation, for instance, but not enough to pay the fee. With the observation that some goods we enjoy have a certain public good nature to them, some would conclude that government must be in the business of providing certain goods or services to us that would not optimally be provided by the private sector. Yet, if we accept this argument blindly, we run the risk of having government take over a lot of what we now consider private enterprise.

However, government also frustrates another important tenet of market efficiency. If the very nature of public goods makes it difficult to extract a fee from Consumer-Investors, who will pay for the services? We will return to this question later, but we may ask another more looming question: If the business of providing public goods is not for profit, what are the criteria the government should use to ensure they provide the good efficiently?

A healthy skepticism

Government agencies must necessarily substitute the profit motive with some alternative objective to guide their enterprises. Without the obvious focus of the profit motive and the constant diligence of capitalists who will lose their investment if the enterprise is not run efficiently, we are left instead with a bureaucratic model of an organization. A bureaucracy is designed to serve some useful economic purpose but without the economic forces buffeting and focusing its operations. Alternative objectives must act as its focus. In the best organizations, we create visions and, at times, missions to focus and benchmark our operations.

The worst organizations end up being run apparently for the benefit of the providers rather than the benefit of the Consumer-Investors. In such organizations, misspent budgets, corruption, low morale, lower efficiency, and very low public confidence result. These organizations often have the goal of budget maximization and employee benefits maximization as the primary measure of success, rather than cost minimization or the efficient provision of public goods. And they give government a bad name.

So unpopular is this bureaucratic tendency of government that the critics in us argue that government cannot "fix" markets. We could argue that we can afford the deadweight loss of an inefficient market, or we can afford the cost of excluding some from a park that has been privatized, because to do otherwise would create even greater losses through bureaucratic ineptitude.

No doubt there is some truth to that argument. Even the most economically casual observer will note that our local Department of Motor Vehicles is not typically a client-friendly bureaucracy. If such an important function were to be privatized, we can imagine a flourish of innovations that would make the process more efficient. For one thing, a private provider recognizes that waiting customers are costly – if not to the company, then certainly to the customer. And a phone call that goes unanswered is a customer lost. But, monopolies, especially not-for-profit monopolies, have a difficult time keeping their focus on the ultimate goals of the organization.

The DMVcratization of governments

Some of government's greatest follies into the marketplace cause us to maintain a visceral bias against public provision of goods or services. This value is likely stronger in the United States than most other countries more accustomed to a greater role of government in commerce. In the United States, government is often prevented from competing, either statutorily or ethically, from providing services in direct competition with private providers.

Regulatory bias and gold plated capital

Let's look at one example where we would agree the government can perform a useful function, but still ultimately distort market decisions. When the United States began electrification more than a century ago, there was a debate about whether the government should provide this most important and most expensive infrastructure, or whether private companies should fill the void. In many countries, it was the government, or corporations owned by the government, that did this. In Canada for instance, such a corporation is called a Crown Corporation. In the United States, more typically a franchise was offered by the government to a private provider to build the electric service. This exclusivity made sense for a couple of reasons. First, it would be unattractive if we simply opened up the byways to as many separate power and telephone poles as there were private companies willing to vie for that prize. Even more problematic, it is likely that the spoils will end up going to one lucky monopolist. At least we avoid redundant over-investment of utility poles on our roads.

To avoid this problem of redundant investment, we chose a model in which we encouraged the formation of a monopoly, and then we regulated that monopoly closely. Our regulations limit the prices monopolies are permitted to charge to ensure that they don't use their monopoly power to gouge the public. We also ensure that the monopolist franchisee earns a sufficient investment on their Producer-Investment to make it worth their while to provide good quality infrastructure. The other costs like labor, materials, and factors of production, are also passed on for the consumer to pay.

This creates a regulatory bias, though. A Producer-Investor facing this regulatory regime will prefer to purchase very good physical capital because that will influence the profit they are permitted to earn. They are more indifferent to their employment of people, though, because their allowed profit is on physical capital, not human capital. Some label this bias as "gold plated capital," also known as the Averch-Johnson effect.[1] Firms regulated in such a way tend to invest in the best plants and machines, knowing they can pass the higher costs onto the consumer. Expensive nuclear power plants of the 1960s and 1970s were, at least in part, a consequence of this bias.

Cat and mouse

The next challenge is to remedy the cat and mouse game that exists between regulators and regulatees. By its very nature, there is a certain mistrust between these two groups. This mistrust manifests itself in one of two ways.

Companies have a tendency to not reveal all to the regulator. Recall that the beauty of the competitive model was predicated on full and complete information. If knowledge is power, too much knowledge in the hands of regulators takes market power and profitability from the profit-making entity. Certainly in most all cases, the private company does not believe the regulator is there to help them, even if the regulator sees it otherwise. And the regulators do have a point. If the public loses confidence in the function being regulated, all private companies and the public will suffer. Regulators have an important public confidence function to prevent the lemons from taking over the marketplace and driving out all the good firms. Nonetheless, a private company might prefer that the regulator focus more on its competitors and less on its operations. This tension is natural, understandable, and problematic.

On the other hand, some private markets redress their concerns by aligning the interests of the regulators with their own interests. Let's look at one common example.

Co-opted regulators

We all want well-built and marketable homes and we recognize the value of local building codes in ensuring that any permanent structure added to our homes is done according to accepted standards. However, much of the quality of a structure is hidden behind walls.

To ensure marketability and safety, government appoints building inspectors to oversee work done on a home to be sure it is done in a way that will protect future owners. Purchasers of homes appreciate this process, even if those building a house wish there was an alternative solution. Recognizing there are more purchasers than builders over the life of a home, we subscribe to the need for arms-length building inspectors. We fear that privatizing such a function may create too cozy a relationship between the builders and the inspectors. Who oversees this entire process though? While it does not sound like the most exciting way to serve the public, we need a committee of concerned citizens that will make sure the building codes are enforceable, reasonable, and cost effective. However, we can always rely on one citizen's group to be willing to serve on such a committee at the drop of a hat.

Building codes committees are often stacked with plumbing, electrical, and building contractors. On one level they are ideal because they really know the industry well. Indeed, they are the industry. And they pass ordinances that require you to only perform work through licensed plumbers, electricians, and building contractors. It is the proverbial fox watching the hen house.

It would be very difficult to prevent this constant attempt to co-opt the regulators, to the point that we often must also create regulators for the regulators. Regulatory bodies often have offices of inspectors general to ensure that their ethics and their relationships with the industry remain on the up and up. When there is so much potential for profit though, the job of an inspector general is a difficult one indeed.

The angels of Wall Street

The potential for mischievous profit is perhaps no more dramatic than in our financial markets. It should not be surprising to expect some of our best regulators to be found in the regulation of financial markets. Regulators, in these industries, are a rare breed of public servants dedicated to an incredibly difficult task. They spend pennies to regulate millions, so the decks are severely stacked against them. And, so, they try to use their resources well, take on the most significant cases, and sometimes create a most public example to deter others, as we witnessed in the prosecution of Martha Stewart for charges relating to insider trading. And these regulators perform this function almost scandal and corruption free.

The deck is stacked against them

We may argue though that, at times, this regulatory function has been inadequate, and almost certainly this has been the case. At the same time, in financial markets so complex and so surrounded by secrecy, it would be hard to imagine a regulatory investment sufficient to prevent some of the problems we have witnessed lately. The rate of innovation of financial products has grown geometrically since the 1980s, while government and regulatory agency budgets have barely grown arithmetically. Regulators cannot keep up.

Even in the best of circumstances, the well-meaning bureaucrat must take great time, care, and research to formulate policy. Good policy is a compromise, providing the public with confidence while still providing the incentive to be creative and innovative. Again, the bureaucrat is out-staffed. Regulations promulgated by a few good policymakers will instantly be torn apart by hundreds of the smartest lawyers and financiers in the country, each trying to discover the clause or loophole that can make their firms rich. There is little incentive in developing considerate regulation and every incentive to profit from the regulation, at best, or legally make the regulation superfluous, at worst.

Brave New Worlds

Policy paralysis aside, there is also the problem of the regulators understanding precisely the nature of an emerging problem. In an economy based on the free market and free enterprise, the premise is that everything is legal unless a law says it is illegal. This is in contrast to a more authoritarian and centralized system in which nothing is legal unless expressly permitted. In FEW countries in which innovation of just about any sort is encouraged, financial markets are just like every other industry in for new products and ideas. Just as a piece of software or a new DVD format may be over-promised and may not perform well, new financial instruments can be ill-conceived.

The classic example is the Credit Crunch of 2007.

A perfect storm

Of course, looking back, we can see the perfect storm coming. The echo children of the baby boom reached the age of home ownership, putting pressure on the housing stock and prices. At the same time, longevity of the retired was increasing and there was a movement afoot to keep these retirees in their homes. Housing prices began to rise and speculative investors jumped on the bandwagon, pushing prices up still further. A slew of shows began to appear on television with a theme of "Flip That House," promising quick returns so long as the speculative bubble continues to grow. There began a whole cottage industry on how to make a killing in real estate with no money down. The strategy falls into that problematic category of "it's okay if few do it, but bad if everybody does it." Such strategies are by definition unsustainable.

Economic prognosticators did not universally recognize the problem. The economists Karl Case and Robert Schiller certainly took note, as did former Federal Reserve Governor Ed Gramlich. Unfortunately they could not convince regulators of sub-prime mortgages or the central banks, despite their high respect among the regulatory community.

The second storm was the innovation of the NINJA (No Income, No Jobs or Assets) loans. These "pyramid" loans were based only on one market fundamental – the loans are safe if housing prices continue to rise. Based on zero down payments and a de-emphasis on income, credit, or character verification, these loans allowed a significant amount of new money to enter the housing market. The new money pushed housing prices up further, giving a temporary reprieve for the NINJA pyramid scheme, at least until the third storm entered the marketplace.

The final piece of the puzzle was the collateralized securities innovation. Packaging these NINJA loans up into bundles and selling their flow of income to investors that would, in return, provide the funds for even more such loans, the originators of these new loans and securities took advantage of one primary weakness in financial markets. New financial instruments do not have the track record to reveal their Achilles heals. The loan originators, the agencies that rate the new securities, and the banks and investment houses that peddled them were all able to profit from this instrument not yet understood. And neither the Fed nor the Securities and Exchange Commission had the foresight, intimate knowledge, or resources to stay ahead of this rapidly burgeoning phenomenon – until it was way too late.

Trying to keep up

Money will move very quickly to profit from such financial innovations, perhaps in a matter of days or weeks. Government regulatory agencies can perhaps respond in weeks or months and the underlying legislation through Congress or state legislatures may take months, years, or sometimes decades. It is this disconnect between the pace of financial innovation and the pace of regulatory innovation that exacerbated these perfect financial storms.

Is there a solution to this perplexing problem? Likely there is not. With tens of trillions of dollars invested in financial capital markets and only hundreds of millions of dollars invested in the institutions that regulate these markets, the odds are stacked against the regulators 100,000:1. And much like the rhetoric following 9/11, the regulators have to get it right each and every time, while the "too clever by one half" crowd must only succeed spectacularly just once to create a problem of mammoth proportions. Also like the 9/11 analogy, the regulators are working with an industry that is necessarily shrouded in secrecy, which is perhaps a less flattering spin than the "proprietary information" term the industry would prefer to label itself.

Solutions to this dilemma must rest with internal ethics watchdogs in their own corporate suites, in combination with stern punishment when an ethical breach translates into a financial meltdown. Unfortunately we again suffer from a principle agent problem. Those most hurt by these meltdowns are not the same individuals or corporations that profit from the schemes. The NINJA originators have their money in the bank, while former Countrywide Home Loans CEO, Angelo Mozilo, left his company with a reported 24 million dollar pension, 20 million dollars in deferred compensation, and almost 6 million dollars in company stock. The bond rating companies too received their commissions offered by the investment banks and the investment banks received their packaging fees for the products they sold to investors. These investors, and now the taxpayers, are left holding the bag, and the government has had to step in to ensure people are not thrown out of their homes.

As we shall see in the next chapter, sometimes a company is just too big to let fail. This simply worsens the principal-agent problem. The agents made their money, the principals are indemnified, and the public, which was not part of either side, is left holding the bag.

20
The Bigger You Are, the Softer You Fall

There is a long tradition of indemnifying the corporate mistakes of the free market system, so long as the mistakes and the corporations are equally massive. The notorious bailout of Chrysler in the early 1980s was, until very recently, the best example in our lifetime. Like all US car companies at the time, it was reeling from years of failure to innovate. The oil price run-up of the late 1970s left the US automobile industry vulnerable to the onslaught of small, fuel-efficient cars from Japan and Germany. These countries never had the luxury of cheap domestic oil and so had always kept fuel efficiency in mind. The oil crisis played into their strengths and held the US automobile industry hostage.

The automobile industry also suffered from its own arrogance and dominance. It no longer felt the need to be innovative or responsive to consumer needs. It was said that what was good for General Motors was good for the country. Instead of dealing with consumer needs, the industry thought they could dictate these needs through marketing. Just as Henry Ford once said you could have any Ford Model T, so long as it was black, Chrysler, too, thought you could buy any car you wanted, so long as it was a K-car. Chrysler realized that they had an advantage over other manufacturers that were allowed to fail – most notably the car manufacturer American Motors. Chrysler was a major employer, employed workers from a major union, and was a major provider of jobs in a politically very significant region of the country. While market Darwinism might be willing to let a large company fail, politics could not afford to have a large number of voters lose their jobs. Consequently, the government agreed to underwrite debt so that Chrysler could afford to borrow to reorganize. At the same time, these threats of failures increased its leverage with unions as it sought concessions from workers too.

For a long time, politics and big business have been necessarily intertwined. Rarely would government intervene for individual homeowners, for small businesses, or any but the largest of enterprises. But, once a company is tallied in the billions or tens of billions, Wall Street has the attention of K Street and Pennsylvania Avenue.

Corporate rescues are again part of the political and editorial vocabulary. For example, Long Term Capital Management (LTCM) was one of the earliest and most notorious of the modern hedge fund era. Founded by a former principal in Salomon Brothers, LTCM had on its board the 1997 Nobel Prize in Economics winners renowned for their contribution to modern financial analysis. And they made money – lots of it. With returns perhaps four times larger than those typically earned in financial markets, LTCM was the darling on Wall Street. Then in 1998 it lost almost five billion dollars in just four months.

Greed gone sour

Their success was again in the category of "too clever by one half." The principals were able to make money by observing that frequently traded bonds will move more quickly to an equilibrium price than less frequently traded (or, in the parlance of economics, more thinly traded) bonds that are otherwise very similar. The movement of the thickly traded bonds was predictive of the direction of their less traded sisters, allowing LTCM to sweep in and buy those thinly traded bonds that would soon rise, and selling short those that would soon fall.

This strategy had two effects. First, it allowed LTCM to profit by pennies at a time, but replicated over hundreds of millions of bonds purchased or sold, thereby creating millions of dollars of profits with almost no risk. Second, this arbitrage strategy also moved the thinly traded bonds closer to equilibrium more quickly.

This strategy did not necessarily create value. The cleverness of LTCM was in extracting the ultimate profits for itself rather than from the slow-moving holders of the bonds. However, nor did LTCM incur costs or use resources that could have gone elsewhere. This strategy then was rather benign until it failed spectacularly.

The amazing success of LTCM induced its principles to find other new and profitable opportunities. Like the company that grows too quickly and finds itself in markets that it knows little about, LTCM found itself developing new investment strategies that bore no resemblance to its original arbitrage bread and butter. They took their same strategy of borrowing a lot of capital to invest it momentarily, profit with a little more capital, and apply the technique to options on stocks, and other similar derivative instruments.

The LTCM strategy could have been successful, on average, were it not for a couple of artifacts. First, because their strategy worked quite well typically, they were able to borrow huge amounts of capital, hoping to profit perhaps as little as a percentage point, but over a matter of days. However, if they were so highly leveraged by the vast amount of borrowed capital, even a loss of a few percentage points would be spectacular.

Second, the strategy works so long as there are no systematic phenomena that adversely affected all market participants. LTCM could not have predicted the first Asian Contagion of 1997 or the threat of Russian default on bonds in 1998. As a consequence of their positions in this critical time, they lost billions, and, perhaps most importantly, they threatened to affect the overall level of market confidence. The fear was that if a bunch of smart Nobel Prize winners could lose almost everything, then surely the market is not very safe for the average investor either. While smart money might have known better, the bread and butter of investment houses is the confidence you and I have in the marketplace. Financial markets could not afford the specter of a major failure of Long Term Capital Management.

The first response was for the industry to take care of its own as an example of enlightened capitalism. A consortium of financiers, including the world's richest man, Warren Buffett, offered to buy out LTCM. The principals thought they could do better though, and indeed the Federal Reserve Bank of New York organized an injection of almost four billion dollars, bankrolled by major global investment banks, in exchange for a 90% equity share.

While crisis was averted and the market remained liquid, this willingness to intervene opened a Pandora's box. If very large funds are permitted to profit almost without bounds, but will be bailed out if they lose equally spectacularly, these funds come to believe they are indemnified from downside risk. This is the moral hazard we have come to know from earlier chapters. If one is indemnified from downside risk, one may engage in risky behaviors that would otherwise be avoided.

Privatized Profits and Socialized Losses

Let's fast-forward ten years later to the most recent outbreaks of financial meltdowns. The recent bout of bailouts arose from the Credit Crunch. When Consumer-Investors learned that a lot of risky mortgages were mixed in with top grade mortgages in packaged mortgage-backed securities, they realized that the assets were not nearly as secure as they had originally thought. There was a flight of capital from those risky assets to less risky assets and a lot of investors were left holding the bag with losses rising to hundreds of millions of dollars.

This virus spread to other markets too because it is the ability to obtain mortgage credit that fuels home purchases and hence home demand and housing prices. As prices plunge, existing mortgages become even more risky, foreclosures increase, and the Consumer-Investor, who makes up 70% of our economy, feels poorer. This vicious cycle reinforces itself, and spirals downward until some entity, or more likely a collective group of entities, manages to re-establish market confidence. Perhaps the worst thing for market confidence is a constant stream of news about investment house failure after failure. It is marginally better to hear about a steady stream of investment house bailouts.

What do these major investment and huge mortgage funds have in common? Bear Stearns, Citigroup, Morgan Stanley, Carlisle Group, Northern Rock, Merrill Lynch, Union Bank of Switzerland (UBS), Nationwide Financial, and Goldman Sachs are no longer the major funds and sources of capital that sweep up smaller competitors to create mammoth stores of wealth and capital. Instead, they are huge financial firms that are regularly candidates for bailouts by governments, government and central bank funds, and other banks and financial houses. A veritable who's who of finances, these companies are just some of the latest to be too big to fail.

Up to the Bear Stearns bailout of 2008, governments had been reluctant to participate in these bailouts, perhaps fearing the re-establishment of a precedent that could encourage moral hazard. The constant flow of the need for such action is likely to so tap the willingness of large solvent funds to continue to bail-out these companies that the federal government may be forced to respond. For the time being though, it is interesting to pause for a moment and understand both why and how large funds can afford to indemnify, for a price in the form of an equity share, the mistakes of these once-powerhouses of global finances.

The how and why

Let us begin with the how. The scale of the current sub-prime mortgage crisis is in the hundreds of billions of dollars, perhaps even in the trillions of dollars. Who could possibly have the wealth sitting around to buy up huge chunks of the US financial markets? Well, who has been attracting the bulk of new wealth arising from globalization? The Asian countries, by strength of their strong exports to the US consumer market and the oil exporting nations, from the near insatiable demand for oil by the rapidly growing Second Economic World, are amassing huge surpluses.

What can they do with a huge number of US dollars coming in and so few goods and services they want to buy from the United States? If some would say the US economy is spending beyond its means, it is perhaps more accurate to observe the US is spending because others are willing to lend it the money – for now. In return, the United States is sacrificing its own financial autonomy and potency, and the Second Economic World is happy to oblige.

If FEW trade and budget deficits are fueling SEW surpluses, why are these large funds, owned by the Chinese, Singaporean, Saudi Arabian, or even the British governments, so willing to keep propping up these financial houses? Very simply, it is good for business. Recall when America sneezes, the world catches a cold. The hint of a recession, or even less than robust growth, can throw world markets into disarray. Some argue that the Chinese even hold their currency artificially low to keep affordable the prices of their products landed in the United States. And if the Chinese own so much US equity, and so many bonds, the decline of the value of the US dollar now proportionally affects the value of its own holdings.

In the past, the United States worked closely with the OPEC leaders to ensure that oil was priced right for the oil exporting nations while at the same time keeping the US economy, and hence demand for oil, healthy. It is not that this argument lacks current cachet. Rather, it is perhaps that things have gotten away from us so quickly that there seems to be little that any one entity can do to put the Genie back in the bottle – except perhaps the Chinese.

At one time, and in the spirit of economic enlightenment when the Group of Eight (G8) highly industrialized nations recognized their mutual interdependence, ministers of finance would coordinate such policies as interest rates and exchange rates. The goal was to keep the US dollar within a nice range, or band, vis-à-vis other major currencies. The ultimate goal was to keep the US economy strong and preserve it as the engine of the economies of the First Economic World.[1]

Ironically, the Global Financial Meltdown is bringing some unity to the world finance leaders. The Group of Eight nations, augmented by participants from China, and elsewhere, are now meeting more regularly to discuss their mutual interdependence and the need to solve global problems with global initiatives. These discussions are healthy, but difficult.

Some new players

A couple of phenomena not directly related to healthy economies have disrupted this delicate coalition of mutual enlightenment. First, there are now some significant new players. The BRIC nations of Brazil, Russia, India, and China now represent the rapid growth countries of the Second Economic World. Also on these sidelines are the oil rich countries like Saudi Arabia, Venezuela, Iran, and others. There is a growing lack of appreciation for mutual interdependence. Rather, the institutions of economic cooperation, borne out of the rebuilding following the First and then the Second World Wars, have been slow to absorb these new Second Economic World countries.

Second, the United States has, in effect, pursued an isolationist foreign policy, making it now more difficult to pursue a cooperative economic policy. It may also be emotionally difficult for the United States economy to ask for help for many reasons. The United States has maintained a reputation as the world's economic superpower. And to ask for help might not project an image of strength.

Even if the United States were to ask for help, it would still have to endure some gloating as others ask why we would let things get so out of hand and so affect economies worldwide as a consequence of the Credit Crisis virus. Foreign finance ministers might also claim that they have problems of their own, too sizeable to worry about taking care of the US problems first.

Finally, some may ask what can be done at this point. If very high oil prices are choking the US economy, some of the high prices are because oil is denominated in a rapidly depreciating US dollar. A good part of rising oil prices is from a falling US dollar and a good chunk of the explanation for the rest of the rise in oil prices is that capital is fleeing troubled financial markets into presumably safer commodity markets, like oil. OPEC managers will correctly point out that there is not an imbalance between the actual supply and demand for oil. In this case, oil prices are rising not for reasons of supply and demand, but instead for reasons of market speculation and capital flight. And little can be done by foreign finance ministers or by foreign governments about this phenomenon.

Why isn't this news?

There may be one additional reason for the lack of market confidence or perhaps more correctly, the lack of a concerted effort to restore market confidence. The US domestic economy has not been a pressing national interest, at least in the United States, upon until very recently.

While the economy has not repeated the heights of growth and innovation of the 1990s, unemployment has remained very low and steady and inflation has been in check. The economic life has been fair, if not good, as the country's collective attention has been instead directed to wars in Iraq and Afghanistan, and the perennial issue of illegal immigration. There has been little discussion of domestic economics, perhaps arising from a certain and almost legendary comfort with the financial stewardship of the Federal Reserve Chairman Alan Greenspan.

To attempt now to offer economic leadership is to fall on deaf ears. Over two terms of President Bush, the country grew accustomed to a president who did not view himself as an economic commander in chief. And just as a child does not listen to the advice of parents speaking beyond their experience, when President Bush spoke on the economy, Consumer-investors no longer listened. Add to that a reluctance in a lame duck Republican president to mention the "recession" word, and in doing so disadvantage a Republican presidential candidate during an election year, and the domestic economy was left to rely on a relatively new Federal Reserve Board chairman for its economic leadership.

Our economic commander-in-chief

It of course remains an open issue whether the political leader of a nation should also be an economic leader. Perhaps herein lies an ideological split. Many Democrats are accused of having too large a propensity to interfere with the economy, while many Republicans are accused of relying too much on the beauty of the free market. No doubt the correct position is somewhere between these extremes, but that fine balance point has not yet been discovered.

It would be too glib to say that the right balance is just enough, but not too much. The balance point shifts with each force to buffet the economy. There can be no easy answer to such complex questions, especially when financial markets are innovating much more quickly than they can even adjust and are much for government to keep up with. There are more broad principles though, which could be embraced by either faction that will be discussed later.

Add to the mix a legitimate allegiance of either party to the fairness secured for their base supporters, and the issue of free market efficiency becomes even more complicated and politicized. Of course, we could instead have economists be our political leaders, except for two problems. One is that economists are often accused of being charisma-challenged.

And the economic focus on overall market efficiency leaves abandoned the very important function of politics to decide how to fairly divide the spoils of economic success. Politics is by its very nature political, and apolitical economics have little to offer in that discussion. Finally, economists are people too, and often, perhaps very often, confuse their economic policy prescriptions with their political conclusions. We will return later to the theme of politics masquerading as economics.

As a consequence, the issue of the proper intervention into free markets is complicated, indeed. And so it is inevitable that bailouts will always be considered as highly politically charged, especially when they are few and far between and are likely to be invoked only in the case of very large, and consequently, very wealthy financial entities. It is perhaps true that we cannot afford the one or two behemoths to fall, even if we are at a loss sometimes with what to do for the many.

This same argument can quite accurately be made on behalf of the Consumer-Investor. Of course, no single individual has as much at stake as a mammoth corporation and its shareholders. But, while we will bailout a large corporation to protect confidence in financial markets, salvaging a large number of Consumer-Investors can have equally large effects on the economy.

The trick with either bailout is to balance the overall effects on the economy with the dangerous signals that result when we indemnify poor choices. We can ill afford to generate moral hazard, so solutions require risk sharing of some sort. If we can do this, no side of the transaction gets off scot-free, while the innocents of the economy are held more or less harmless for the imprudence of others.

21
It's Downright Criminal

A bailout in the best or circumstances is a sticky issue. Bailouts when there has been evidence of criminal activity is yet another. It is important not to confuse the two.

When firms profit spectacularly because they rely on the judgment of some very potent and powerful individuals, the ability to also fail spectacularly increases substantially. Let us look at the instances when huge financial failures are increasingly created by rogue individuals in critical positions. We'll first differentiate these, though, from financial problems caused by mistake or by misguided ethics.

Mistakes and bets on the direction of movements of the market are part of the Darwinist evolution of a business and an economy. Taking risks is essential for innovation. Of course, when risk taking succeeds, one is called brilliant, and when it fails, one is left holding the bag. If the successes are bigger than the failures, overall success is assured. The art of business is to ensure there are more successes than failures.

The legal system is designed to ensure that innocent parties are not affected by the follies of others. Statutes can protect property rights but cannot possibly anticipate every potential human folly. Few violations of the rights of others are so problematic that they threaten the safety or security of us all, so few human or business interactions violate criminal statutes. Many more affect other innocent parties that are nonetheless, and narrowly, affected by a business decision. These interactions gone wrong can be remedied through suits in civil courts. And a third category of business interactions must be guided by our internal compass of right and wrong. Our ethics must necessarily govern this vast majority of business interactions. It is this gray area between unambiguous right and absolute wrong where business people may venture.

A case for business ethics

Every professor of business ethics has heard the inevitable comparison of business ethics to military intelligence or jumbo shrimp. Oxymorons aside, there are many tests and frameworks for determining what is ethically right. The philosopher Immanuel Kant warned us about the human tendency to rationalize to ourselves our preferred decision.[1] He drew our attention to the inconvenient truth of what would result if everybody made the same decision. For instance, I would not want everyone to cheat on their taxes, so I should not cheat on mine. This is the maxim of the universal law, and the tenet of the golden rule that we should do unto others what we would have them do unto us.

A Kant contemporary named John Rawls warns us of the danger of the situational ethic.[2] Human nature as it is, we are not surprised when someone who is wealthy recommends lower capital gains taxes or one who is poor recommends we tax the rich. It is more interesting and Rawlsian to determine what tax system each would recommend if they did not know in advance whether the luck of the draw would determine they are rich or poor.

Another approach is the New York Times test. Except for those few cases in which publishing our decisions would harm others or permit others to profit without commensurate effort, each of our decisions should be able to endure everyone knowing it. If we make good, ethical decisions, we should have no problem with these decisions being published on the front page of the Times. If the publicity from our decision would cause us a pang in our solar plexus, then it is likely ethically wrong, even if it may be legally defensible.

Most transactions that are at arm's length, follow good policies, or are made under full disclosure, do not violate the tenets of business ethics. The looming threat of well-founded lawsuits also disciplines the shady practices that perhaps diminish the rights of others, or are made with such secrecy that one must wonder whose interests are being advanced. Civil and corporate lawyers play an important role in creating an acute awareness of the effect of one's action on others. Of course, overzealous lawyers, who may themselves behave unethically through their zeal, may create a bias that sometimes has a chilling effect on difficult but good decisions.

Transactions that rise to the level of criminality are more problematic. It is the very nature of criminal behavior that induces its perpetrators to operate in secrecy. Because so much effort is devoted to secrecy and detection of the crime is never perfect, remedy must go far beyond mere compensation and must include punitive damages as a deterrent.

The corruption contagion

Following the political excesses of Watergate, there were waves of business excesses, some of which rose to criminality. Insider traders of the 1980s, from Ivan Boesky to Michael Milken and their many contemporaries were first treated as heroes yet subsequently disgraced. Years in jail, and millions of dollars of fines did not allow these individuals to recover their reputations. Yet if it afforded them good speaking fees to counsel a myriad of budding students of business about what not to do, and perhaps inspired just a few about what they could get away with if perhaps they are just a bit more clever. These lessons seem to be repeated every decade, with meltdowns at WorldCom, Adelphi, and Enron in the 1990s, and Society Generale in the 2000s.

The new and interesting phenomenon is the ability of a rogue trader to bring down whole corporations and with it the wealth of thousands of shareholders. The first of this recent wave of rogue traders was Nick Leeson, a trader that brought down Barings PLC, Britain's (then) oldest investment bank. Mr. Leeson found himself making tens of millions of dollars on behalf of his employer by the age of 25 and earning a salary of more than 300,000 dollars, including bonuses. His run of good luck as general manager of a new futures market desk in Singapore ended when his attempts to cover up and remedy some mistakes created bigger and bigger mistakes. While he claimed he simply went down a wrong path one step at a time, it was later discovered that he somehow managed to sock away millions of dollars in secret various international bank accounts.

In the final account, losses exceeded more than a billion dollars, forcing his employer into bankruptcy. Leeson fled and was eventually found and jailed in 1995. He was released from jail after four years, and now is the chief executive officer (CEO) of a soccer team in Ireland. His story of rogue trader to soccer CEO is the stuff of the dinner speaking circuit. Who says crime doesn't pay?

History seems to repeat itself, although the size of the transgressions continues to grow. Jerome Kerviel was recently apprehended for losing almost ten billion dollars in his capacity as a trader at Societe Generale in 2007. While the full story has yet to emerge, it is still further evidence that the systems are not, and some would argue cannot be, in place to prevent huge damage from those who lack a moral compass. In an industry where you are a hero until you make a colossal loss, the system seems destined to repeat its notorious history.

What would induce one to take such risks with another's money? Michael Douglas starred as Gordon Gekko in the movie *Wall Street*. In the most memorable moment, and inspired by a similar speech reputably made by Ivan Boesky at the University of California Berkley, Gecko espouses the beauty of greed. Gekko believed in productive destruction – taking a company and breaking it up into pieces under the assumption that the sum of its parts is sometimes greater than the whole, even if shareholders or workers lose in this necessary evolutionary process. Gekko was motivated by greed – which, in his mind is good – and presumably had been the catalyst for the capitalist system since the early part of the industrial revolution.

The extremeness of Gekko's speech is that it does not define where greed should end. Greed without limit falls into criminality, as Mr. Leeson and Mr. Kerviel perhaps now attest. But, while greed is the seventh deadly sin for the individual, it is something ignored by the firms who otherwise profit from the successful missteps of their agents. Mr. Leeson and Mr. Kerviel were given expanded authority, autonomy, and reward because they were bringing to their firms huge profits. They were not vilified until their employers lost huge sums. The system unfortunately remains blind when profits are to be had, and looks for scapegoats when losses mount. And a new generation of future rogue traders sees the watches and cars of successful traders and wants to emulate their lifestyles, and perhaps even their situational ethic.

When ethics strays into criminality

Can we get a handle on this seemingly inconsistent ethic that often strays into criminality? Perhaps there are two lessons to learn. One is that if something appears too good or comes too easily, perhaps it is dishonest or unethical. If strategies must be secretive to be successful, do we do more than violate the premise of competitive markets that rely on perfect information? Perhaps we too often use secrecy as a shield to disguise unethical behavior that can stray into criminal behavior.

What would the financial world look like if we lifted every rock? While certainly individuals would like to keep their financial affairs private, the overall state of anyone's finances is rarely private these days. Just ask the fundraiser at your college alumni office just how private your assets are. What would we then have to lose if we could witness every market transaction, and the forces moving every hedge fund? For sure, this transparency would have a chilling effect for the tiny minority of transactions that genuinely need to keep a strategy secret. The gains overall, though, from greater transparency must dramatically out swamp the problems this might create for some.

Just like most other market transactions, at least before the anonymity of the Internet, financial market transactions may be exposed, but the underlying motivations of any market participant will remain forever in their private minds. Greater transparency of every transaction would allow us to see who is benefiting at each step, and by how much. It would allow us to better understand the risks of instruments that fully disclose, yet not aggregate to such a degree that we know so little about so much, or nothing about everything.

Perhaps most importantly, we could truly see the difference between participants who are buying or selling based on the very nature of the security sold, and those rather that are buying and selling in an effort to encourage less informed participants to follow suit in a predictable way. By some measures, half of the speculation that makes markets soar and plunge are highly leveraged hedge funds that profit by leading when they know the rest will follow. Just as a camera on every corner has made London safer, perhaps a computer screen immediately broadcasting every transaction would restore trust and honesty to financial markets. Certainly the technology that allows anyone to trade anywhere at any time, instantly, will also allow us to easily track and monitor every transaction just as efficiently. This will only be possible if we can put the collective good of the market ahead of the private greed of a few.

If the names, positions, and pattern of trade for every transactor were instantly known, would there be any negative consequences? Already it is possible to see the volume of each trade transacted. Transparency not only in the quantity of trades, but also in the transactors, would simply further add to market information. If the Efficient Market Hypothesis is based on the price of a security reflecting all available information, this additional transparency can only act to improve market efficiency.

While the worst transgressors would likely prefer to remain anonymous, it seems likely that they would still participate if their trading became public. Revealing their in-again and out-again strategies might make their strategies less effective, but it could only improve overall market efficiency. Meanwhile, the trades that are long term and based on market fundamentals will likely go unaffected by this policy – as they have nothing to hide.

Of course, we must protect our freedom of life, liberty, and the pursuit of happiness. Such a right to pursue is not absolute though. It was formulated under the belief that an individual free to pursue happiness and inventiveness is good for the economy and for all. It did not anticipate that freedom and privacy would instead create an industry of gamesmanship that comes at the expense, rather than furtherance, of an expanded economic pie. The test should perhaps be whether the activity benefits the market overall.

The economy is a wonderful enabler that permits us to pursue our interests, at a cost. The cost might be taxation, the laws that ensure fair commerce, and the necessity to preserve the rights of others. We do not have a right to participate in a given market – instead, we are given the privilege to do so, as long as we follow the rules. Full transparency is perhaps a price we can afford.

22
Somebody's Hedging

The reforms arising from the Great Depression and panics before and since, have created a body of regulations designed to keep together Consumer-Investors and their money.

Remember George Bailey and his best efforts on the part of his members in *It's a Wonderful Life*? While George undoubtedly knew a little more about financial markets than the average Consumer-Investor, he knew much less than the Wall Street traders who could watch the market gyrate on those days before and after the Great Crash in October 1929.

Given the technologies of the day, it was probably best that banks did not engage in stock market trading. One good reason is that there were 30,000 banks before the Great Depression, but only 15,000 a few years later. There was just not enough expertise around to protect the hard-earned money of the Consumer-Investor. So, banks were asked to get out of the business of trading in securities.

As a consequence of the Stock Market Crash, a wave of banking regulations culminated in the Banking Act of 1933, popularly knows as the Glass-Steagall Act, after its congressional sponsors. One part of the Act required banks to create a firewall between its household and commercial banking operations, and investment banking. Banks in effect had to rely on the return of their community investments (mortgages and loans) to pay the interest on savings accounts and provide a return to their shareholders. Banks were also prohibited by Regulation Q from paying interest on checking accounts. This imposition was not problematic given prevailing interest rates were only two or three percent per annum, anyway.

Unanticipated consequences

Like every regulation, one cannot anticipate every state of the world. However, these regulations worked pretty well for almost 50 years.

The high inflation arising from the first OPEC oil crisis exposed the Achilles Heal of Regulation Q. As a rise in oil prices induced a secondary rise in the price of goods derived from oil, Consumer-Investors began to demand more in wages. These wages gave rise to greater increases in prices, and pretty soon inflation was out of control.

Nobody will save their money in a bank that cannot offer an interest rate that is sufficient to maintain purchasing power. When inflation of 15% easily exceeds the interest rate, banks must offer perhaps an 18% return on accounts to induce people to save rather than to spend on something of lasting value quickly, before it is too late.

Something has to give. Banks in response began to offer novel new alternatives to checking accounts, like "money market" accounts that could earn a higher interest rate because they were not considered checking accounts.

This era also beckoned in the widespread development and use of mutual funds. A mutual fund is simply a pool of funds collected from many Consumer-Investors and managed by a professional investor. This innovation became very popular because it allowed Consumer-Investors to make more sophisticated investment decisions, for a fee, while freeing them up from having to educate themselves in all the knowledge necessary to protect and enhance our investments.

The creation of an accessible and alternative store of value created a crisis in the banking industry on the one hand and spawned a whole industry of self help books for Consumer-Investors and for mutual fund managers on the other. Either way, the banking industry was beginning to suffer a liquidity problem. They were facing an exodus of their short-term funds, but they could not easily shed their long-term liabilities, just as George Bailey experienced in the run on his bank.

We know that many of the biggest institutions in our economy are too big to fail and banks are bigger than most. In this case, it was Regulation Q that was the root of their problems, primarily because no regulator could have anticipated the need to provide double-digit interest rates way back in the 1930s. Congress could not repeal Regulation Q quickly enough, and did so. Money flooded out of the banking industry and into new fangled instruments, turning many that were conservative savers with banks into new money moguls.

Around the same time, the collapse of oil prices, and the subsequent collapse of real estate values in oil producing states, created the Savings and Loans (S&L) crisis. The long-term assets of S&L's were tied to the value of mortgages on property that was no longer worth as much. And the S&L's were caught out with long-term assets gone bad and with the exodus of short-term cash as people preferred to invest in something with a better return.

Perhaps it would not be too unfair at this point to note that the banking industry was not complaining about Regulation Q when they were demanding high interest rates on the money they lent to Consumer-Investors but were "prevented" from offering high interest rates on our checking accounts. The difference was just pure profit. Once the Consumer-Investor caught on though, banks clamored for deregulation and they got it.

Soon the genie was out of the bottle. The taste of high returns in money market mutual funds and a broad-spread speculation on gold and silver made high financiers of us all. The illegal market manipulation of world silver prices by the wealthy Texan Hunt Brothers in the late 1970s also produced the first market bubble in recent history. Many more would follow.

We could view these developments as the democratization of financial markets. Democracies rely on the collective wisdom of the many to make decisions for the common good. History is riddled with collective wisdom gone wrong and market participation by the masses is surely no exception. If markets come to respond to information poorly, making the market larger may only make the problems bigger.

There's a new fund in town

Another spin on this familiar story is that the market became segmented into two groups – smart money and our money. The smart money pooled to invent a new type of investment, called "Hedge Funds." These hedge funds are fast becoming the money market mutual funds of the 1980s and regulators are trying to make sure this does not happen.

The definition of a hedge fund is simple enough, and has nothing to do with "hedging one's bets." A hedge fund is a pool of money from a small number of wealthy partners, and often a substantially larger loan from a bank, permitting the fund to be highly leveraged. Accounting for up to 50% or more of activity in some markets on some days, and catering primarily to the wealthy, these hedge funds are the new smart money. They have thrived because they work on the fringes of financial markets, able to pursue strategies not available to traditional brokerage houses or mutual funds because they are considered funds not open to the public. They profit from market inefficiencies, and indeed have an incentive to create market inefficiencies from which they can subsequently profit. By catering only to a select group of wealthier investors, they bypass the protections created by the Securities and Exchange Commission and others for the benefit of the typical Consumer-Investor.

For instance, hedge funds are able to short sell. This short selling is selling a stock the fund does not have. You can think of this as the fund having temporarily borrowed the security from a long-term investor. The hedge fund manager believes the security price will fall, if perhaps for no other reason then our observation that their aggressive selling must portend to problems in the underlying security. Once the security price falls, the hedge fund can buy the shares it previously borrowed and sold, return these stocks to the original owner, and pocket the difference. So long as this is all done quickly enough, the fund would not even need to borrow the securities in the first place, and assumes little risk, especially given their market power to influence prices so profoundly. This selling short of stocks one neither has or borrowed is called " naked short selling." Such naked short selling is only illegal if done fraudulently. It is akin to betting at a casino table without having to purchase any chips.

Another profitable strategy is to engage in futures, swaps, or options, each a sophisticated financial instrument that is highly leveraged. The leveraging is much like our margin discussion earlier, but to a much greater extent. If the hedge fund can essentially borrow and put only ten cents of their own money up for every dollar invested, they can multiply their returns by a factor of ten. In reality, the funds often borrow up to 97 cents of every dollar invested, allowing the funds to double in value for just a 3% rise in the value of the investments.

These sophisticated investment strategies produce spectacular returns to the private, and often secretive, investors. So large are the returns that hedge fund managers typically earn the "2 and 20," meaning managers collect 2% of the investment off the top, and 20% of the returns, which is very lucrative compensation when compared to typical mutual funds. For instance, in 2007, hedge fund managers were compensated more than 17 billion dollars for their efforts, with one manager compensated almost 2 billion dollars alone for his year's effort.

To further skirt regulation, hedge funds are typically established in such regulation havens as the Grand Cayman Islands or the Bahamas. Of course, while the fund may be domiciled in such havens, they can be managed from anywhere as a consequence of modern investment technologies and the Internet.

The regulatory environment in the United States that enabled this greater flexibility for hedge fund investors arose from the Investment Act of 1940. This act exempted funds with 100 or fewer sufficiently well-healed investors from the scrutiny and protections afforded for more public investment funds.

Recently, the US Securities and Exchange Commission (SEC) recognized the inherent risks of hedge funds to less-than-sophisticated Consumer-Investors and has attempted to bring hedge funds under greater regulation. The regulations exempting hedge funds from closer scrutiny specified clients with a net worth in excess of five million dollars. While large, this level of assets is becoming more common as retirement funds grow, people live longer and retire later, and housing values in some areas grow to astronomical levels.

As a consequence, the number of hedge funds has grown far faster than the SEC's ability to keep up with them all. The SEC made the sensible decision to regulate based on a risk-management strategy, focusing on those funds that were larger than most. However, the US Court of Appeals rejected this discriminatory approach, forcing the SEC to retrench and reformulate its regulatory approach. This defeat places the SEC even further behind the regulatory eight ball.

In the interest of free markets, we might impose the criterion of hedge fund buyer beware. Caveat emptor does not save the rest of us from the damage a huge hedge fund can inflict on global financial markets. As we discussed, the dominant hedge fund called Long Term Capital Management (LTCM) suffered spectacular losses in 1998 that threatened the entire market. And once again, a federal agency facilitated a bailout.

After years of incredibly double-digit profits, the LTCM hedge fund made a spectacular bet that went sour, losing more than four billion dollars in a few short months. The fund could not pay its creditors and the Fed stepped in by orchestrating a bailout of almost four billion dollars in order to prevent a wider market collapse and loss of market confidence.

While the Fed obviously is concerned about the role of hedge funds in increasing market volatility, and the SEC is running fast to stay ahead of, or not too far behind, this growing investment vehicle, Europe's version of the Fed is fast becoming the most strident voice warning the public and the market about the risks of hedge funds.

The European Central Bank (ECB) recognizes that the seemingly coordinated activity and pattern of activity of hedge funds can destabilize markets, while at the same time creating predictable profits for those hedge fund managers. The strident calls from the ECB have received greater credibility as we all witness the colossal losses of some hedge funds that were exposed to the recent meltdown of mortgage-backed securities. While the failure of some hedge funds had to be written off by major investment banks, the Fed also stepped in with injections of tens of millions of dollars to ensure the market for long-term mortgage instruments did not collapse completely.

Most recently, and unprecedented, the US Fed went beyond coordinating a bailout, and, for the first time in history, actually pumped taxpayer money into reorganizing one of the top five investment banks to prevent its failure. Bear Stearns was over-exposed in the mortgage-backed securities that arose from the sub-prime mortgage debacle. However, the investment banking industry is notoriously incestuous. It became quickly apparent that if Bear Stearns fell, it would also jeopardize many other investors and investment banks. Despite the calls to let those who invested poorly fail, and not create another problem of moral hazard, the Fed felt this situation was just potentially too damaging to financial markets. They forced a merger, and the Fed also promised to more fully regulate this previously less scrutinized sector. In doing so, it has brought investment banking into a fold that had previously been reserved for commercial banks.

Covert and tacit collusion

One of the reasons why markets fail to perform well is because big participants can manipulate prices. We discussed earlier the inefficiencies of monopolies. One side of a market can act as a monopoly even if constituted by more than one firm. An oligopoly is defined as a small number of firms that collectively act like a monopoly. An oligopoly could even have a large number of follower firms that take the lead from one dominant leader. Economists have been concerned about participants that can collectively collude to act as a monopoly. Blatant and overt collusion to frustrate the marketplace is illegal under modern anti-trust laws. However, covert collusion is much more difficult to detect, and colluders are not inclined to advertise their behavior. This is especially true in the secretive and cloistered world of hedge funds.

Even more problematic is de facto collusion to hamper competition. I argued that good price information helps improve market decisions. Ironically enough, could the advertising of prices also be used to prevent competition and create higher returns for one side of the market? Consider two examples.

Price leadership – another game of cat and mouse

One example of tacit price fixing is the system of listing airfares. Pioneered decades ago by American Airlines, the system also provided an easy way for airlines to compare prices and to easily detect if any airline is deviating from a standard market price. If one airline drops its price, it can then expect all airlines in the same market to match the price drop, meaning the first airline has lost its advantage of selling more seats but at a lower cost. Alternatively, an airline can experiment by pushing its price in a market up a bit and see if its competitors follow. In other words, price advertising can be viewed as a way to coordinate prices and collude subtly, rather than compete in prices.

Another example of this might be the collusion of gas station pricing. By posting their prices on large signs, a station can send a signal to other gas stations that it is not cheating in the market price discipline. Such tacit signaling among more sophisticated players can result in higher prices for the insiders but without any overt or covert agreements.

Following the example of price leadership described in the airline or gas station industries, a large hedge fund can signal to the market that the fund believes the market to be over-valued and will be taken down to equilibrium. The hedge fund can "dump" some stock, and watch as many followers mimic their lead. Once the stock drops enough, the hedge fund can aggressively buy. As others also mimic this action, the stock is driven back up. The early movers, that is, the hedge funds, make a handsome profit with almost no risk, and without tying up their capital for a significant length of time.

Hedge funds can accomplish the same goal simply because their actions are transparent to insiders, but opaque to the Consumer-Investor. This is good for the hedge funds, but troubling to the regulators. By increasing profits for the colluders, those on the outside receive lower than average returns, and market confidence suffers.

Investor confidence – the essential ingredient

Financial markets depend crucially on investor confidence, as previous chapters describe. There is likely a role for more sophisticated trading strategies that are the basis of hedge fund investments. Well-informed investors with a risk profile and sufficient capital to engage in riskier investments in exchange for a higher return ought to be permitted to pursue their strategies.

Hedge funds may then serve a useful purpose. However, if their primary advantage is that they can squeeze out greater returns for their well-healed Consumer-Investors, but without the ability to increase capital formation to build new plants and expand available production, these tools merely extract greater returns for some by reducing the return for the typical Consumer-Investor. Market confidence is eroded and capital is diverted away from these financial markets.

More problematic, though, is the corollary of Gresham's Law. In the historic formulation, he observed that counterfeit (bad) money will reduce people's confidence in good money. Similarly, George Akerlof's Nobel Prize winning concept embodied in his paper "The Market for

Lemons" observes that a few lemons in a brand of cars may force the lucky owners of good versions of the car to hold on to their car even if they would otherwise like to sell.[1] This is because buyers will assume that there is a good chance the car for sale is a lemon, even though they are unable to detect that when they purchase the car. No seller of a lemon would ask for a below-market price because that would signal their car is inferior. And no seller of a good version of the car would sell their car at the market price because the market price is discounted because of the lemons. The market breaks down because Consumer-Investors lose confidence in the quality of the product. It is this concern of a breakdown in market confidence that induces the Fed and the SEC to ensure consumer confidence in the marketplace.

The cost of regulation

It seems likely that while the cost of regulation is high in absolute terms, the cost of regulation is not very high in terms relative to the size of financial markets. Returns on financial markets are very competitive though, measured in basis points of one one-hundredth of a percentage point. Any additional transaction cost that takes its cut out of market profits will discourage market participation. For this reason, regulatory costs are typically not paid as a tax on each market transaction. Instead, regulators are typically funded from government coffers under the insight that a breakdown in the financial marketplace will tear at the fabric of the economy and hurt us all.

In other words, we believe that regulation of financial markets is a public good especially when the public must at times step in to pick up the pieces of colossal financial failures. All benefit from the regulation because markets are made more efficient and the decision not to impose a transaction tax ensures the greatest liquidity in these market transactions. As with many public goods, the government is in the best position to regulate on our collective behalf. This maintains the integrity of the financial marketplace and avoids the specter of an industry that claims to regulate itself.

The job of a regulator could not be any more complex. The instruments, funds, and participants they are trying to regulate are varied, growing rapidly, and strive for secrecy to protect their proprietary strategies. Further frustrating the regulator is the role of technology, allowing participants to do their thing from almost anywhere and with near anonymity. It is this role of technology we discuss next.

23
Markets and Technology – The Great Enabler or the Great Disabler?

Technology has changed the world of financial markets. It has certainly changed the life of brokers and the brokerage industry itself. Has it changed the fundamental way in which markets operate? Absolutely.

There are a number of dimensions to this technology. Of course, any information relevant to the market is now available everywhere in the world, simultaneously. The ability to do market research, to analyze results, and to quickly respond to new information contributes to efficient markets. It is unlikely that this information innovation makes markets any more efficient in the long run. However, markets can now re-establish equilibrium much more quickly following the release of new information. In other words, the time it takes to arrive at the long run is now very short indeed.

Perhaps one disadvantage of this information innovation is the difficulty in establishing whether information is good. Just as we have discussed Gresham's Law and the Market for Lemons, bad information may distract the market and may induce analysts to be more skeptical of the reliability of any information, be it good or bad. When information was less instantaneous, there was a greater incentive to get the story right rather than simply get the story. With the rapid quantity of information generated, it is more difficult to discern its quality.

The ability to more easily disseminate investment information also creates an opportunity for new enterprises to raise capital. With instantaneous market information worldwide, there are also more opportunities to raise capital worldwide. While this potential exists today and is improving all the time, there remain significant barriers to capital movements, especially in the Second Economic World.

However, technological and informational innovations occur much more rapidly than the ability of our institutions to evolve. Less mature financial markets do not have the sufficiently well-developed regulatory environment necessary to ensure financial information is reported accurately. Governments also have not universally embraced mobile international capital, favoring domestic investment over foreign investment from a nationalistic perspective.

While the ability to access good investment opportunities is improved almost daily through new technologies, it will likely take decades to establish the mature regulatory regimes and investment policies necessary to fully take advantage of these opportunities. All the while, technology improves, creating a perpetual game of catch up.

This is not just a problem in the emerging Second Economic World. We have seen earlier the problems with the creation of new financial instruments and investment opportunities in mortgage markets that were not met with sufficiently adapted regulatory structure, creating the Credit Crunch of 2007 and the crises that followed.

Tools of the trade

Technology also creates analytic tools for traders that surpass the analytic capabilities of even the major investment banks just a decade ago. This level of analytics has produced a whole new type of analysis and has spawned the day trader.

Four decades ago only the largest investment banks could afford mainframe computers that would assist in the statistical analysis of a security price and could perform projections of earnings growth much more quickly than the typical Consumer-Investor. These innovations allowed big firms to better understand the implications of subtle changes in market conditions.

Three decades ago, investment banks could use the capital asset pricing model to determine if a security was overpriced or underpriced compared to its level of risk. With the widespread use of personal computers 25 years ago just about any investor could adopt these tools.

Two decades ago, even a moderately sophisticated investor could employ many of the tools that the large investment banks had at their disposal. Nobel Prize winning tools developed by Black, Merton, and Scholes, and previously used to great effect by such analytics powerhouses at Long Term Capital Management could now be adopted by smaller investors. This technology dispersion was essentially complete a decade ago.

The tools were now in place to popularize a new investment strategy. The bread-and-butter investment technique has been Fundamentals Analysis. This approach is based on the rational investor model and assumes that earnings, earnings growth, interest rates, and other firm, industry, and market specific variables ultimately determine the market price. Teams of analysts perform company and industry specific research and translate their research into stock price predictions.

This form of analysis is highly specialized and labor intensive, and gives the advantage to the large investment banks that can afford to employ the teams of researchers, and pool the research to help other teams in the bank. Small investors can purchase similar research, but can not get access to the intensive and broad-based research that only the large investors could afford. Small investors can purchase reports generated by a growing industry of private research companies, or be guided by analysts that might publish investment newsletters. It was not a level playing field however.

Enter the day trader

With the widespread use of powerful personal computers, a new type of analysis called Technical Analysis became more widespread. Rather than basing the market price on various microeconomic or macroeconomic factors, technical analysis takes past trends in prices as a predictor of future trends. In the absence of news that could cause a permanent shift in prices, technical analysis instead identifies if a price is a little below or a little above its recent history. If higher, a trader can sell short, in essence, borrowing the stock today to sell it today, and replacing the borrowed stock tomorrow by buying it back at its lower price. If the price is a little lower than the recent history suggests, a trader could of course buy the stock and sell it once the price rises.

This technical analysis strategy is not a buy-and-hold strategy. It is based more on market psychologies rather than market fundamentals. It is designed to take advantage of small differences in prices from one minute, hour, or day, to the next. Actually, if a market is only open for eight hours, and a trader works for perhaps nine or ten hours per day, it becomes risky to hold a stock overnight. News or market movements can occur anytime and a trader employing technical analysis has to stay on top of any movement that takes the price away from its historic price trend. As a consequence, these traders only trade during the day, and often liquidate their positions at the end of the day. A new occupation, called the Day Trader, was born.

Day trading could not have occurred were it not for the ability to obtain instantaneous trading information anywhere and at any time. Also necessary is the ability to retrieve historic prices for stocks and to be able to buy and sell stocks over the Internet at low cost. All of this was possible a decade ago and tens of thousands of average investors became day traders, sometimes trading millions of dollars of securities a day, perhaps buying a 1,000 shares of their favorite stock, selling them half an hour later, and repeating this pattern a number of times a day. If the trader could make only a dime per share on each transaction, they could easily make hundreds of dollars an hour, from the comfort of their favorite computer chair. By the end of the day, they would close their positions and start fresh again the next day.

The democratization of trading

Day trading was perhaps also a microcosm of the strategies some hedge fund managers had already discovered. At any given time there may be only a handful of traders actively watching and trading a particular stock. Like a game of poker, traders can bid or sell against each other, trying to create the impression of growing market momentum in one direction or another. Bluffing, putting our feelers, creating excitement through bidding pace, and similar strategies poker players also use, and have become the tools of the trade.

Of course, because the bids and asks are anonymous, there is no role for the poker face. The experience that allows a poker player to understand human psychology became just as important for the day trader. While the trader might need 50 or 100,000 dollars to invest for the day, they might be able to eek out 1,000 dollars a day in profits. After covering the 20 dollars or so of interest due each day if they had to borrow 100,000 dollars in capital, the profits were good, indeed, for those that could excel in this daily cat and mouse game.

So profitable was this, for some, that an accompanying industry of day trading workshops at local convention centers and meeting halls became popular. Just like the get-rich-quick flip-that-house workshops that arose before the bust of the mortgage market, hundreds of thousands of small investors laid down their 1,000 dollars to learn how to make money just like the big investment banks. If we do the math, perhaps it was most lucrative to tap into the hundred million dollar workshop industry rather than the day trading industry. Of course, only one in ten might discover they could succeed in day trading. For a while though, there was a big industry built up on the dream of financial freedom.

Using 100,000 dollars of borrowed money to try to make 100 dollars at a time through nickel and dime movements in prices is precisely what hedge funds do, but with a hundred million, or almost a hundred billion, dollars at a time. But, it is not for the faint at heart. A good profit of 3,000 dollars might be balanced off with a sizeable loss of 2,500 dollars a moment later. Gamblers fueled by the adrenaline rush found out that they could get their kicks in the comfort of their own home. And tens of thousands did.

With more traders, from hedge funds to day traders, employing this get in and get out strategy, the enabling technologies began to create some market dysfunction. Without the steadying influence and reflection that only time brings, markets became jumpy and volatile. Without some innovations that discourage trading based on psychology and tiny movements, this volatility is likely here to stay. And with markets now relying as much or more on psychology rather than market fundamentals, wild swings and overreactions could be the norm rather than the exception.

It would be unfair to conclude that technology is a bad thing. Technology is only a tool and we must adopt every tool that proves useful if we want to avoid the destiny of the Luddites. A better approach is to develop responses to the unfortunate symptoms that a technology creates so we do not throw out the baby with the bathwater as a response to some unfortunate consequences.

If the issue is the adoption of strategies designed to take advantage of market psychology rather than market fundamentals, perhaps we should more fully publicize who is practicing what strategy. We know, for instance, that potential insider traders must report their transactions to the Securities and Exchange Commission and this information is subsequently published. Perhaps all trades by insiders should be immediately published. Surely in this world of instantaneous information, this would not be difficult to accomplish. If we publish the names and financial positions of every corporate insider, market information would be improved and the ability to replicate the trades of these individuals would be possible.

If hedge fund trades had to be delayed for five minutes to create sufficient time for others to absorb the information, then this might be better yet. One might argue that even an insider has the right to trade the stock of the company that employs them. Certainly delayed and publicized trades would not violate this proposition and would do nothing to inhibit long-term returns or trades.

Of course, an insider is always free to trade in stocks of companies other than his or her own. As mentioned elsewhere, while traders would obviously prefer to remain anonymous, using information technologies to better inform the public would not likely decrease the level of long-term investment. And it is obvious that market information is bound to improve.

E-trading – around the world in thirty milliseconds

Before we leave the topic of technology, let's spend a moment on the intricacies of E-trading. Before the electronic trading innovation, orders were transmitted to specialists working on the floor of an exchange. The specialist would manage the orders and set a price that approximately equated supply and demand. Parallel to the traditional labor-intensive exchange were market makers, large brokerage middlemen that held in inventory commonly exchanged stocks and who could offer an alternative to the exchange, but at a price that might represent 100 dollars for a typical transaction. That was because stocks would be denominated in eighths or sixteenths of a dollar and the "spread" of an eighth or a sixteenth between the bid and the ask price could represent the price a market maker could extract.

With the popularization of Internet-based electronic trading, firms like E-Trade or Charles Schwab agreed to route trades through these market makers. The electronic brokerage house might charge only 9.95 dollars for a trade, but would be given a cut of the 100 dollar profit the market maker earns.

Small investors began to demand trading without middlemen and trading floors began to accommodate. The National Association of Securities Dealers Automated Quotient, or NASDAQ for short, is an exchange that has led the way toward all electronic trading, replacing floor trading specialists with computers that would match supply and demand, all the while showing the more sophisticated trader the bid and ask requests by the various participants. Outside of the trading floors, various electronic "islands" also formed that would perform this same matching function, even when the traditional exchanges were closed.

There has recently been a convergence of these functions as exchanges adopt new technologies and merge with other exchanges around the world. Most significantly, the venerable New York Stock Exchange announced a merger with Archipelago, one of the premier electronic islands in 2005. This largest exchange merger ever to that point was prompted by new Securities and Exchange Commission rules that required exchanges to execute trades at the best possible price, even if it forces them to use the services of competitors. Responding to the same climate, NASDAQ announced a merger with the electronic island Instinet in that same week.

With the New York Stock Exchange's subsequent merger with a European market, securities access is becoming global and the majority of all trades now completely electronic. A five hour time difference between Europe and New York and a three hour time difference between the New York Stock Exchange and partners on the West Coast of North America means that trading can be conducted for 15 or 16 hours of the day. Further partnerships in Australia, Asia, and India will make 24 hour electronic trading on open exchanges a reality.

A common theme is the enabling of technology to create efficiencies and instantaneous activity worldwide. There remain significant hurdles in the creation of common practices, regulations, and reporting requirements that allow capital to become truly fluid. Sovereign tax and investment policies also prevent true capital mobility.

As the electronic innovations provide solutions to challenges we did not even know were problems until now, it becomes apparent that new problems emerge. In the next chapter we discuss the extent to which the free flow of information may not necessarily create better information, and whether more information is always helpful.

Part VI
Politics and Perceptions

We observed earlier that the government plays a crucial role in our economic destiny, for better or worse. With this potency comes political mischief too. This creates an onus on citizens to be able to judge whether a government is behaving with economic responsibility or political pragmatism. We all have a role to play, with the media the conduit for most of our information. We next discuss the interaction between politics, the media, and the economically educated citizen. From this discussion flow some recommendations that will help us shape and improve our economic destiny.

24 Panics, Politics, and the Media

The information technology revolution has not only affected financial markets. The Internet and television financial news has fundamentally changed access to the market, for good or for bad.

As markets increasingly become driven by group psychology, and the psychology is increasingly influenced by global events, the news media has become a major participant. At the same time and for the same technology-driven reasons that have so transformed financial markets, the news media has itself been transformed. The print medium, previously the bastion of thoughtful political and economic analysis, has become a secondary source, and now seeks an online presence to maintain its relevancy.

Are markets apolitical?

Let's first ask if markets behave differently under the coarsest of political measures. How does the market compare under US Democratic or Republican presidencies over the past 80 years? Since October 1, 1928 to March 14, 2008, the Dow Jones Industrial Average has risen from 240 to 11,951, adjusted for dividends and splits. Over the same period, Republicans and Democrats have each occupied the White House for 40 years. Surprisingly, the increases in the Dow Jones Industrial Average have averaged 1.6% per year under Republican presidencies, and 8.2% per year under Democratic presidencies. Perhaps even more surprising is that the average Federal deficit under Republicans (in 2007 dollars) was 136.7 billion dollars, almost double that of the 70.3 billion dollars under Democratic presidents. As a share of GDP, this is 2.5% under Republicans and 2.0% under Democrats. Finally, average real GDP growth has been 1.89% under Republicans and 5.87% under Democratic presidents. While many more forces are likely at work, some may conclude that politics does indeed affect financial markets.

Another piece of evidence for the influence of political news on financial markets is the ubiquitous display of CNN, Fox News, or MSNBC in executive suites and financial floors. At the same time, more specialized cable financial news channels have erupted, offering 24 hour financial news and commentary, just as their political news siblings.

It would be difficult to draw conclusions regarding the reasons for the seemingly counterintuitive result that Democratic presidents are associated with more rapid growth than their political counterparts. Perhaps it may lie with the contradiction that, while individual business people prefer less regulation than more, the overall financial sector may benefit from greater scrutiny than less.

Economic leadership and the media

One service the press and news services have offered ever since the fireside chats of President Franklin Roosevelt is the opportunity for our leaders to use the media to access, inspire, or even cajole the entire voting population. While one could argue that the amplification of the president's pulpit does not necessarily inform the citizenry, it does allow the president to very clearly state the direction in which he or she is leading the country. If one of the most important leadership mandates is the health of the domestic economy, the president has the opportunity to lead through rhetoric and by offering a clear economic vision. The importance of this power cannot be overstated.

Beyond the efficiency by which the media can take the president's domestic economic agenda to the people, does the media well serve its purpose of educating the citizenry? Regulators who have economics degrees and years of relevant business experience are barely able to keep up with financial innovations, as the failings of the Credit Crunch will attest. It is perhaps unreasonable to expect that the media has the expertise to truly perform the function of providing an economic education for the citizenry.

Nonetheless, there is a thirst for economic education. We all sense that our financial future may be controlled by others. Therefore, we must secure our own future by making good economic and financial decisions. This is especially true as more people believe that a viable social security system will not guarantee their secure retirement. We should all make an effort to understand the economy. Our economic future depends on it. And our primary source of economic education remains the print and cable news media.

There was a time when the media took its role to inform and educate very seriously. Indeed, prior to and during the Kennedy era, the media took great pride in its role of withholding information deemed not in the public's best interest to know. In the past there were few media outlets, and this paternalistic collusion was easier to coordinate. Now, given the number of news outlets competing for the attention of the public, a marketplace for news has replaced the news oligopoly. It is in the nature of modern television media that stories must be simplified and sufficiently short to fit into neat 15 second, 30 second, or 2-minute analyses. While that same 30 second economic or financial news could be repeated a dozen times in a day, it will never likely become a more thoughtful or better researched piece lasting perhaps 5 to 15 minutes.

There are, of course, some nice exceptions to the rule. For instance, Paul Solman regularly produces very thoughtful pieces lasting 10 to 15 minutes on important economic phenomena for the Jim Lehrer News Hour on U.S. public television. His pieces may be the best example of news that is simultaneously an economic education. Unfortunately, he is but one of hundreds of commonly broadcast financial reporters and the exception rather than the rule.

The well-informed economic citizen

It is inevitable that the Consumer-Investors of economic news must be more economically educated, more discerning, and more thoughtful about the wealth of financial information, good and bad, that they receive every day. Even many of the most sophisticated citizens likely fail to fully comprehend and successfully absorb all relevant information they receive each day. Unfortunately, this failure is at our peril, especially given the importance of the Consumer-Investor on our mutual economic health.

While I advocate for the creation of an economically educated Consumer-Investor, I realize that the media is likely to continue to dilute its content, at least until the Consumer-Investor insists on better information. A most troubling tendency is the trend to have citizens make their own news. Viewers are now encouraged to submit video and on-the-scenes commentary to breaking news. In the interest of timeliness and scoops, these pieces often reach the air without the filter of an experienced reporter trained in the ethics of journalism.

Adding to this problem is a growing role for sensational or self-promoting commentators, rather than thoughtful and well-educated ones. At play is the penchant to have the extremes duke it out over the issues, be they legal, political, or financial. Exposing the extremes of a complex issue does not necessarily educate the viewer though, especially if the viewer cannot fully understand the arguments. Instead, the average viewer leaves the discussion believing there is significant disagreement and controversy, even if the subject is well understood and agreed upon by a vast majority of the practitioners.

Another growing tendency is to ask uninformed viewers what they believe, and allow their beliefs to become the news itself. For instance, a number of months before economists were willing to adopt a consensus view that the economy is in a recession, a cable news source reported that their informal poll shows 61% of Americans believe we were in a recession. This statistic is economically meaningless unless it is complemented with an explanation of how Consumer-Investor perceptions might somehow influence the economy. By elevating polls of the uninformed to the category of news, the media does a tremendous disservice by dumbing down an important and complex topic.

While a recession is definitional and not an issue determined by a vote or survey, it is true that our beliefs of whether we are in a recession will dramatically affect the possibility of falling into a recession. Amplifying the notion of impending doom then becomes a self-fulfilling prophecy, especially in the absence of effective messages to the contrary from leaders who could truly make a difference.

While the power of rhetoric by our leaders is a common theme for this book and the subject of a chapter, there is no doubt that this power can only be diluted by false, misleading, or irrelevant news created not to inform but to sensationalize. Such a democratization of the news is not healthy if it is not informed and truly representative. A poll by a reputable polling agency would not be considered valid if it only enumerated those that wanted to be called. This selection bias is a constant concern for those that want to ensure the relevancy and value of the information gleaned.

While it seems necessary to further educate the economic citizenry, the challenges are becoming more significant. Certainly competition among the news media and our inability to discern between a polished reporter that is well trained in the issue and an equally polished reporter who is not, the media will likely continue in the bias of style over substance. Until we place a premium on substance, the media will likely continue to spiral downward, just as Gresham's Law suggests that bad money forces out good money.

Compounding this dismal prophecy is that financial markets are becoming increasingly complex and the demographics and growth rates of the Second Economic World are becoming increasingly powerful. Civilization is at a crossroads that does not have a parallel in the modern era. Perhaps not since the Industrial Revolution has a whole new class of global citizens been on the verge of a convergence into the economic superpowers that have been the First Economic World.

If we are to successfully navigate this inevitable convergence, we must place a premium on thoughtful discourse. Of course, the convergence will occur even if we are unable to fully integrate its institutions and anticipate its challenges. The difference will be in the degree of discomfort uncertainties and posturing may create – mostly for the Consumer-Investors in the First Economic World.

25
The Only Thing We Have to Fear is Fear Itself

Franklin Delano Roosevelt (FDR) was the first economic commander in chief of the modern era. It is ironic that his first economic action once he was inaugurated on March 4, 1933 was to promptly shut down banks and financial markets for two weeks. Everyone needs a holiday once in a while, but this bank holiday was of absolute necessity. As discussed, there was a terrible run on the banks that threatened the industry, with half the banks in the United States wiped out between the years 1929 to 1933.

It was not just the bank holiday that created order. The first of the famous FDR fireside chats that began on March 12, 1933 became the blueprint for a new level of engagement between government and the Consumer-Investor. The stage was set well before FDR, as President Herbert Hoover was notorious for his faith in the market's ability to fix itself and his skepticism of government involvement in the affairs of the marketplace. President Hoover did not arrive at this conclusion by chance. The Roaring Twenties was a decade of excess and in such excess everyone believed they could succeed based on their wiles, through a sense of social and economic Darwinism that was widely held.

Indeed, President Roosevelt did not campaign so much on what he would do, perhaps in fear that the need for radical change would be just too radical, and perhaps because he did not yet know what he was going to do. It is instructive to read the text of his speech from his Inaugural Address on March 4, 1933:

> I am certain that my fellow Americans expect that on my induction into the Presidency I will address them with a candor and a decision which the present situation of our people impel. This is preeminently the time to speak the truth, the whole truth, frankly and boldly. Nor need we shrink from honestly facing conditions in our country

today. This great Nation will endure as it has endured, will revive and will prosper. So, first of all, let me assert my firm belief that the only thing we have to fear is fear itself – nameless, unreasoning, unjustified terror which paralyzes needed efforts to convert retreat into advance. In every dark hour of our national life a leadership of frankness and vigor has met with that understanding and support of the people themselves which is essential to victory. I am convinced that you will again give that support to leadership in these critical days.

In such a spirit on my part and on yours we face our common difficulties. They concern, thank God, only material things. Values have shrunken to fantastic levels; taxes have risen; our ability to pay has fallen; government of all kinds is faced by serious curtailment of income; the means of exchange are frozen in the currents of trade; the withered leaves of industrial enterprise lie on every side; farmers find no markets for their produce; the savings of many years in thousands of families are gone.

More important, a host of unemployed citizens face the grim problem of existence and an equally great number toil with little return. Only a foolish optimist can deny the dark realities of the moment.

Yet our distress comes from no failure of substance. We are stricken by no plague of locusts. Compared with the perils which our forefathers conquered because they believed and were not afraid, we have still much to be thankful for. Nature still offers her bounty and human efforts have multiplied it. Plenty is at our doorstep, but a generous use of it languishes in the very sight of the supply. Primarily this is because the rulers of the exchange of mankind's goods have failed, through their own stubbornness and their own incompetence, have admitted their failure, and abdicated. Practices of the unscrupulous money changers stand indicted in the court of public opinion, rejected by the hearts and minds of men.

True they have tried, but their efforts have been cast in the pattern of an outworn tradition. Faced by failure of credit they have proposed only the lending of more money. Stripped of the lure of profit by which to induce our people to follow their false leadership, they have resorted to exhortations, pleading tearfully for restored confidence. They know only the rules of a generation of self-seekers. They have no vision, and when there is no vision the people perish.

The money changers have fled from their high seats in the temple of our civilization. We may now restore that temple to the ancient truths. The measure of the restoration lies in the extent to which we apply social values more noble than mere monetary profit.

Happiness lies not in the mere possession of money; it lies in the joy of achievement, in the thrill of creative effort. The joy and moral stimulation of work no longer must be forgotten in the mad chase of evanescent profits. These dark days will be worth all they cost us if they teach us that our true destiny is not to be ministered unto but to minister to ourselves and to our fellow men.

Recognition of the falsity of material wealth as the standard of success goes hand in hand with the abandonment of the false belief that public office and high political position are to be valued only by the standards of pride of place and personal profit; and there must be an end to a conduct in banking and in business which too often has given to a sacred trust the likeness of callous and selfish wrongdoing. Small wonder that confidence languishes, for it thrives only on honesty, on honor, on the sacredness of obligations, on faithful protection, on unselfish performance; without them it cannot live.

Restoration calls, however, not for changes in ethics alone. This Nation asks for action, and action now.

Our greatest primary task is to put people to work. This is no unsolvable problem if we face it wisely and courageously. It can be accomplished in part by direct recruiting by the Government itself, treating the task as we would treat the emergency of a war, but at the same time, through this employment, accomplishing greatly needed projects to stimulate and reorganize the use of our natural resources.

Hand in hand with this we must frankly recognize the overbalance of population in our industrial centers and, by engaging on a national scale in a redistribution, endeavor to provide a better use of the land for those best fitted for the land. The task can be helped by definite efforts to raise the values of agricultural products and with this the power to purchase the output of our cities. It can be helped by preventing realistically the tragedy of the growing loss through foreclosure of our small homes and our farms. It can be helped by insistence that the Federal, State, and local governments act forthwith on the demand that their cost be drastically reduced. It can be helped by the unifying of relief activities which today are often scattered, uneconomical, and unequal. It can be helped by national planning for and supervision of all forms of transportation and of communications and other utilities which have a definitely public character. There are many ways in which it can be helped, but it can never be helped merely by talking about it. We must act and act quickly.

Finally, in our progress toward a resumption of work we require two safeguards against a return of the evils of the old order; there must be a strict supervision of all banking and credits and investments; there must be an end to speculation with other people's money, and there must be provision for an adequate but sound currency.

There are the lines of attack. I shall presently urge upon a new Congress in special session detailed measures for their fulfillment, and I shall seek the immediate assistance of the several States.

Through this program of action we address ourselves to putting our own national house in order and making income balance outgo. Our international trade relations, though vastly important, are in point of time and necessity secondary to the establishment of a sound national economy. I favor as a practical policy the putting of first things first. I shall spare no effort to restore world trade by international economic readjustment, but the emergency at home cannot wait on that accomplishment.

The basic thought that guides these specific means of national recovery is not narrowly nationalistic. It is the insistence, as a first consideration, upon the interdependence of the various elements in all parts of the United States – a recognition of the old and permanently important manifestation of the American spirit of the pioneer. It is the way to recovery. It is the immediate way. It is the strongest assurance that the recovery will endure.

In the field of world policy I would dedicate this Nation to the policy of the good neighbor – the neighbor who resolutely respects himself and, because he does so, respects the rights of others – the neighbor who respects his obligations and respects the sanctity of his agreements in and with a world of neighbors.

If I read the temper of our people correctly, we now realize as we have never realized before our interdependence on each other; that we can not merely take but we must give as well; that if we are to go forward, we must move as a trained and loyal army willing to sacrifice for the good of a common discipline, because without such discipline no progress is made, no leadership becomes effective. We are, I know, ready and willing to submit our lives and property to such discipline, because it makes possible a leadership which aims at a larger good. This I propose to offer, pledging that the larger purposes will bind upon us all as a sacred obligation with a unity of duty hitherto evoked only in time of armed strife.

> With this pledge taken, I assume unhesitatingly the leadership of this great army of our people dedicated to a disciplined attack upon our common problems.
>
> Action in this image and to this end is feasible under the form of government which we have inherited from our ancestors. Our Constitution is so simple and practical that it is possible always to meet extraordinary needs by changes in emphasis and arrangement without loss of essential form. That is why our constitutional system has proved itself the most superbly enduring political mechanism the modern world has produced. It has met every stress of vast expansion of territory, of foreign wars, of bitter internal strife, of world relations.

These prophetic words could just as well be uttered today. It is not because the situation is now as dire, because it is not, nor because we fail to understand the forces at work. We probably have a much better grasp of the situation than FDR could have during the dawning days of Keynesian Economics. Rather, it is because FDR was asserting a notion that the government could, through force of rhetoric, educate the populace about the economy, and in doing so, shine a light where fear once prevailed.

These words may also be the most powerful offered by a President in a century, but with the economic flourish as President Kennedy's, "Ask not what the country can do for you. Ask what you can do for the country," and not unlike the political clout of President Reagan's, "Mister Gorbachev, tear down this wall."

Like many good speeches, listeners recognized at the time that they were experiencing something truly important. And like all important speeches, FDR's words were transformational, telling a nation not necessarily what it wanted to hear, but rather what it needed to hear.

More than simple rhetoric

The FDR's rhetoric worked. Prior to the inauguration and the market holiday, hordes of Consumer-Investors withdrew their cash and squirreled it under their mattresses and in their cookie jars. Their actions, each individually rational, but collectively devastating, almost brought down the entire financial system.

The first day markets reopened following FDR's speech, the public returned half of their cash to the banking system and the stock market experienced the largest single day rise in its history. The results were not just a flash in the pan, but were permanent. The market never again fell to the level it was before FDR performed his daring and successful experiment in rhetorical flourish. It was the cold shower the public needed to pull itself out of its self-induced panic.

One could argue that this gesture was more than rhetoric. In his executive order declaring a bank holiday, the President claimed that confidence could be restored as each bank was audited. It is obvious, though, that there could not be enough bank auditors on the entire planet to audit each bank in the country over a two-week period. No matter. Confidence was restored because someone was willing to take charge and ward off the animal spirits that brought markets to their knees.

In the week that followed the inauguration, Congress, too, was led. It swiftly passed the Emergency Banking Act of 1933, the Federal Reserve guaranteed financial liquidity and in essence, created the precursor to deposit insurance. A little rhetoric and a little insurance went a long way.

The FDR's ideas were not entirely unique. Individual states had oversight on state chartered banks and some of these states experimented with bank holidays for the same reasons, but with limited or dubious success. Federal agencies also toyed with solutions, but each agency in isolation concluded that they did not have the mandate or potency to solve the problem in isolation. Success could not occur unless all agencies, jurisdictions, and citizens cooperated in concert. And only the President could corral these diverse groups, especially the public.

Following his inaugural address, and in the period of the banking holiday, FDR again spoke directly to his citizens in a fireside chat on March 12, 1933. Just eight days into office, FDR directly broached the most complex of topics by beginning his speech with the words "My friends, I want to talk for a few minutes with the people of the United States about banking – with the comparatively few who understand the mechanics of banking, but more particularly with the overwhelming majority of you who use banks for the making of deposits and the drawing of checks."

After the speech, the sense was that the President spoke to the nation on a personal level, with a reassuring tone. He accepted his responsibility as the Economic Commander in Chief of the nation and the country responded just as he hoped.

It was not just the public who heard his message, though. Financiers who were profiting from the uncertainty, or who were responding to their baser instincts, also heard the message and were willing to do their part, too. Indeed, the message may have been framed for the public, but it was squarely and assertively delivered to the financial industry.

We want to be led

Perhaps one of the most interesting facets of this dramatic economic transformation was that few challenged FDR's authority. FDR was able to pass a banking act that gave the executive branch almost dictatorial power over an entire industry because he filled a leadership vacuum.

It would be too easy to conclude though that rhetoric was sufficient to avert a growing crisis. The power of rhetoric served two functions. It got everybody's attention, not the least of who were the leaders of financial markets. And it was backed with serious reform that added credibility to the President's words.

Mere rhetoric cannot transform a nation if we can rationally expect our institutions will not respond in substantive ways. Credible rhetoric requires a proverbial line in the sand. It was the ensuing legislation that immediately and decisively followed the rhetoric that backed up words with action. In doing so, the President demonstrated that there is no undoing of his words for individual profit.

The government must demonstrate that it stands shoulder to shoulder with the citizens and will do whatever is in anyone's, or perhaps everyone's power, to remedy the situation. While a "put a shoulder to the problem" approach might violate ideologies, it is a necessarily pragmatic solution to a problem that might indeed someday fix itself.

26 Do Stimulus Packages Work?

Of course, while the President's inaugural words in 1933 were words the nation needed, it was only the first volley in the war against recession and depression. What followed the Emergency Banking Act of 1933 was a series of initiatives designed to stimulate the economy. The question remains, though – do Keynesian fiscal stimulus policies work?

There have been ten post-World War II recessions in the United States, defined by two consecutive quarters of a decline in the gross domestic product (GDP). It is perhaps reassuring that in almost every incidence, the Federal Reserve expressed concern about impending recessions, and vetted the range of possible solutions.

These recessions, in 1953, 1957, 1960, 1969, 1973, 1980, 1981, 1990, 2001, and likely 2007/2008, all attracted the attention of perhaps the world's pre-eminent collective wisdom on the health of the economy. However, not in all circumstances were the resulting policies the same.

In these more than 60 years since World War II, nine of ten recessions began during a Republican presidency. There were sixteen presidential terms in this period, seven of which were Democratic presidencies, and nine Republican presidencies. Four of these recessions under a Republican president occurred the year after a Democratic presidency ended, preventing us from drawing any firm conclusions about the propensity for politics to influence recessions.

A brief history of recessions

In the first of these recessions, the aftermath of the Korean War resulted in a decline in government sponsored war spending. The Eisenhower administration did not substitute the decrease in war spending with a corresponding increase in fiscal spending. It did repeal the tax increases instituted during the Korean War, though. And this was felt by the Eisenhower administration to be a significant anti-recessionary policy decision.

The 1957 recession was countered, perhaps as planned or perhaps fortuitously, by a ramp-up in defense spending to renew a battered defense establishment and to prepare for the emerging Cold War. However, it is interesting to note that President Eisenhower had become quite ambivalent to increased governmental spending. At the end of his second term, he warned the nation of the dangers of being co-opted by a new economic force he was first to identify – the Military Industrial Complex. Instead, he was much more comfortable with policies of expanded federal spending in roads, schools, and hospitals, and, most notably, in the creation of the US Interstate Highway system. His concern about the military and defense industry playing too large a part in economic expansion was partly frustrated, though. The Defense Department played a significant role in designing and coordinating the construction of the Interstate Highway system.

The administration also induced the Congress to extend unemployment benefits in recessionary times, and in doing so strengthened an automatic built-in stabilizer. These stabilizers automatically pump spending and consumption into the economy whenever unemployment is on the rise, thereby creating a more immediate fiscal response not so dependent on the recognition of an impending recession by government or the central bank. These three prongs of fiscal policy were the most concerted and effective in an era with a Republican president who campaigned on economic prosperity, in the form of a car in every garage and a chicken in every pot.

Soon after his inauguration in 1961, President John F. Kennedy recognized an inherited recession as gross domestic product peaked following the Eisenhower administration. Kennedy accelerated federal government spending and tax cuts and he, too, extended unemployment compensation benefits. He also immediately began to search for a large federal project that may even eclipse Eisenhower's successful initiation of the Interstate Highway system. In essence, he was adopting the three-pronged approach of his Republican predecessor.

The large fiscal projects explored by the Kennedy administration were wide-ranging. Common to all was the premise that the economy should harness the creativity of science and stimulate further science to sew the seeds of a bright technological future. The result of the Kennedy fiscal exploration was to send a man to the moon and safely back in the decade. This program stimulated educational spending, science, and technology, including military technology. This was indeed the most significant and consequential federal fiscal project since perhaps the building of canals or the pyramids.

The 1969 recession came in the midst of spending to fuel the Vietnam War. This increase in spending, in debt, and in the money to fuel the spending, was recognized by the newly elected President Richard M. Nixon administration as inflationary. As a consequence, the Nixon administration was reticent to increase spending still further for fear of stagflation, the simultaneous occurrence of both economic stagnation and inflation.

The Nixon administration did respond in dramatic fashion a year later. However, their response was focused on inflation rather than growing unemployment and recession. The administration imposed wage and price controls to curb inflation and reasoned that this would create some leeway for tax cuts and imports surcharges. This New Economic Policy may also have been an attempt to redress an unpopular presidency during an unpopular war.

President Nixon was unsuccessful in putting the economy on a growth path that would arrest the recession. He was also unsuccessful in bringing the inflationary climate under control. Economic troubles compounded by 1973, by which time the Nixon administration was embroiled in political scandal and international isolationism. It is not surprising that the Nixon administration did not mount a concerted response to the recession of 1973 until it was too late.

It was not until the Tax Reduction Act of 1975 that a concerted anti-recessionary policy was adopted. This Act provided significant tax rebates, increases in future standard deductions, and augmented a minor extension in unemployment compensation benefits with an expansion of Social Security benefits. However, the Nixon and Ford administrations appeared opposed to the Eisenhower and Kennedyesque expansions of public infrastructure as a tool of fiscal policy, leaving it to Democratic President Carter to propose and pass educational and public works programs to remedy an increasingly gloomy economic outlook.

While President Carter may have kept the worst of the recession at bay for a few more years, he did so at the cost of a spiraling inflation. Double-digit inflation created double-digit interest rates and private investment began to suffer. A brief recession reappeared in 1980. Carter had recognized that fiscal policy becomes dangerous when inflation becomes institutionalized. The widespread use of Cost of Living Allowances in labor contracts meant any price increase was almost immediately translated into a wage increase, inducing a further round of price increases, and so on. While President Carter was reticent to make inflationary pressures worse through increased spending, he was also reluctant in an election year to make the painful adjustments to wring institutionalized inflation out of the system.

A series of incomplete and disjoint measures in the 1970s and a failure to effectively coordinate both fiscal and monetary policy put newly elected President Reagan in a difficult position. When the fourth recession in a dozen years set in just as President Ronald Regan assured office in 1981, he responded with tax cutbacks and tax reform, an increase in federal spending, often in the form of increased defense spending, and a burgeoning public debt.

Reagan was attempting to sew the seeds of long-term growth, acknowledging that it may be at the expense of the short term. It would not be improper to conclude that the motivation for these policies was ideological rather than economic. However, an ambitious Federal Reserve was willing to raise interest rates to reduce inflation and economic activity in the short run and their perseverance was successful, if painful.

It's the economy, stupid

President Reagan's vice president and successor, President George Herbert Walker Bush, was almost entirely unresponsive to a recession that began a year after he assumed office in 1989. The President's lack of effectiveness was not insignificantly due to a resistant Congress dominated by members of the Democratic Party. However, some accused President Bush of economic elusiveness, prompting his successor, President Bill Clinton, to campaign in 1992 on the slogan "It's the Economy, Stupid."

Upon Clinton's election, there was a greater drive for the middle, and optimism on the part of Consumer-Investors. What followed was the creation of a climate for high technology investment that transformed recessions into the longest peacetime expansion and federal budget deficits into surpluses.

Near the end of the Clinton era, recessionary forces reappeared. While the recession officially occurred in 2001 on the watch of newly elected President George Bush the Junior, the seeds of the recession likely began as the economy needed to take a breath from an unprecedented long expansion. A stock market bubble had popped, mostly in the high technology sector, and the optimism of Consumer-Investors likewise suffered.

But while recession was beginning, pessimism took hold in a dramatic fashion when terrorists loyal to Osama Bin Laden flew jet airplanes into the World Trade Center in New York City, the Pentagon, and a field in Shanksville, Pennsylvania. Even before that fateful day, the stock market began to fall, and has dipped in 2008 below the high set for the Dow Jones Industrial Average on May 13, 1999, almost a decade earlier.

When nobody was looking

The recession that likely began in 2007 is perhaps the most complex of them all. Invoked in this recession is a dramatic increase in oil prices to over 140 dollars a barrel and its concomitant effect on inflation, rising food prices because of the higher energy prices. The US Congress also passed a misguided policy to reduce only marginally our dependence on oil through a federal policy designed to create a wholesale expansion of comparatively expensive ethanol production from corn. This latter effort drove up agricultural prices for all crops, further exacerbating inflation.

At the same time, the Credit Crunch, which has been so central to this analysis, created absolute panic in domestic financial markets, induced a large downward correction in the stock market, and caused investors to flee from US denominated assets. This dramatic movement out of the US dollar caused oil prices to rise further as it is also denominated in the less valuable US dollar. This increase in oil prices, and a movement to commodities as a store of value further fueled inflation, limiting the resolve of the Federal Reserve Board to quickly and with confidence create a viable monetary strategy.

While the Federal Reserve Board suffered a certain policy paralysis as it was pulled in two different policy directions, the oddest reaction was the failure of the Federal Government to respond. This failure to coordinate an effective fiscal policy seemed less motivated by the fear of inflation that hamstrung Reagan in 1981. Rather, it is more reminiscent of a disconnect with the domestic economy reminiscent of President Bush Senior. The political dialogue since 2001 had been dominated by the wars in Iraq and Afghanistan, leaving little recognition of an increasingly precarious domestic economy.

One obvious reason is that the severe instabilities in financial markets were not broadly identified sufficiently early and unemployment remained consistently low. Another is a strong Reaganesque ideological bent by the Bush administration that the government cannot and should not interfere with the economy. The President's inherent focus on international over domestic issues, and his cultural distance from the plight of the unemployed likely influenced his aloofness.

Finally, in an effort to protect the president from critics, President Bush rarely speaks to increasingly hostile crowds. So that his popularity is not further impaired from historic lows, he is reticent to speak on a failing domestic economy. Over time he has become increasingly isolated from the public consensus. He eventually proposed a tax break amounting to somewhere around 1% of the gross domestic product, to be paid out perhaps six to nine months after many believe the recession may have begun. This policy has generally been regarded as too little and too late, and had already been deemed inadequate months after it was proposed, and months before it was to be distributed.

The common component of all these recessions is the correct identification, more or less quickly, of the Federal Reserve, and the failure of the branches of the federal government to cooperate on prompt and effective fiscal policy. Administrations and Congress seem to develop ideologically based rather than pragmatic economic policy.

These cases also almost universally generated the concern on the part of the Fed to balance anti-recessionary monetary policies with a concern for the effect these policies may have on inflation. Especially in 1980, 1981, and 2007, inflationary pressures arising from oil price-induced shocks gave the Fed pause.

One cannot help but wonder if a greater coordination of fiscal and monetary policy is necessary. Such cooperation has given other FEW nations like Canada and many European countries consistent and stable economic growth. However, while the parliamentary system lends itself well to strong economic leadership, the US federal system is designed around checks and balances and political battles between two ideologically distinct parties.

It would not be unreasonable to argue that monetary policy is better positioned to respond quickly and effectively, and is better tooled in economics to develop coherent policies. Most economists agree that well timed and well modulated interest rate strategies by the Federal Reserve are the most effective tools to abate recessions, with effective fiscal policy much more difficult given the competing interests of elected officials. However, the point most missed and the opportunity least often exploited is the power of sound monetary policy in concert with the credible statements, both rhetorically and fiscally, from the executive branch.

Such a lack of quick and concerted economic policy by the executive branch should not be surprising. So much energy is appropriately devoted by the Presidency to international issues. After all, it is only on the popular US television program "The West Wing" that the president is a Nobel Prize winning economist. And if it is unusual for financial reporters to have formal training in economics, it is perhaps even more unlikely for members of Congress to have an economics education. This is perhaps one more reason that economics is deemed the dismal science.

27
When Politics Gets in the Way of Good Ole' Common Sense

On the one hand, there are those that believe government is the problem and have never met a tax cut they did not like. If the economy is thriving, it is time to cut taxes, and if the economy is tanking, it is imperative that we cut taxes, immediately. On the other hand, there are those that believe government is the solution and it is always a good time to increase taxes for the wealthy. Presumably, these two sets of views cannot simultaneously be correct, and it is likely that neither approach is ever wholly correct.

Recognizing these dichotomies and consistent with the prevailing notion of checks and balances in the First Economic World countries, we have wisely kept central banks of the executive and legislative branches. This independence, though, prevents us from coordinating economic policy to a degree that is common in many other First Economic World nations. Instead, we have run domestic economic policies that have created budget deficits in 31 of the past 35 years, through booms and recessions alike. Is it possible then that our political agendas are masquerading as economic policy?

A wolf in sheep's clothing

Confusing politics and economics is quite natural. Economics is essentially the study of efficient use of resources to meet human needs. Doing so makes the economic pie as large as possible for a given level of resource usage. There remain two additional questions though.

First, how much of our resources should we use today at the expense of generations tomorrow? Second, how do we divide up the economic pie? These questions, though, are decidedly beyond the scope of economics. Instead, economists must rely on the political system to create a consensus of present versus future and who gets what now. And these decisions can only be made through the political process, for want of any other way to somehow aggregate the collective wishes of the Consumer-Investor.

The complex interaction between economics and politics is not easily bridged. Recall the response of President Reagan to the recessions of the early 1980s. His response was to not worry about government spending to counteract an inevitable downturn in the business cycle. Instead, he preferred to sow the seeds for long-term economic growth. Of course, we know now that his prescription, known then as Supply Side Economics and regarded now as a failure, was ultimately poor social science. However, his intuition that we should promote long-term economic growth was sound.

Can we have the best of both worlds – long-term economic growth and short-term economic stabilization policy? Probably, but politics gets in the way. Let's look at some of the wedges that seem to be driving this great divide.

Recall the fundamental observation of John Maynard Keynes that while the economy will likely re-establish equilibrium in the long run as classical economists have always suggested, there is simply no way to determine how long it takes to arrive there. Faith in the power for the market to correct itself is a faith that this correction is sufficiently timely. It is not misguided to have faith in eventuality, but nor is this faith a panacea for current problems.

Government to the rescue?

On the other hand, faith that government can quickly and efficiently solve our economic problems each and every time is equally misguided. Government is often big and unwieldy and it, as likely as not, responds politically when it should respond economically. There is just no mechanism that finely tunes our economic intuition like spending our own money to improve our own lot. Something is lost when a bureaucrat is charged with putting forward their best effort to spend the public's money for the public good.

For centuries, businesses have been wrestling over how to solve this principal-agent problem. Government is relatively new to this problem, and does so with so many challenges because they do not have the focus of the profit motive that is the basis for private industry. It is difficult to simultaneously view the role of government as efficiently providing public services but also generating the maximum number of public sector jobs. At times, though, it may be the only possible provider of public services as private firms simply cannot generate a pricing formula that would permit it to do so efficiently.

There is a class of public services that perhaps could be privatized. For instance, we could privatize the parks or the department of motor vehicles, along the principles government may formulate. To ensure fairness though, the government may still determine pricing and if this pricing generates a loss, the government may need to pay the firm on a cost-plus basis. Doing so though places a private firm at the same disadvantage as a government agency. With its success unrelated to the revenue generated, it too loses the focus that a direct economic interest in a successful outcome provides.

If we can recognize first that government engaging in meeting our economic needs is never perfect but also never entirely out of line, and if we agree that government inaction sometimes has drastic consequences, then there is a balance somewhere between the two extremes.

A backhanded compliment

Even those that suffer government reluctantly admit that central banks perform a useful function. Central banks are quasi-governmental agencies, so it is assumed that there is some role for government intervention in the economy. The art is to be able to provide for just the right market intervention when necessary and to stop when government has intervened enough. As mentioned earlier, there has been more government activity than government revenue in 31 of the past 35 years, implying that it is difficult or impossible to turn government down or off when necessary.

Some of the problem is that government inherently creates life of its own. By its very nature, it often occupies a monopoly of services, does not respond to the forces of perfect competition, and loses its focus as an efficient producer of a service done only for as long as necessary. Just as with its private industry counterparts, a government monopoly is less responsive to the needs of the Consumer-Investor, and instead develops a need to feed itself and to exist in perpetuity. This is likely the root of the frustration that some have with government, a frustration they likely also share with monopolies of all types.

Were we able to solve this seemingly intractable problem that government agencies begin to serve the agency rather than the public, and in perpetuity rather than temporarily, we would still be left with another legitimate problem. When activities are provided based not on the revealed demand of the marketplace, but rather on the power of politics, we must rely on imperfect democracies to somehow aggregate our wishes.

Casting aside the very real problems of politicians properly representing the needs of the citizenry rather than those who can most guarantee their re-election, we are still left with the optimal provision of public services through democracy. But, while we each make careful decisions regarding which car to buy or house to purchase, our single vote bears the responsibility for making thousands of choices simultaneously on our behalf.

This impossibility of representing all of our common needs with a single vote perhaps explains why the majority of us engage fully in our own purchases or job decisions, but only a minority of us votes. Even more problematic, most of those affected by our long-term political decisions cannot vote because they are not yet born or have not reached the age of majority.

There is a further complication to the notion that each of our votes is aggregated to represent our collective preferences for the production and division of public goods. Even assuming everyone exercises their franchise to vote, some votes speak louder than others. Political contributions act to amplify one's vote or, more correctly, amplify the message of one's preferred representative.

The constitutions and amendments of the FEW countries enshrine the right to free speech, and political speech perhaps ought to be the most free. The founders strove to ensure that the person standing on the corner could broadcast a message as far as his or her voice could carry. This right could not have anticipated the mass media we have today. Now we can stretch our voice to hundreds of millions, rather than hundreds of people. Money is the great amplifier and it gives greatest amplification to the wealthiest. If the division of public goods also highlights a division of classes, those with a greater ability to pay are destined to have greater command on decisions of government that may favor their interests. Of course, some could also claim that to squelch this reality would also be to squelch the premise that those in a free market economy cannot use their wealth in the pursuit of their own happiness. This freedom is a tenet of the Declaration of Independence – in life, liberty, and the pursuit of happiness.

An impossibility theorem

The Nobel Prize winning economist Kenneth Arrow has proved that there cannot be a perfect democratic system that can properly, fairly, and efficiently aggregate our individual wishes.[1] Arrow's Impossibility Theorem describes the paradox of democracy when a political platform necessarily bundles a whole series of positions. If each position could instead be defined in a way in which we each have one preferred choice and if we could instead vote on each position separately, as in the spirit of a New England Town Meeting, efficiency of political decision-making is restored.

However, it is in the nature of the representative democracy that we cannot each vote on each issue and hence government by definition becomes a clash of simplified ideals rather than a complex set of decisions for which we all participate. A view of politics as simplified and with these necessarily competing ideals creates the inherent tension of politics.

If the political system is defined based on competing and often extreme ideologies, can we salvage this intrinsic conflict in the best interest of economics? The solution would likely require us to more strictly adhere to a shared value of what government should and should not do.

Perhaps we can agree that a federal government should not be viewed as representing primarily regional or state concerns, unless an overarching premise affecting us all is violated. Likewise, state government should not reach so far as to affect localities, unless again it is important to preserve a mutually shared value or generate a mutual common good, like education or interstate roads, for example.

The premise is to create decision making that is as close as possible to those it affects, while preserving a level playing field we all cherish, a strong economy that benefits us all, or an economy of scale that that allows us to benefit from the efficiency of a larger entity.

Striking a balance

A greater adherence to the need of government to address the public's need when it truly makes sense and to resist the temptation to grow government when it does not, might be the appropriate criteria for optimal government. In this way, the government would be expected to always raise sufficient revenue, but would spend more only when more spending serves the economic interest and spend less otherwise. On average, the government would maintain a balanced budget and could save for a rainy day to even out the vagaries of the business cycle.

However, one problem remains. This economic view of the world is based on generating efficiency in the provision of public wants and needs and in the coordination of economic activity when coordination failures would cause us all to suffer. An alternate role of government is in the distribution of the fruits of the modern economy. Under the assumption that civilization creates the institutions that so benefit the economy, it is fair to ask for those that benefit most to pay for infrastructure and institutions.

It is this alternative view of government as redistributors of income that we treat next. Of course, everyone strikes a different balance between economics and politics. It is most challenging to separate one's economic perspective from their ideological beliefs. These beliefs often are influenced by one's economic position in life, and political beliefs are often subjugated to this economic reality. Nonetheless, we can create a tax system designed to optimize economic efficiency and the size of the economic pie, and rely on the political system to redistribute wealth if necessary.

28
The Taxman Cometh

> In this world nothing can be said to be certain, except death and taxes.
>
> From a letter to Jean-Baptists Le Roy, in *The Works of Benjamin Franklin*, 1817, Ch. 4

And this is a good thing.

Government is in a unique position to do those things that we agree are in our collective interest and then to use the power of taxation to force us to pay for them. Recall our earlier discussion of public goods – those items that benefit us all, without diminishing any of our mutual enjoyment. For instance, most all agree that some form of national defense is necessary and we all benefit from a secure border. Likewise, those living downstream from a flooding river might agree that a dam is a good thing.

There is a problem though. If I know you are likely to pay for it even if I cannot, I may not want to reveal to you my true valuation, in hopes I can ride on your coat tails. This creates a problem for a private entity that must build a border or a dam and then somehow coerce the beneficiaries into paying for it.

These are the instances that government can be most effective. Our concerns with bureaucratic inefficiency arising from a lack of discipline the profit motive typically provides. Still, government can use its unique power of taxation to force us to pay for some goods we need.

Obviously, only a small share of the goods produced has these characteristics. The challenge is to prevent government from compounding the market failure, as we discussed earlier. Even then, the market failure inefficiencies must be compared with the inefficiencies that arise in government when profit is not the motive. If we decide that the government should be in the pension and insurance business, the licensing business, sometimes the utility business, or the education business, we are implicitly deciding that some sort of market failure exists and government co-opting of the industry is necessary.

Death and taxes

Taxes, at least to some degree, are inevitable. The range of goods and services that government ought to provide from either a public goods or a market failure perspective is debatable. And industrialized nations differ in this range of gross domestic product devoted to government-provided goods and services. Highly centrally planned economies could be perhaps close to 100% government controlled, while the most free market countries might have direct government involvement in 5% to 10% of commerce.

This wide range suggests that different types of government serve different functions. As a consequence, the tax system serves two mutually impossible functions. One is to generate the right level of revenue to permit it to efficiently and optimally provide the services citizens collectively demand, even if we may be reluctant to say so. The other is to take from one voting bloc of society and give to another. There can never, by definition, be universal agreement on this latter definition.

Let us discuss for a moment the tax fairness issue and then devote the remainder of the chapter to tax efficiency issues.

If a society creates the infrastructure that permits commerce to thrive, it is fair to ask for those who benefit to pay for the infrastructure and institutions. Under a head tax, all pay an equal amount toward government infrastructure, regardless of an individual's ability to pay. The theory is that we all use roads, so we should all pay for them equally. For some things, like a government provided toll road, this might be the simplest strategy. However, any such price will exclude some who only marginally benefit from the road, even though it would cost society nothing more to let these individuals use it for free. If we force everyone to pay for the road, those who don't have a compelling need for it feel that they are subsidizing those who do.

Types of taxes

Under a head tax, all pay an equal amount toward the institutions and infrastructure government provides regardless of the extent they individually benefit. Under a neutral tax as a common percentage of our income, all would pay an equal proportion of their fruits, again regardless of the benefits they receive, but under the assumption that those who earn more either benefit more or have a greater capacity to contribute more. Finally, under a progressive tax system, all pay based on their ability to pay, with a proportionally greater burden placed on the wealthier because it is assumed their burden is equal even if they pay proportionally more.

To tax in a way that is unassociated with the benefit you might receive is considered unfair. It would be considered a regressive tax because low-income individuals would then be paying a much greater share of their income on a tax than a high-income citizen. As a rough approximation, we sometimes decide that those who benefit more from publicly provided infrastructure are those who earn higher income. If time is money, those who earn more may also place more value on the travel-time savings a good road provides. And if the value of our time is proportional to our income, such infrastructures should perhaps be paid for in proportion to each of our income. This is the argument for a neutral tax.

Some may even take the argument still further by postulating that we should all feel the same pain or burden from the tax if we all extract the same enjoyment. For instance, we may all enjoy the vista from a national park facility in the Grand Canyon, regardless of our income. If we all benefit likewise, perhaps we should all be burdened with a tax that "hurts" the same amount. A million dollar fee might hurt the world's richest person as much as a dollar fee might hurt the world's poorest. If taxes are designed to equalize burden and if each dollar earned means less (diminishing marginal utility) to those who are wealthier, the tax system should create an increasing burden as income rises.

This progressive tax system is indeed what many countries use. Low incomes, up to a certain threshold might pay little or no taxes and the highest income taxpayers might pay a rate close to 50% or more, once Federal, State, local and perhaps even property and sales taxes are factored in.

A neutral or a progressive tax, then, is a form of income redistribution in a way. It is not simply taking from Peter to pay Paul, although some countries even do that. Instead, it is taking more from Peter than Paul, but giving both the same level and types of services in return. In doing so, at least one measure of equity is at least approximately restored because it can be argued that it is only fair for those with the greatest capacity to give back to society to be giving more.

A Randian argument

As with any measure of fairness, there are those who will counter this argument. If all enjoy publicly provided goods the same amount (roughly), so why should a high-income earner be permitted to keep only 50 cents of every dollar earned, when a poorer person might get to keep every penny they earn?

Some would even take the argument still further. Ayn Rand and her devotees argue that the overall well being of society is very much supported by that same creativity and inventiveness that also made the rich wealthy. Perhaps the rich should be able to keep every penny and maybe more. Certainly to tax away the fruits of one's creativity will take away some of the incentive to be creative. And yet, the sweat of that economically creative class does the economy wonders and should be encouraged, not discouraged through taxation. Even the most ardent devotee of the Randian argument may eventually agree that a flat percentage tax on everyone is in some sense fair, or at least not too unfair, and is certainly beautiful in its simplicity, stability, ease of application, and predictability. This flat tax does have a counterpart in today's political discussion. If we assume that most Consumer-Investors consume most of what they earn, then a tax on all things consumed is equivalent to a neutral tax on income. It is an easier tax to administer because it allows us to abolish taxing treasuries, for instance. It has been calculated that perhaps a 20% tax on all consumption, with the eradication of the income tax, would be sufficient to support most government functions.

The European Economic Community and many of the First Economic World countries have supplemented their income tax system with a Consumption or Value-Added Tax to good effect. In doing so, citizens still have the incentive to work because they are not taxed on income. It also has other benefits. By deferring consumption by instead saving, you are deferring taxation. The delayed taxation is then a relative subsidy to savings, which allows countries to more easily mobilize savings from Consumer-Investors. This translates into greater growth.

A consumption tax also preserves the relative prices of all goods and services. A fundamental theorem on the efficiency of markets is that the market-determined price of a good should not be distorted relative to other prices, unless it ought to be distorted to correct externalities. A consumption tax treats all goods and services equally, and thereby maintains the proper relative prices.

Some are concerned that such a consumption tax, while good in its simplicity and good because it no longer reduces the incentive to work, is not so good in its neutrality. Countries cope with this by giving a tax rebate back to those on low income who had to pay a consumption tax all year. How do we know how much they paid in consumption taxes though? If they are low income, it is believed that they consume everything they earn.

Even if they did not, it would not be difficult for us to figure out how much they earn, and deduct from that the only thing they could have done with their earnings – namely to save. The difference is consumption, and we can then quickly calculate how much consumption taxes they paid. They could then be rebated all or a portion of their consumption depending on our society's preferences for income redistribution.

Efficiency over fairness

So far we have been describing the need to tax fairly and to not penalize an individual's effort to work more. Are there other legitimate uses for the tax system beyond fairness and incentives to work more?

A tax simply adds to the price of an activity, while a subsidy reduces its price. Put simply, if we want more of a certain activity, we can subsidize it to decrease its cost. Alternately, if we want people to do less of something, we can tax it.

We may also want to determine if people are sensitive to price changes. For instance, if we wanted to raise revenue for the government, and did not want to use an income tax, we could simply look for something people really want or need and tax that. There are types of goods or services that people need very much and because of this need, their consumption of the good or service is insensitive to price changes. We described such goods and services earlier as price inelastic. Raising the price of such goods, through the imposition of a tax on that class of goods alone, will not change an individual's consumption of an inelastic good, but will absorb wealth that causes a decrease in consumption of all other goods.

This is not to say that these citizens are not hurt by price changes – just that they have no choice but to pay. For instance, if there are life-saving medicines, we could tax them knowing people would be willing to pay the tax rather than perish. While this may be considered ruthless, it is what economists call non-distorting because it does not dramatically affect their decision to buy the drug – even if it reduces their income and hence reduces the amount of all the other normal goods they would buy.

There are other candidates for taxation that do not have this unfortunate aspect. For instance, any activity that is addictive would not be much distorted by the tax. The tax would also have the benefit of discouraging future participants in the addictive behavior, while perhaps once in a while inducing the addict him or herself to cease consumption of the good. We could also use some of the revenue from the tax to ameliorate the cost of the addictive behavior, by paying for drug rehabilitation or family counseling centers, stop smoking programs, health care for those suffering from second hand smoke, or domestic violence programs that cope with the ravages of excessive drinking. In this sense, part of the tax is simply helping to pay up front for the long-term costs society will incur. In economics lingo, the tax should then at least cover the negative externality induced on society.

Many economists take this rehabilitative effect of tax revenue even further. Recognizing that humans regularly engage in diverse activities, some of which harm the user and others, they recommend that the more harmful of these activities be taxed rather than prohibited. For instance, even those as associated with conservatism, such as conservative economist Milton Friedman, former Fed Chairman Paul Volcker, Financier George Soros, President Reagan's former Secretary of State George Schultz,[1] and police associations recommend legalizing some lesser drugs. The reasoning is that while criminalization is certainly a deterrent, its ultimate effect is to drive the illicit drug price up, in effect, taxing users. However, these premiums, or taxes, do not accrue to government left to fix the associated problems, but rather to the illegal drug trade, who are not likely to report their ill-gotten gains to the Internal Revenue Service. Legalizing these drugs removes the black market and the criminal element and probably does little one way or the other in affecting the addictive behavior.

Certain other activities might be considered positive and, hence, we may want to encourage them with our tax system through subsidies. Residents are encouraged to buy a home by the provision that they can use their mortgage interest payment to reduce their taxes. Deductions that encourage home ownership, education, alternative energy usage, farming, retirement savings, and many other activities deemed desirable receive favorable tax deductions or, in essence, subsidies from society. Subsidies occur because society places a value on such activities and uses tax incentives to encourage them.

The tax code has created a complex, indeed often too complex, system to encourage investment. While these incentives are imperfect, they share a common principle that is often elucidated. They encourage the Consumer-Investor to save and to invest to expand the productive capacity of the economy. They also have the side effect of offering tax burden reductions to those who are the most likely to benefit from such provisions – mainly those with higher incomes – and so are often accused of favoring the wealthy. While this artifact goes against the accepted principle of tax progressivity, it appeals to the Randians who believe those who mobilize capital in society should be rewarded rather than discouraged.

It is a fair question to ask if deferred or reduced taxes on the gains in value of investment capital truly expand our economy's capacity to produce. Certainly venture capital raised, or capital invested in homes built, or inventory produced, is investment in the economic sense. However, land that becomes more valuable through a speculative bubble or stocks that are bid up in a stock market bubble do not necessarily translate into greater future production.

It would be difficult to discern between capital gains we might want to subsidize that are in truly productive capacity-expanding categories, and those that are not. If the vast majority of capital gains are not productive capacity gains, the tax as redistributive, from all and to the investor class, rather than an instrument that expands the economic pie.

The same argument of redistribution may equally be levied at low corporate dividend tax rates. Dividends are profits a firm returns to its owners, rather than re-injects into their corporate capacity. As a consequence, dividends are instead of, rather than contributing to, the productive capacity of the economy. Some rationalize this by claiming that the recipients of dividends and the tax savings they receive are more likely to do something with the tax savings that will benefit the economy overall. Again, that may be the case if the dividends were reinvested into other forms of productive capacity, but not if they are simply used to further inflate the speculative bubble.

Double taxation

Another argument on reduced taxation from income derived from dividends is that the corporation paying out the dividends has already been heavily taxed. Indeed, US corporations pay upwards of 40% on their net profits. Remaining profits further distributed is taxed a second time by Consumer-Investor recipients. Under the principle that one should be taxed only once, some argue for reduced or even zero dividend taxation.

Instead, it would make sense to not tax corporate earnings at all. Ultimately, corporations are making goods that we consume. To tax corporate earnings is to simply force their prices higher, which will be passed on to the Consumer-Investor anyway. Additionally, offshore companies are even given a competitive advantage. If their nation's corporate tax rate is lower than the US tax rate, they can sell goods in our country without the same tax burden our companies must bear. To add insult to corporate injury, domestic companies are not only put at a disadvantage in their own countries, but are also disadvantaged in competing abroad with companies who must pay lower taxes.

Global tax harmonization

One way around this problem is international tax harmonization. Already the tax community understands how to calculate corporate taxes based on whether their activities are benefiting from, or destined to, a market in a given tax state within a country. If so, they bear the tax burden for those state activities as would other corporations competing in the state. Taking this principle further, we could use international tax apportionment to ensure offshore companies pay a share of taxes based on how much they sell in the United States, just as a domestic corporation would. US corporations will then be treated abroad just as their competition in these other countries would compete.

Some progressive countries, most notably Ireland, have enjoyed great success by competing for international trade. Ireland decided for economic strategy reasons to charge very low corporate taxes. In doing so, they found they could attract much new economic activity and have their companies compete effectively world-wide.

Certainly the reduction of taxes on domestic corporations sounds like a radical and unfair proposal that violates our sense of fairness in dividing the economic pie. Instead the focus ought to be how to effectively expand the economic pie and then use other mechanisms that can then restore fairness without reducing international competitiveness. This is a reach however, until we realize that some of the largest corporations in the country pay millions of dollars per year to manage, reduce, and often even eliminate their corporate taxation obligations.

Nothing is gained by devoting resources into non-productive enterprises that put effort into shifting tax burdens. A simple consumption tax would reduce this gamesmanship.

Tax policy as fiscal policy

Economic history has demonstrated that tax rebates can stimulate the economy, especially if they are well tailored to enhance domestic consumption and investment. Can tax policy in itself act as a stimulus? Recall the popular definition of a recession is two quarters of negative growth. Tax policy stimulates economic efficiency, spurs growth, and may help end a recession. Such policies should reverse though in times of economic prosperity. Indeed, tax policy should be directed toward maximizing efficiency and, at times, ending a recession.

A well-tuned tax policy makes the economy more receptive to both fiscal and monetary policy. Good tax policy induces individuals to make decisions for sound business reasons rather than tax reasons. For instance, an artifact of the US tax code motivates individuals to sell stock that has declined in value just before the end of the tax year. If they do so, they can offset capital gains accrued at other times in the year. If they do not, they may have a difficult time deducting the costs imposed by the capital loss, even if they are certainly taxed for the profits from a capital gain. Without more rational treatment of capital gains and losses, at least some portion of stock sales and purchases are motivated by factors completely unrelated to the formation of capital to produce goods and services.

29
An Educated Global Citizen*

If you are a child in a SEW country, and the first generation educated for a new global world, you will approach the challenge of rapid technology development not wondering what has changed, but thirsty to be part of the change. It is that same zest to succeed in a new world that brought waves of immigrants from China and Ireland and then Italy, Germany, Hungary, India, and Eastern Europe to the United States. For these immigrants, everything was new, and so they embraced the change with an almost evangelical zeal. They succeeded and insisted their children succeed, in turn.

Those thrust into their first generation of change know nothing but change and don't have the expectations or entitlements of a past heritage to fall back on. They work hard, they are open to opportunity without entitlement, and they almost can't help but succeed in an economy that will increasingly demand these qualities.

This, of course, has ramifications for our education system. Our parents argue that there is nothing more valuable in the upbringing of a young person than education. Today I might argue that there is nothing more essential for the economy than education, in all of its varied forms. At the same time, there is perhaps nothing more dynamic, in flux, and in constant need of reinventing itself.

A little uncomfortable

This need to reinvent education is a little uncomfortable. After all, the institution of education is one of the oldest and most revered institutions in society, with a mission as noble as society itself. Another venerated institution, society's various forms of faith and worship, shares much with education. Both are storehouses of knowledge and history and both offer direction, guidance, and contemplation to those who subscribe. Those that commit to service do so for noble reasons and serve in a challenging environment at relatively low pay when compared to other sectors of society. Both practitioners are offered more than average flexibility in how they go about practicing what they preach. And while some of the teachings may have changed, education and faith both use modalities that have not changed in their essence for millennia.

Over the long history of education, society has remained essentially unchanged for millennia – up until the last few centuries, and especially the last few decades. But, new forces buffet us in education as we cope with a knowledge base that is dramatically expanding, a population that is demanding a different mix of skill sets so they can keep up with the changing global economies. Add to that a student body that often comes with some skills already more adapted to the new economy than those of their educators.

Even in this new economy, it seems likely that the tradition of an older generation teaching a younger generation will remain. Educating requires a certain seasoning and experience, an ability to see the forest through the trees, and to boil an immense body of knowledge down to the essence. While the younger generation seems increasingly able to absorb huge amounts of information, it is the role of an educator to synthesize the vast information around us in a meaningful way. For that reason, the model of one generation educating another will most surely remain.

However, the academy can do a better job in its role of synthesizer. As an example, consider the plight of the automotive industry. The year 2008 marks the hundredth anniversary of the Ford Model T, a car built by a company that epitomized the new industrial concept of the assembly line. While the idea was not completely original, borrowed from the way animals were slaughtered as they moved along a conveyor belt or a "disassembly line," it was revolutionary in industry because it allowed a car to be manufactured every 90 minutes – faster than ever before.

The model succeeded less because it brought the cars-in-progress to the trades people but rather because workers were converted to highly productive specialists, resulting in somewhat higher wages and much higher profits. Soon Ford quickly garnered 90% of the market share for cars worldwide. The new manufacturing model relied on extreme specialization to create efficiencies and these efficiencies put a car in every garage and a chicken in every pot. But, this specialization also created isolation and hampered creativity.

Education also practices extreme specialization. My specialty, the economics of information, is a barrier to holding down a meaningful conversation with a scholar studying econometrics, much less one studying English Drama Before Shakespeare. Of course, these silos, often within silos contained in silos, are very conducive to sharp focus on a narrow discipline, just as the Ford worker became the world's expert in dropping a crankshaft into a crankcase.

But, just as the Ford worker had little idea what happened 30 feet further down the assembly line, our increased specialization means we are losing sight of the forest for the wood. Sometimes now a professor discovers what is taught in another course by asking his or her students rather than colleagues. The education assembly line can also be intellectually isolating.

Sixty years ago, in post-war Japan, General Macarthur invited Professor Edward Deming to help rebuild Japanese industry. Deming's 14 Points[1] were primarily centered on the need to create communications and cross-disciplinary awareness in an increasingly specialized process. The concept of Kaizen Teams, or "quality circles," in which a group of specialists would collaborate around a function rather than a specialization, created new perspectives and insights, and ultimately new efficiencies and quality.

Toyota used this approach to great advantage and has now supplanted General Motors as the world's leading automobile manufacturer. So successful were the teachings of Deming and others on the value of collaboration and cross-disciplinary manufacturing that Ford invited Deming to teach US industry about his methods 35 years after he helped transform Japanese manufacturing, and the world.

Have we learned to make connections?

Education can learn from the revolutions sweeping the world through collaboration. The market demands collaboration and cooperation, and we are now seeing growing demand for our institutions of higher education to provide the cross-disciplinary education global commerce requires.

30
Let's Build a Better Mousetrap

Many saw our most recent financial meltdown coming. Increased volatility in global financial markets were the early warnings of discomfort, just as farmers claim jittery livestock and wildlife are precursors to earthquakes and volcanic eruptions. These early warnings though did not seem to prepare us to quickly clean up the mess.

When the market began to implode, and when we finally accepted that the plunge would be deeper and longer than others of late, the Fed and central banks around the world jumped in to plug the leaking dyke. None of the measures were more than stop-gap, including an anemic fiscal stimulus package that was too little and far too late. Each measure provided just enough of a glimmer of hope to very temporarily appease a very grumpy financial market. None, though, has been the panacea that restores investor confidence.

The interesting question is why our responses have been so anemic and indecisive. There seems to be a great reluctance to profoundly redesign or regulate the market, even when we see all the damage done and consumer confidence fall to levels comparable to the Great Depression.

Our collective reluctance is anchored in political philosophy rather than policy pragmatism. This is the nation of the better mousetrap. Our policies are formulated around the premise that free markets encourage innovation, innovation encourages economic growth, and growth translates into prosperity. It is an Ayn Rand sense of encouragement of the entrepreneur who will create new wealth for all.

This philosophy of the unfettered innovator certainly fueled the Industrial Revolution and the booms of the twentieth century. They do not apply to innovations in financial markets, though. Here's why.

We encourage innovation when it translates into growth. At the same time, we recognize that growth may not be evenly distributed, so we use tax policy to redistribute the growth. Knowing we can ameliorate economic displacement or the inequities of growth through public policy allows us to preserve the baby and the bathwater.

The new instruments in financial markets do not translate into a bigger economic pie. Much of the antics of hedge funds are designed to divert market wealth toward the smart money. The vast majority of their efforts are sophisticated attempts to snatch another's slice of the pie rather than creating a larger economic pie.

Why is this a problem? Never before has so much effort and so many clever minds devoted so much time and valuable resources to manipulation financial wealth rather than enterprises that are economically productive. Their creation of wealth is our loss of wealth. In the end, there are no new inventions, no new homes, and no new chickens in every pot. There is just new cynicism. Imagine what we could do as an economy if we diverted the energies of all these clever financial innovators into really building better mousetraps.

A twelve-step program toward a vision 2020

One can only be hopeful, and take past successes as a predictor of a resilient present and a bright future. If there is one defining quality that has emerged time and time again since the Industrial Revolution, it is the resilience and creativity of the FEW economies. This resiliency and creativity has also shown the Second Economic World how to emulate the FEW success. The SEW countries may actually excel where others could vanquish, because the SEW countries invest highly in education and are prepared to do whatever is necessary to succeed. The success of the FEW countries will depend on their ability to reinvent themselves as they have done time and again.

I would like to take what we have learned about the need to expand the economic pie, rather than fight over its pieces, and use this spirit as a basis for an economic vision that will allow us to succeed in a converged First and Second Economic World.

Let us first grasp what the future might look like.

The assumptions

Within the lifetime of most people alive today, the First Economic World will go from about one billion inhabitants to about six billion inhabitants. Perhaps a quarter of the world will remain less developed, but they too will join the path of global economic convergence.

By the year 2020, the world's biggest economy, biggest bank, biggest company, largest English speaking population, and most engineers, doctors, and scientists will likely be in China.

In the year 2020, there will simply not be enough of the commodities we use so intensively today.

With the convergence of the First Economic World, most people on the planet will have moved from a goods-dependent economy to a services-dependent global economy, with many more services delivered via a new and much faster Internet. There will be more computing power in a 2020 personal computer than existed on the planet two generations earlier.

China and India will have developed a technical intellectual stock that eclipses the First Economic World.

People will be more mobile, less loyal to their employer, more multi-tasking, more globally aware and footloose, and will need to be much, much more adaptable and prepared for change.

Change is the new normal.

Most specialized knowledge we will teach in our colleges will be obsolete before they graduate. We have to learn to teach to learn.

If the nineteenth century was the Century of England, and the twentieth century was America's Century, the twenty-first century will belong to China and India.

If we accept these assumptions and roll up our sleeves to prepare for a new and dynamic future, there are some economic changes that must take place. As the world becomes a much more complicated place, we will have to better understand how the economy works. If we do not, we leave ourselves more prone to the shenanigans of smart money or dogmatic leaders.

The innovations

Innovation one: education reform

These realities have ramifications for our education system. Our parents argue that there is nothing more valuable in the upbringing of a young person than education. Today I might argue that there is nothing more essential for the economy than education in all of its varied forms. At the same time, there is perhaps nothing more dynamic, in flux, and in constant need of reinventing itself.

Education can learn from the revolutions sweeping the world. Rather than courses of study in increasingly obscure areas of business, how about a course or two that gives our students what they need to know to deal with the Customer, the Banker, Venture Capitalist, Production Foreman, Politician, Scientist, or the Regulator? Could we present our theories in a way that is best packaged for our students to receive and absorb the material, rather than as homage to the specialty to which we as scholars devote all of our energies? Perhaps we could have our courses team-taught by a few experts, each offering their color, so we eventually paint a richer picture for our students.

As we go to our students rather than have our students come to us, we can more directly provide them with the information they need to be successful. This new model would not simply fill their heads with greater and greater detail because we must fill up a 3-credit course with 45 hours of material. Instead, we need to think about education in a fundamentally different way – based less on what a specialist thinks the student needs and more along the lines of a collaborative exercise between scholars from different disciplines. Let us go from Henry Ford's vision of offering a car of any color so long as it is black to giving students the tools they need to compete in an increasingly Technicolor world. The market demands collaboration and cooperation, and we are now seeing growing demand for our institutions of higher education to provide the cross-disciplinary education global citizens require.

The future will be in this much more responsive, tailored, adaptable, and interdisciplinary style of education. That is the way innovators and companies think, or need to think, in our future.

We also have to be more educated economic citizens so we can seize control of our own financial destiny. We are now too prone to the manipulations of sophisticated smart money. They profit from volatility, and are increasingly accused of generating volatility. Our public officials are little better educated than us in the intricacies of modern financial markets. If we don't ask for better, they likely won't offer.

Innovation two: a new energy policy

It is inevitable that the hydrocarbon-based economy will be transformed. This is less because the world will run out of hydrocarbons, but that we will be forced to adopt new technologies. The price of hydrocarbons will rise sufficiently to make other technologies more cost effective. At 140 dollars for a barrel of oil, wind power and some potential solar power technologies become cost effective. If global warming concerns cause the imposition of a carbon tax on the use of carbon dioxide-generating energy sources, technologies known as alternative today will be traditional tomorrow.

There is a tremendous technology curve that must be navigated to succeed in the energy race. This research and development intensive industry will give a tremendous advantage to those countries, companies, and colleges that get two steps ahead in technologies we all will need.

Germany in particular has embraced this economic reality. The German government has offered a 25 year guaranteed price for any Consumer-Investor who would like to become an energy producer. This price at first seemed so exorbitant that many thought it was unrealistically generous.

Farmers began to augment their agricultural income with energy production income as a consequence of the generous prices offered. While the guaranteed price was sufficiently large to produce a wave of production, research, and innovation, the price no longer seems so exorbitant at current oil prices.

While Germany, India, and others have fully engaged in the new energy economy, there is still room for a new Kennedyesque-scale plan to make gold out of green technologies. Just as with the moon race, the green race will guarantee our economic future while at the same time stimulate our science and engineering education and create spin-offs for other new technologies not even imagined yet. And while the entire moon mission cost 125 billion in today's dollars, the increased cost of oil to the U.S. alone in the past few years could equal that endeavor six times over – every year!

The FEW community is tinkering with some energy technologies. Unfortunately, we are perhaps engaging in the politics rather than the economics of energy. For instance, US tax and industrial policy subsidizes oil much more than it subsidizes technologies that will sooner or later replace oil. It subsidizes ethanol production, which unfortunately requires a significant amount of oil to produce a gallon of ethanol, while at the same time bidding up prices of all agricultural food crops. This is good for farmers but not good for Consumer-Investors, and likely not good for energy independence in the final analysis.

Some FEW countries are also investing somewhat in the hydrogen economy. However, hydrogen is not an energy source, but rather is an energy storage medium. Lighter than air and having long since dispersed in the atmosphere, hydrogen is created primarily by the use of electricity to electrolyze water. We can then transport the hydrogen to market with relatively little transmission or storage loss and recover the electricity in a fuel cell at some significant efficiency loss. While hydrogen should then not be regarded as an alternative energy source, as it still requires affordable electricity, it can play a role in energy storage and transportation. We are on the verge of relatively inexpensive solar power, with its economic viability enhanced as oil becomes more expensive. Hydrogen as a storage and transportation mechanism, in conjunction with economically viable solar and wind power, may provide the backstop technology growing nations need, and the opportunity for FEW countries to conduct research in the next energy revolution.

Innovation three: a coordinated industrial policy

Modern industrial policy was borne out of the wild and wooly era of the early industrial revolution. Fears of a few industrialists dominating commerce and oil in the nineteenth century produced a rash of laws preventing collusion. With each law came imaginative ways to circumvent the law. A law that prevented industrialists from colluding induced them to instead form trusts, essentially large holding companies that shared a common economic interest and destiny. As a consequence, most industrial policy was designed mindful of the "anti-trust laws."

Countries that industrialized after the US nineteenth-century experience did not create the same barriers to corporate cooperation that is inherent in the US industrial public policy. For instance, MITI, the Japanese government's Ministry for International Trade and Industry, had an explicit industrial policy that brought together major Japanese corporations to cooperate on innovation and infant industries. South Korea adopted this model and the start-up Airbus consortium in Europe is now going toe to toe with Boeing, the icon of aviation innovation.

While industrial and even international cooperation is becoming the norm, even through direct governmental partnerships, such a twenty-first century policy is shunned in the United States. This is likely an area that will need regulatory reform. Gone are the days when an Edison can innovate in a small lab and produce the phonograph, photographs, generators, and electric lights. To avoid falling behind, a modern corporation might need to earn as many patents in a year as Thomas Edison earned in his lifetime. Patents protecting an innovation for 17 to 25 years create rewards to innovation but they also create barriers to cooperation. We must recognize that patent and industrial policy borne of the realities of the nineteenth century may need to be remade to cope with the realities of the twenty-first century. We will likely need to arrive to a point where government, educational, and multi-corporation industrial partnerships are prized rather than shunned.

Innovation four: tax policy

The tax code is amazingly complex, derived from waves and waves of new tax policy, layered one on top of another. A good idea designed by a clever and well-meaning legislator is usurped by 100 of a country's smartest tax lawyers even before the ink is dry. The more cynical among us might claim that the new tax laws are formulated with greater regard for lobbyists than the size of the country's economic pie. Too often tax policy is focused on class wars, with each striving for a share of the other's piece of the pie, without regard to the costs that such jockeying incurs overall.

It is time for the tax code to be dramatically simplified and redesigned by apolitical economists with no obvious axe to grind, to create a level playing field for the economy to grow. There ought to be room for incentives to engage in those activities that will provide for long-term economic growth. For the first round, there should perhaps be only a single goal – How will each provision further long-term economic growth?

It would be naïve to imagine that a coherent and progressive economic policy contained within a tax code would not invoke titanic political battles. If we could learn to keep it simple and effective, and use other more transparent and more temporary measures to redistribute the income that politics will inevitably want to pass, we can keep our nations on a path for economic growth.

Innovation five: coordinated monetary and fiscal policy

Fortunately, most central banks of the First Economic World are relatively autonomous. Since their founding, politicians have been wary of a Fed that could be influenced by the executive branch. There is nothing like some good economic news to ensure a party gets re-elected and neither party wants to concede that gift to the other. As a consequence, there is little room for explicit coordination of monetary and fiscal policy. Indeed, some economists argue that monetary policy has been mostly successful in spite of contradictory or unhelpful fiscal policy.

It is difficult for legislators to delegate their fiscal authority to a central bank governor unelected by its citizens. For example, the US Executive Branch has little economic power but the veto pen and temporary Executive Orders. This creates barriers to the concentration of economic power sufficiently to replicate the success of Ministries of Finance in parliamentary systems. It is also unlikely that the Congress will delegate its power of the purse to technocrats under their control or under executive control. As a consequence, while one could imagine an enlightened Congress that passes policies to create an environment for economic success, it is unlikely that the Federal government could successfully create the significant and direct partnerships found in Europe, Japan, and China.

Were the FEW nations able to conduct coordinated monetary policy, we would find that its policy was much more effective, and at little cost. The beauty of monetary policy is that it does not require significant public resources. The monetary authorities essentially have their hands on the throttle of the economic engine and can throttle down very effectively, and throttle up with a bit more difficulty, rather quickly.

If our monetary policy was layered with some carefully timed fiscal policy designed to add credibility and magnify its effectiveness, the results would be much stronger. Especially in today's market, it is confidence that we must maintain. This confidence is easier to obtain if it is clear the various agencies of public policy will work together to ensure the economy stays on an even trajectory. If the confidence can be maintained, these agencies in reality will have to do little more than reassure an occasionally jittery public.

As an analogy, we can look to the example of the Federal Deposit Insurance Corporation (FDIC). This government corporation was part of the 1933 initiatives hailed in by President Roosevelt to lend confidence in financial markets. It insured the Consumer-Investor's bank deposits were secure, today up to 100,000 dollars per account. The mere existence of the fund lends confidence to the banking industry. As a consequence, the runs on the bank so common in 1932 and 1933 are largely averted, at little cost to the government.

Such fiscal policies need only assure the Consumer-Investor that the government will do whatever is necessary to keep markets solvent and functioning. This simple gesture is usually all that is necessary. If we wait too long before re-establishing confidence, we may pay a higher price.

For instance, in the current Credit Crunch, homes secured by sub-prime mortgages are threatened with foreclosure. The social, economic, and monetary costs of these foreclosures are exorbitant. The costs do not only inflict the owners of these homes. All home prices will be depressed for years if an inventory of boarded-up homes is suddenly created. Tens of millions of households that never participated in the sub-prime debacle will have much of their housing equity wiped out, and with it, their nest eggs for retirement.

We simply cannot afford for this to happen. It may be costly to fix the sub-prime crisis, but it will be far more costly to fix the financial lives of innocent bystanders. While one could make a philosophical argument about how the markets simply must fix themselves, the pragmatic solution requires recognition and a fiscal response, as politically distasteful as that might be to some. And to "wait and see" just causes more collateral damage to manifest.

This fiscal policy in support of monetary policy must be quick and decisive, and if so, the monetary policy can be most effective, and the fiscal cost often little more than some confident and well placed words. However, each day we wait is another day of economic hardship and uncertainty and one more arrow permanently removed from the monetary quiver.

We must also renew international economic coordination. While financial crises are now global, solutions remain local. When a global crisis is severe enough to bring down a nation's economy, the country will try to lower interest rates to stimulate economic growth. In the absence of international coordination of monetary policy, this causes their currency to worsen, raising prices and inducing stagflation. Other nations may have the incentive to keep this nation's currency strong, thereby nipping in the bud a crisis that could spill out across borders.

Innovation six: a manageable public debt

The annual federal budget deficit of any nation cannot be permanently in the red. Unless there is some massive project that will place a country on a growth trajectory and generate more than its fair share of surpluses in the future, we are simply mortgaging our children's future for our fiscal imprudence. In other words, we should systematically add to the national debt only if it is an investment that will pay good dividends in the future.

Instead, the US government has run a deficit in 31 of the last 35 years, through booms and busts alike. In such an environment of mounting debt, there is no saving for a rainy day. Prolonged or intense fiscal stabilization policy becomes difficult.

This is not to say that we should never run a deficit. A well-tailored fiscal policy, working in orchestration with monetary policy, will incur a deficit of perhaps half a percent of the gross domestic product in the depths of the troughs in the business cycle. This might amount to an annual deficit of 100 billion dollars or so, or approximately 300 or 400 dollars per resident.

The multiplier will then kick in to ensure growth can be maintained even during the steepest downturns we typically see. This 300 or 400 dollar deficit per person will then be made up with an equal surplus a few years later when the economy is at a peak in the business cycle.

In other words, tax revenues should once in a while exceed outlays as we save for a rainy day. In reality, we almost never run a surplus anymore. Rather than running the occasional deficit that might amount to a few 100 dollars per capita, balanced with a surplus later, our current level of debt in the United States is 100 times larger, at over 30,000 dollars per person and growing very rapidly.

The consequences of running perennial deficits and creating mounting debt, in good times and in bad, is that we lose our latitude to conduct effective fiscal policy, and we rob the investment market of badly needed funds. With a US public debt nearing 10 trillion dollars, the investment community has lost the access to funds that can expand the productive capacity of the nation.

Just the interest payment drain of about 500 billion dollars each year to service the debt crowds out private investment that would dramatically improve our national competitive position. It would also provide for all the liquidity necessary to avert the financial crises that have been afflicting first the United States and then the world financial markets.

Innovation seven: a perception of ethics

A number of ethical meltdowns have eroded public confidence in our business and financial institutions. While the ethical breaches very rarely escalate to criminality, there is a strong public perception unethical behavior is now rampant.

The Sarbanes-Oxley law and its international equivalents are good attempts to ensure that chief executive officers accept responsibility for their corporate decisions. However, insider trading, failure in fiduciary responsibility, and corporate governance accountability are still problematic. We must re-establish the balance between the corporate interest and the public interest. It is important to remember that corporations are entities created by public policy and must be held to a much higher standard than they would perhaps prefer.

With all the benefits created for corporations and all the resources provided by society to allow corporations to do their business, it is not unreasonable to ask for greater accountability, greater transparency, and a greater adherence to ethical behavior. This must become a corporate culture rather than a corporate pain.

Innovation eight: compensation reform

Markets have become increasingly cynical at the same time as executives have become increasingly well compensated. What can we do to lend greater confidence to the market and to weed out cynicism of our institutions? For one thing, we must ensure that those receiving the rewards are also bearing their share of the risk. This problem certainly became apparent in the sub-prime led Credit Crunch. We may want to revisit corporate executive compensation schemes, too. If the majority of compensation is in the form of stock options, executives can earn astronomical sums when times are good but still receive a very generous base pay when times are bad.

In effect, executives benefit from upside risk but are not penalized from downside risk. The Consumer-Investor receives a lower return on the upside because executives then take their cut, and the Consumer-Investor is also invariably left holding the bag when times are bad. Assumption of risk to sharpen one's decision-making of course requires assumption of risk even when things are bad. To do otherwise creates externalities, a perverse system of incentives, and increased market cynicism. And none of these are healthy if we want to create an efficient financial market.

It seems likely that the solutions to this dilemma must rest with internal ethics watchdogs in their own corporate suites, in combination with stern punishment when an ethical breech translates into a financial meltdown. Unfortunately, we again suffer from a principle agent problem. Those most hurt by these meltdowns are not the same individuals or corporations that profit from the schemes. The NINJA (No Income No Job or Asset) sub-prime mortgage originators have their money in the bank, while former Countrywide Home Loans' CEO, Angelo Mozilo, left the company with a 24 million dollar pension, 20 million dollars in deferred compensation, and almost 6 million dollars in company stock. The bond rating companies received their commissions offered by the investment banks and the investment banks received their packaging fees for the products they sold to investors. The investors were left holding the bag. The government has had to step in to ensure people are not thrown out of their homes and taxpayers have ultimately lost perhaps a trillion dollars or more of wealth. We can ill afford another mammoth financial scandal that some may be hatching in the shadows beyond the bright lights of transparency and ethics.

Innovation nine: regulatory reform

Just as industrial strategies have become increasingly sophisticated and complex, so too have financial markets. But, while the increasingly complex industrial strategies are a reflection of a style of commerce that is highly oriented toward new technologies and the creation and refinement of new products, too much attention is now devoted to generating paper wealth over real wealth.

There are definitely new financial instruments that make markets more efficient and stable. The challenge for regulators is in knowing the difference between true financial innovation and smoke-and-mirrors tricks designed to make some better off at the expense of others. This is a colossal challenge, given the resources attracted to the financial smoke-and-mirrors industry to try to garner someone else's piece of the pie, compared with the limited regulatory resources we muster to devote to preventing this phenomenon from happening.

A second challenge is to re-establish the long run as the primary objective of financial and industrial strategy. A focus only on short-run success creates a willingness to doctor performance that will give very good short-run results even if it will consequently generate very poor long-run results. Corporations seem to harbor the perennial hope that the chicken will never come home to roost because the poor long-run results can be negated by some new short-run trick that will cover up the short sighted policy. Some corporations have become quite adept at cobbling a corporate strategy out of a series of short-run tricks, as we saw most painfully with Enron.

Such a strategy is very risky, and any misstep or surprise places otherwise good people in a difficult position to try an ethically questionable quick fix. Of course, they can rationalize to themselves that they are doing this only to save the shareholders and workers of the company from a painful financial reality. But, these desperate and short-sighted acts invariably fail, leaving shareholders, workers, and often the general public to pay the price.

What can we do besides putting in good money after bad by creating new layers of regulators to keep an eye on vastly greater numbers of financial tricksters? We need much more transparency and much less anonymity in financial dealings. While there will obviously be a great deal of reluctance on the part of those that rely on the smoke-and-mirrors, the economy overall will benefit.

We know that trade secrets are an essential protection to encourage productive innovation. Nobody would innovate unless they are afforded the protection to secure for themselves a share of the new economic wealth they create. But, such protections are unwarranted if there is no productive innovation. Why would we ensure financial secrecy if the secrecy only benefits the tricksters determined to divert existing wealth to their pile?

Few markets are anonymous. For most of us, someone sufficiently determined can discover every economic transaction we make. Most purchases we make need not be kept secret because they are not strategic. I argue that few financial transactions are truly strategic, but rather are tactical. Ironically enough, the truly strategic transactions in financial markets do require full Securities and Exchange Commission reporting if they are designed, for instance, with a corporate takeover in mind.

Let us observe every move a hedge fund makes. If we individually make tactical financial transactions in the hopes of benefiting from a rising market, our very public purchases could only act to bring the market up quicker and allow us to realize our hopes sooner. If financial markets are truly information efficient as theorists assume, then full market transparency can only enhance this efficiency. With such transparency, smoke-and-mirrors will no longer work. We can then redivert all that effort and the efforts of all those very smart financiers into building the better mousetrap.

Finally, much of the volatility in some shares comes from the practice of naked short selling. Short selling tries to profit by selling shares now, with the expectation that the price will fall further, at which time you can buy them back. Because you intend to buy back the shares later, you can even borrow some shares temporarily. Naked short selling is doing this without having borrowed the shares in the first place. Just as check kiting, the practice of writing a check on an account with insufficient funds in the hope you can cover the debit before the check clears, is illegal, so should naked short selling. If someone is able to sell a product, including a security, they should have possession or ownership of the product they are selling. Continuing to allow the shady practice of short selling adds significantly greater downward price instability to an already volatile market.

Innovation ten: infrastructure investment

We must be prepared to invest in our own collective future. Some of that infrastructure can only be provided by government because of its public goods nature. The legal infrastructure has to be improved to ensure that commerce can compete fairly and can focus on making, and not just cutting, the pie.

Perhaps most importantly though, we must invest in the human capital of our citizens. The strength of most First Economic World nations is derived from ingenuity and hard work. Few of these countries have large and sustainable endowments of the other factors of production. And as we move away from a goods oriented economy to a service oriented economy, the investment in our people will become even more important.

This investment in human capital is not something that individuals usually have the capacity, the foresight, or the desire to do all on their own. There is a certain publicness of their education. A well-educated workforce is collectively more productive and happier, lives longer, and has lower rates of crime.

From this we all benefit. We all have a stake in each of our educations because we all enjoy the lifelong fruits. As a consequence, economic theory tells us we will likely under invest in education if left to our own devices. We must recognize the value of a subsidized education, knowing full well that we will get back every dollar, and more, through taxation of our productive citizenry.

Innovation eleven: legal and political reform

The Magna Carta and US Constitution were amazing documents. Together with the words of the Declaration of Independence, they created rights for humans and for property and permitted a middle class to engage in free markets and pursue happiness. The legal system has gone through tremendous modifications in the centuries since, but it still necessarily relies on some precedents that are now outdated.

For instance, the legal system must enforce certain anti-trust provisions that no longer make sense and it protects patents in ways that do not sufficiently differentiate between the categories of innovations seeking patent protection. The bias is the protection of individual rights in an economy that is increasingly collective in its interest and interactions.

Legislators will have to lead this charge though. An economically sophisticated and educated government is essential. However, we must also figure out a way to put aside provincial interests in the overall interest of our mutual economic future. Strong leaders that can educate as well as legislate will play an important role in the necessary economic and political reforms.

Innovation twelve: an economically empowered citizenry

Perhaps the most important innovation of all is the need for a well-informed economic citizen. Just as little knowledge of our automobile sets us up as a mark for an unscrupulous mechanic, ignorance of the economy will permit those with an obvious axe to grind to take advantage of the system. Already this is happening to a large degree. One or two hedge funds may, on a given day, dominate trading in an important stock. They can take the market down and bring it up, almost at will, and we are taken for a ride. When these organizations fail colossally, the rest of the economy must pick up the pieces, while the principles are often completely indemnified.

Corporations speak with too loud a voice in government and pass legislation designed to benefit them. There is little defense against such a co-opting of legislation. They have the resources to make a case that sounds reasoned and thoughtful to legislators and they can spend millions getting their economic message out.

The Consumer-Investor, even in aggregate, cannot mount an effective counter-argument. All too often, the special interest legislation passes, without making our collective pie any larger or efficient. On the contrary, it is often the case that the economy is less efficient after special interest legislation. And if the special interest secures a gain, this must mean that the Consumer-Investor taxpayer incurs a loss.

We can only avoid this natural tendency by recognizing the problem and educating our legislators and the media. If we demand better legislation and more informed media coverage of economic issues, we will eventually get it. As we educate ourselves and others, we will also find that we make more informed decisions on our own behalf to secure our family's economic future.

31
Conclusions

As we conclude this book, we have come full circle. We began with the goal of explaining why we are currently experiencing a dangerous economic meltdown. Talking this through, we realized a certain economic education is necessary to do justice to the intricacies of a complicated and nuanced economy. As we explained the economy and the institutions that make it function or cause it to fail, it became apparent that we will succeed only if we can wrest control of our own economic destiny.

The range of topics covered here would not typically be contained in one college level economics course. We have spent time on the microeconomics of commodity pricing, the macroeconomics of monetary policy and banking, Keynesian theory, modern finance theory, the provision of public goods and taxation theory, political economy, economics and law, stabilization theory, growth theory, demographics, development economics, and environmental economics. Each of these topics is often a course in itself, and in total could constitute an entire major in economics.

One short book cannot substitute for a complete course of study of the macroeconomy. Hopefully I provided you with a better understanding of the ways the modern economy is tied together and imparted some intellectual tools to sort some of these phenomena out for yourself.

We also began this book discussing the profound frustration with the ways in which modern financial markets function. While there will still be frustration with the lack of political and economic leadership, we should be much more optimistic that we can collectively determine our own economic future. In isolation, each of the forces that frustrate the economy and our future seem daunting. In sum, they seem overwhelming. There is hope though. The common theme of the current financial dysfunction is the fact that our economic future is being done to us rather than with us. We should be assured now that this need not be the case.

We shouldn't underestimate the scale of the challenges in creating an economically literate citizenry. The fact is, though, that we don't all have to be uber-economic-citizens. Rather, if enough of us have a good grasp of the modern economy, there will be one less place to hide for those that want to create a good living at our expense through their creation of smoke-and-mirrors finances.

Well intentioned and well informed people can make good decisions that allow them to pursue their own happiness. And the world is a big enough and a tolerant enough place to let that happen, so long as individual actions do not impinge on the happiness of others. When they do, systems should be in place to compensate those adversely affected, or prevent those who are impinging. There is incredible value in coordinating our efforts in an educated and enlightened way so we do not suffer from the Paradox of Thrift, the negative externalities, the smoke-and-mirrors, and the efforts of some to devote huge amounts of energy to capturing a bigger piece of the pie for themselves rather than helping us create a bigger pie.

Finally, both education and information is the key. In my own academic research in the economics of information, I have come to realize that the critical assumption of the competitive ideal is in the access to good information. We see what happens when bad money forces out good, bad mortgage instruments destroy an entire financial sector, when bad players make all corporate citizens suspect, and when leaders aren't honest with the public about the direction in which they would like to take us.

My solution would be in dramatically enhanced transparency in those decisions that will eventually affect us all. This is not at odds with personal freedoms or privacy. Rarely, if ever, would a personal freedom issue affect an entire economy. Rather, this is about the need to have the information necessary to understand what is truly happening.

With the right to be informed though, comes the responsibility to use that franchise to promote the ideal society and economy our forefathers envisioned. This will be no easy task. The modern economy is very complex, as we have seen. And we are confronted now with the convergence of the First and Second Economic Worlds. This creates a diversity of peoples that we have never quite had to deal with before, especially as the traditional First Economic World becomes the minority in the new relationship. However, change is the new constancy, and I have confidence that we can collectively rise to the occasion. Perhaps confidence in our ability to work together to converge our economic worlds is the only viable strategy. This convergence is going to occur whether or not we decide to participate. That realization should certainly make participation all the more appealing.

One can never underestimate the resilience of creative people willing to take their own economic future in their hands. The world is a different place now, and will likely change more in the next two generations than it did in the previous hundred generations. And labor will likely attain a new position in the mix, with much of what we once did obsolete, and much of what we need to do somewhat destabilizing. Our children now sense that we are, perhaps more than ever, in control of, and responsible for our own economic destiny. The sooner we absorb this new economic reality, the better.

32
Where Are We Now?

This past year has been without parallel since the Great Crash and the Great Depression. It seems that no market has remained untouched. The world's publicly traded companies and partnerships have lost almost half of their value, from a peak of almost $60 trillion, to a little over $30 trillion now. If we look at the value of the world's stock markets and housing markets, almost half of the wealth has evaporated. We now talk in tens of trillions of dollars of international losses, and we don't know if the bleeding has finished.

Perhaps the most reassuring aspect of the global economic response to the financial meltdown is the shared leadership worldwide. How did we find ourselves on this path of unprecedented global market intervention? We are very much a victim of our own success. The rapid wealth creation of the 1990s and 2000s inevitably found its way into rising housing values. At the same time, a push to increase the rate of home ownership in the United States and elsewhere added fuel to the fire. There were exorbitant profits to be had by all and, in such an economic culture, nobody asks questions that would bring the party to an end.

And party we did. Mortgage companies like Countrywide in the United States and Northern Rock in the United Kingdom made it too easy for anybody to realize the dream of home ownership. Many that could not afford home ownership were lulled into the home buying contagion, with the confidence that they could always sell for a handsome profit if they ever found themselves on the ropes. But once the bubble popped, the home ownership dream became a nightmare. It is this nightmare that still haunts us today and portends to a severe global recession.

The rapid decline of Countrywide and Northern Rock in the face of mounting mortgage defaults is a tale of two different market philosophies.

The US response to the bankruptcy of Countrywide was to have it absorbed by Bank of America. The UK took a more multidimensional approach. When building society Bradford and Bingley's subprime mortgage exposure forced it into illiquidity, Spain's Grupo Santander bought some of its operations for less than ten cents on the dollar. However, other parts of its business, and of the Northern Rock building society, were nationalized by the British government through a new arms-length government-owned corporation called U.K. Financial Investments Limited.

The British Government was quick to step in and protect retail accounts of these leading banking entities, as early as the Fall of 2007. This is contrary to the actions of the US monetary authorities, which took a hands-off approach until March of 2008. A greater willingness of the British government to explore nationalization, while their US counterparts adhered to free market principles, allowed the United Kingdom to gain early experience with private-public partnerships as a solution to the private market failures.

The shoes continued to drop though. The Wall Street brokerage house Lehman Brothers was parceled out to the major British bank Barclays. American International Group, a major underwriter of the notorious credit default swaps that created huge liabilities for investment houses and investors alike, was eventually bailed out to the tune of $143 billion by the US Treasury, while the mounting losses of Icesave, the online banking wing of the Icelandic bank Landsbanki, were bailed out by the Dutch and UK finance ministers.

Even the International Monetary Fund, long considered the last resort lender to developing countries, responded to pleas from Argentina, Estonia, Iceland, Hungary, Latvia, Lithuania, Pakistan, Russia, South Africa, Turkey, and the Ukraine. It seems that no country was immune to the threat of bankruptcy in an environment where credit became nonexistent.

These examples of British, European, and international public interventions catapulted UK Prime Minister (and former finance minister) Gordon Brown as the emerging global economic leader. The United States was eventually forced to adopt a similar interventionist strategy to preserve the integrity to the US banking industry and free up what had by the fall of 2008 become an almost complete freezing-up of US and worldwide credit.

The US responses began well after the first European interventions. In the week of March 16, 2008, the Federal Reserve Board facilitated the bailout of Bear Stearns, one of the world's most revered investment banks. By making an unprecedented foray into the investment banking sector, the Fed departed from its traditional role of limiting its efforts to commercial banking. The next day, the Fed again decreased the interest rate it charges for short-term loans to commercial banks to 2.25%, with another quarter percentage point cut a month later.

The Fed was responding to an already alarming crisis in credit markets that by January of 2008 was wreaking havoc in world stock markets. Dramatic declines in the Hang Seng Index of China and the Nikkei in Japan reverberated through Europe and onto Wall Street. Investors worldwide hung on every word and gesture from the as-yet untested Chairman of the US Federal Reserve Board, Ben Bernanke. His willingness to broker a buyout of Bear Stearns and his announcement of a reduced federal funds rate caused the stock market to soar in a day by more than it had any day in five years. The next day, with no quick Fed fix to ward off the market pall, the Dow Jones Industrial Average again slumped by 300 points, wiping out much of the enthusiasm generated just a day before. Predictably, markets the world over had fits. We ushered in an era when any reprieve from a market decline was short-lived, and market volatility ruled the day.

Since then though, the Bear Stearns bailout and the 300 point drop seem like minor bumps on a pothole strewn road. The severe global stock market meltdown in October of 2008 induced the US Federal Reserve Open Market Committee to implement an emergency 0.5% rate cut, followed three weeks later with a further 0.5% rate cut at its regular October meeting. The Fed's interest rate has since dropped effectively to 0%. This places the Federal Funds Rate at a historically low level, lower than the rate in the Great Depression and World War II. The Fed has almost used up its ability to encourage banks to borrow, and is perilously near a Keynesian liquidity trap.

The US Congress also approved an unprecedented $700 Billion bailout package designed to reestablish integrity and confidence in US financial markets, in return for government ownership of newly issued preferred shares in US banks. These funds are being used to create liquidity in first and second tier US banks, and to encourage some buyouts of weaker tier three and tier four banks. This public encouragement in economic Darwinism is also unprecedented, and has inspired the likes of free-marketers such as former Fed Chairman Alan Greenspan to indicate we are all interventionists now.

The Fed and the US Treasury have bought stakes in, and brokered shot-gun marriages of, many more multibillion dollar corporations. And it has injected, or shall soon inject, about a trillion dollars into the US economy. Regulators and Central Banks around the world have done likewise, in a spirit of international monetary economic coordination not seen since Bretton Woods. Still, the Dow Jones Industrial Average has declined as much in a year as it did in the first year of the Great Crash of 1929. But while the market continued to fall for a couple more years in the Great Depression, we remain unsure how much further it will fall this time.

It is understandable that markets have become unnerved and people are scared. These numbers now bandied around are unprecedented in size. People have a difficult time absorbing figures that bear little relation to their own world. In the United States alone, stimulus packages total about two trillion dollars. Nations the world over, from China to the European Economic Community, and international lending organizations like the International Monetary Fund are working in concert to lower interest rates and provide for fiscal stimuli. The world has never before seen such a concerted and expensive rescue package.

And yet, the challenge remains daunting and the outcome uncertain. Export-oriented countries like China, Japan, and Korea have suffered dramatically on the news of reduced US consumption. The Hang Seng Index in China has dropped precipitously, and Japan's Nikkei 225 index reached its lowest level on record. These losses exceed even the losses on Wall Street, and represent vanishing nest eggs of middle class workers the world over. Once the economic security of the consumer-investor is threatened, we respond emotionally, motivated by fear of loss rather than logic. It is natural for us to wonder what is going on, what might happen next, and how it might affect us.

It is now clear that we have entered a global recession that is likely to be deep and prolonged, compared to the short and mild recessions of the past quarter century. We have discovered that dramatic drops in housing values, in combination with the decline in wealth in the stock markets, have an effect on consumption. For instance, US consumers decrease their consumption by about $60 for every $1,000 fall in housing value, and another $40 for each $1,000 fall in stock value. The decline in consumption alone in the United States may account for a 5% drop in spending. This drop is much greater than the stopgap efforts that offered US taxpayers tax rebates in the Spring of 2008 and the initiatives being implemented worldwide. While unprecedented and massive, fiscal efforts up to now have filled only a small share of the spending gap.

As a consequence, nations worldwide have begun reporting their first quarter of negative growth. Most economists now agree we are currently in a severe and likely long recession. Few economists believe we will pull out before 2010.

The Fed and central banks the world over have not needed to cope with the current decline in financial market confidence since the Great Depression. While many now realize that the failure of regulation to keep up with new-fangled financial products is largely responsible for this current mess, spending too much time on blame doesn't get us any further toward solving it. Perhaps history offers us some insights. Confidence in financial markets was shaken with the Great Crash of 1929. The immediate effects of that crash on market performance and confidence were only a little larger than what we are seeing today.

What we perhaps ought to understand is why things continued to deteriorate between 1929 and 1932. First, we did not have a well-functioning Federal Reserve System that viewed the maintenance of financial stability as perhaps their primary objective. We also had a prevailing philosophy in the President Herbert Hoover administration that the market should be left to its own devices. Hoover was monitoring the situation but did not believe the turmoil could last as long as it did.

Modern Keynesian macroeconomics has since taught us that the economy is well capable of long periods of persistent and dramatic recession or depression, but these studies were in their infancy in 1930. Finally, there was a tradition of lack of government involvement in economic affairs that prevailed throughout the Roaring Twenties. But, while the Fed tried to do whatever it could, without the support and reinforcement by the Economic Commander in Chief, the Fed's actions were deemed not credible.

Will things get as bad this time around? I don't think so. While perhaps we have done far too little far too late, the cries are getting louder and louder. And it has not taken four years for these clarion calls to be heard. My only fear is that the Fed has used almost all their monetary arrows in their quiver somewhat futilely, given the lack of a concerted fiscal policy response. There is not much more the Fed will be able to do at this point. We do have the attention of policymakers the world over though, and they are injecting unprecedented amounts of cash in concert into the banking system to thaw the lending freeze brought on by banker caution and pessimism.

There is a broad acceptance though that the unfettered deregulation of the last decades has put too much blind faith in complex markets. There is now broader worldwide appreciation for the need to reform regulatory oversight and encourage a much greater degree of transparency in markets. Only then can we demonstrate to the marketplace that nothing is as important as securing our collective economic future. If we can lend that confidence to financial markets and the economic citizens, it is likely that we will have to do little more. Markets and citizens are incredibly resilient if the financial environment is sound, reasonably optimistic, and well regulated. At least for this moment in history, we recognize that private markets operate in the public trust. We may be witnessing the end of the era in which we turn a blind eye when profits are lucrative because we now know the public coffers must indemnify markets from the most severe losses.

We even see some optimism returning. While we are still met with more bankruptcies, financial scandals, layoffs, and declining wealth, there is finally recognition of the seriousness of the problem and elected leaders show the resolve to do something about. This recognition is important. Without willing consumers ready to reinvest in the economy, we cannot move forward. While there will likely be considerable pain yet, and we all are braced for another tough year or two, there is finally some glimmer of light at the end of the tunnel. And that will make all the difference.

Notes

2 The Beauty (and the Beast) of Free Markets

1. See http://www.gpoaccess.gov/constitution/pdf2002/023.pdf at page 1473, accessed July 17, 2008. The US Constitution and its amendments stood as the first constitution of economic empowerment, and struck a new balance between the powers of the State and the individual.
2. See Garrett Hardin, "The Tragedy of the Commons," *Science*, Vol. 162, No. 3859 (December 13, 1968), pp. 1243–1248. This article nicely formulates an economic principle that public goods are not afforded the same care as those that are privately owned.
3. R.G. Lipsey and Kelvin Lancaster, "The General Theory of Second Best," *The Review of Economic Studies*, Vol. 24, No. 1 (1956–1957), pp. 11–32. The First Fundamental Theorem of Welfare Economics states that a competitive equilibrium is efficient. Lipsey and Lancaster observed that a violation of competiveness in any one market creates a series of other market distortions that must be corrected.
4. Tiebout, C., "A Pure Theory of Local Expenditures," *The Journal of Political Economy*, Vol. 64, No. 5 (1956), pp. 416–424. This seminal paper describes how the analogy of choice for goods can be extended to the optimal provision of public services as well.

3 The Post-Industrial Revolution and the Transforming Economies

1. Jean-Baptiste Say, "A Treatise on Political Economy, or the Production, Distribution and Consumption of Wealth," 1803. Say was one of a tradition of economic philosophers, which included Adam Smith and John Stuart Mill, that marveled in the workings of the modern economy. While Mill went on to discuss the important role of government to correct market failings, Say's main conclusion was that "supply creates its own demand." This notion acted as the basis for the self-correcting Classical model.
2. Keynes, John Maynard, *The General Theory of Employment, Interest and Money* (New York: Harcourt, Brace and Company, 1936). Many readers enjoy Keynes' eloquent writing style, and his ability to describe complex economic phenomena in words rather than graphs and equations. His writings are remarkably relevant today.

6 The World Threw a Party

1. Kuznets, Simon, "Economic Growth and Income Inequality," *American Economic Review* Vol. XLV (1955), pp. 1–28. Kuznets was one of the pioneers of the field of Economic Development.
2. Kuznets, "Economic Growth and Income Inequality."
3. Malthus, Thomas, *"An Essay On The Principle Of Population"* (1798). Malthus too was concerned about development economics, and about the ability of an economy to meet growing resource needs. His prophecy of feast and famine has been ameliorated by technological and production improvements.
4. http://www.un.org/esa/population/publications/sixbillion/sixbilpart1.pdf, accessed July 17, 2008. The United Nations Population Division is the recognized authority in global population dynamics.
5. http://www.un.org/esa/population/publications/wup2007/2007WUP_ExecSum_web.pdf, accessed July 17, 2008.

8 Progress Marches On

1. Schumpeter, Joseph A. *The Theory of Economic Development*. Cambridge: Harvard University Press. (New York: Oxford University Press, [1934] 1961.) First published in German, 1912.Schumpeter predated Keynes as he sought to understand why economies do not remain on an even keel, and instead oscillate up and down over time, but hopefully on an increasing trend.

9 Fill 'Er Up

1. *Economist Online*, April 7, 2008.

10 Gold, Oil, and Dollars, and the Decline of an Economic Superpower

1. www.competitvealternatives.com, accessed July 17, 2008.

11 Too Clever by One Half

1. http://www.federalreserve.gov/BoardDocs/Speeches/2000/20001206.htm. Prof. Gramlich passed away in 2007, but not before our recognition of his important contribution to the need to oversee markets. He was known as one of the most progressive of Federal Reserve Board members.

16 The Timely Death of Supply Side Economics

1. Solow, R.M., "A contribution to the theory of economic growth," *Quarterly Journal of Economics* Vol. **70** (1956), pp. 65–94. Solow went on to win a Nobel Prize for his contributions to the theory of economic growth.
2. Laffer, A. (June 1, 2004) *The Laffer Cruve, Past, Present and Future*. http://www.heritage.org/Research/Taxes/bg1765.cfm, accessed July 17, 2008. The Heritage Foundation. The Laffer Curve has also been observed by Keynes in his seminal work "The General Theory of Employment, Interest and Money."

17 The Higher You Go, the Farther You Fall

1. Schiller, Robert J. *Market Volatility* (Cambridge, MA: MIT Press,1989). Robert Schiller and his colleague Karl Case are lead researchers in the measurement and understanding of speculative bubbles, in financial and housing markets.
2. N. Kaldor, "A Classificatory Note on the Determination of Equilibrium," *Review of Economic Studies*, Vol. I (February, 1934), pp. 122–136. Kaldor was a contemporary of Keynes, and shared with Keynes a fascination with market equilibria.

19 Asleep at the Switch

1. Averch, Harvey A. and Johnson, Leland L., "Behaviour of the Firm under Regulatory Constraint." *American Economic Review*, Vol. 52 (1962), pp. 1053–1069.

20 The Bigger You Are, the Softer You Fall

1. Klein, Michael, "Playing With the Band: Dynamic Effects of Target Zones in an Open Economy," *International Economic Review*, Vol. 31, No. 4 (November 1990), pp. 757–771. Michael Klein discusses the implications of processes designed to coordinate monetary policies between nations to maintain the value of a lead currency.

21 It's Downright Criminal

1. Kant, Immanuel, translated by James W. Ellington Grounding for the Metaphysics of Morals (Indianapolis: Hackett Publishing, [1785] 1993). There are of course many commentaries on the metaphysics of Kant. This is a nicely accessible example.
2. Rawls, John, *A Theory of Justice* (Cambridge, MA: The Belknap Press of Harvard University Press, 1971). John Rawls and Nobel laureates John Harsanyi and Amartya Sen have created a reawakening in the importance of equity in economic decision making.

22 Somebody's Hedging

1. Akerlof, George A. (1970) "The Market for 'Lemons': Quality Uncertainty and the Market Mechanism," *Quarterly Journal of Economics*, Vol. 84, No. 3 (1970), pp. 488–500. While the title of the paper sounds narrow, this concept of information asymmetries has far reaching implications.

27 When Politics Gets in the Way of Good Ole' Common Sense

1. Arrow, K.J., "A Difficulty in the Concept of Social Welfare," *Journal of Political Economy*, Vol. 58, No. 4 (August 1950), pp. 328–346. Nobel laureate Kenneth Arrow made important contributions in the underlying theory of competitive equilibria, and helped establish elegant proofs of concepts that underpin all of economics.

28 The Taxman Cometh

1. "We Believe the Global War on Drugs is Now Causing More Harm Than Drug Abuse Itself." Public letter in *New York Times*, June 8, 1998, pp. A12–13.

29 An Educated Global Citizen

* This chapter is from Read, Colin, "Building Fords in a Toyota World – Kaizen comes to Education" *Strictly Business*, Sept 2007, with permission of the publication

1. *Deming, W. Edwards, Out of the Crisis (Cambridge, MA: MIT Press, 1986).*

Index

Colin Read has a PhD in economics, a law degree, and a master's degree in business and in taxation. He has taught economics and finance for 25 years, and is currently Dean of a school of business and economics in New York, USA. He has recently published a book on international taxation, appears regularly on a local PBS show on economic development, and is a prolific writer on a variety of economic issues.

www.ingramcontent.com/pod-product-compliance
Ingram Content Group UK Ltd.
Pitfield, Milton Keynes, MK11 3LW, UK
UKHW021019050925
462611UK00012B/1325

* 9 7 8 1 3 4 9 3 0 7 7 0 8 *